The School Wellness Wheel

A Framework
Addressing Trauma,
Culture, and
Mastery to Raise
Student Achievement

Mike Ruyle • Libby Child • Nancy Dome

With Jason Cummins, Brian Farragher,
Crystal Green-Braswell, and Alondra Velasco Ledezma
Foreword by Robert J. Marzano

555 North Morton Street
Bloomington, IN 47404
888.849.0851
FAX: 866.801.1447

email: info@MarzanoResources.com
MarzanoResources.com

Visit **MarzanoResources.com/reproducibles** to download the free reproducibles in this book.

Printed in the United States of America

Library of Congress Cataloging-in-Publication Data

Names: Ruyle, Mike, author. | Child, Libby, author. | Dome, Nancy, author.
Title: The school wellness wheel : a framework addressing trauma, culture, and mastery to raise student achievement / Mike Ruyle, Libby Child, Nancy Dome.
Description: Bloomington, IN : Marzano Resources, [2022] | Includes bibliographical references and index.
Identifiers: LCCN 2021035946 (print) | LCCN 2021035947 (ebook) | ISBN 9781943360611 (paperback) | ISBN 9781943360628 (ebook)
Subjects: LCSH: Children with mental disabilities--Education--United States. | Academic achievement--United States. | Psychic trauma in children--United States. | Culturally relevant pedagogy--United States. | Competency-based education--United States.
Classification: LCC LC4631 .R89 2022 (print) | LCC LC4631 (ebook) | DDC 371.92--dc23
LC record available at https://lccn.loc.gov/2021035946
LC ebook record available at https://lccn.loc.gov/2021035947

Production Team

President and Publisher: Douglas M. Rife
Associate Publisher: Sarah Payne-Mills
Art Director: Rian Anderson
Managing Production Editor: Kendra Slayton
Copy Chief: Jessi Finn
Senior Production Editor: Tonya Maddox Cupp
Content Development Specialist: Amy Rubenstein
Proofreader: Mark Hain
Cover Designer: Rian Anderson
Editorial Assistants: Charlotte Jones, Sarah Ludwig, and Elijah Oates

Acknowledgments

Marzano Resources would like to thank the following reviewers:

Linda Beggs
Cofounder
The Centergy Project
Marietta, Georgia

Brad Rogers
Principal
Lincoln Elementary School
Merrillan, Wisconsin

Bonnie Cazer
Principal
Middlesex Valley Elementary School
Rushville, New York

Ringnolda Jofee' Tremain
PK3–8 Principal
Trinity Basin Preparatory
Fort Worth, Texas

Andrew Grider
Principal
Rodney E. Thompson Middle School
Stafford, Virginia

Steven Weber
Associate Superintendent for Teaching
   and Learning
Fayetteville Public Schools
Fayetteville, Arkansas

David Pillar
Assistant Director
Hoosier Hills Career Center
Bloomington, Indiana

Visit **MarzanoResources.com/reproducibles**
to download the free reproducibles in this book.

Table of Contents

Reproducibles are in italics.

Chapter 3
Culture of Mastery 63

Chapter 4
Culture of Learning 83

About the Authors

Mike Ruyle, EdD, has served as a classroom teacher, athletic coach, school principal, alternative program director, university professor, and school consultant for over thirty years. He led the creation and implementation of personalized, competency-based schools in Montana and California, and is a recognized authority in the areas of assessment practice, mindfulness in classrooms, social justice, and healing-centered schooling. Mike's leadership experience and dynamic presentation style have made him a sought-after national and international speaker for numerous schools, districts, state agencies, and conferences.

Mike is the author of the book *Leading the Evolution: How to Make Personalized Competency-Based Education a Reality*, as well as a coauthor of *Cultivating Mindfulness in the Classroom*, *The New Art and Science of Classroom Assessment*, and *Professional Learning Communities at Work® and High Reliability Schools™: Cultures of Continuous Learning*.

Mike earned bachelor of arts degrees in history and English from the University of San Francisco, as well as master's and doctoral degrees in educational leadership from Montana State University. To learn more about Mike's work, follow @MikeRuyle on Twitter.

Libby Child, MEd, has spent over twenty-seven years in education as a high school special education teacher, a special education program coordinator, and an educational consultant for the Montana Office of Public Instruction in the areas of inclusive education, secondary transition practices for students with special needs, paraeducator development, and co-teaching. Her career has been deeply rooted in the belief that every student deserves an education with dignity and the best possible opportunity to learn and achieve at his or her greatest capacity.

Libby holds a bachelor of arts degree in elementary and special education from Carroll College and a master's degree in educational leadership from Montana State University.

Nancy Dome, EdD, has been supporting children to overcome institutional and systemic barriers and developing educators for over twenty years. Starting her career as a childcare worker, she has worked through the ranks as a classroom teacher, teacher leader, college professor, and cofounder of Epoch Education.

Nancy provides current, accessible, and transformational professional development for educators and students on the topics of equity, critical race theory, and culturally relevant teaching and learning to support the development of the necessary cultural competencies needed to effectively respond to our ever-diversifying world. She also cocreated the RIR protocol, which provides concrete steps to practice interrupting dysfunctional systems and negative behavior through compassionate dialogue using the steps of recognize it, interrupt it, and repair it. Nancy earned her bachelor of arts degree in psychology and master of arts in curriculum and instruction at United States International University, and her doctoral degree in technology and learning at Alliant International University.

Awaachiáookaate' (Jason Cummins, EdD), is an enrolled member of the Apsaalooke Nation and an Indigenous scholar who views education as a means of preserving the story, identity, and culture of communities. As an authority in the area of historical trauma and culturally responsive teaching, Jason has served as an educator and mentor for educational leaders in Native American schools for over a decade. He is a recognized leader in shifting how schools think about Indigenous culture and language and has worked toward the promotion and continuation of the Crow (Apsáalooke) language revival in the Rocky Mountain region.

Jason is a Clark Scholar and was one of fifteen principals selected nationwide to attend the first annual Principals at ED in Washington, D.C., and provided feedback for Every Student Success Act (ESSA). He has been honored as educator of the year by the Montana Indian Education Association and is a school leader. He coauthored *Safe Zones, Dangerous Leadership: Decolonial Leadership in Settler-Colonial School Contexts* with Ethan Chang and *In Reciprocity: Responses to Critiques of Indigenous Methodologies,* with Sweeney Windchief, Cheryl Polacek, Michael Munson, and Mary Ulrich. Jason has also served as a guest editor for *Journal of School Leadership* and supports programs and schools as an Indigenous leadership consultant. Jason began his academic career at Little Big Horn Tribal College and earned masters and doctoral degrees in educational leadership from Montana State University.

Jason and his wife, Velvett, have been married for over twenty-six years and live in the ancestral homeland of the Apsáalooke Nation, where they have four adult sons and two grandchildren.

Brian Farragher, MSW, MBA, is a thirty-year veteran of managing residential treatment centers. He led the development of the Sanctuary Institute, a trauma-informed care training and consultation service to disseminate the Sanctuary Model. In the first seven years of operation, the Institute trained over 270 organizations in twenty-six states and seven countries and achieved 2.5 million in revenue.

Brian has coauthored two books with Dr. Sandra L. Bloom—*Destroying Sanctuary: The Crisis in Human Service Delivery Systems* and *Restoring Sanctuary: A New Operating System for Trauma-Informed Systems of Care.* He is also the author of many articles on developing trauma-sensitive treatment programs and reducing the use of physical interventions in residential settings. As a thought leader in this space, Brian has presented at regional, national, and international conferences.

In January 2009, Brian received the Samuel Gerson Nordlinger Child Welfare Leadership Award, presented by the Alliance for Strong Families and Communities, which recognizes individuals who make outstanding contributions to the child welfare field, advancing quality services for children and families.

Brian earned a master of business administration from the Hagan School of Business at Iona College and a master of social work from Fordham University School of Social Work.

Crystal Green-Braswell, EdS, a twenty-one year veteran educator, currently serves as a middle school assistant principal in the Little Rock School District in Little Rock, Arkansas. During her twenty-one years in education, she has served a variety of populations. She is armed with the sincere belief that with the right climate and culture, every school can succeed. Dedicated to being a servant educator-leader, her mission is to change the world one educator at a time. Crystal earned a bachelor's degree in special education, a master's degree in adult education, and a specialist degree in education leadership from Arkansas State University.

Alondra Velasco Ledezma, PhD, has spent over fifteen years in education, serving as a classroom teacher, curriculum specialist, and as the Mexican program director at the American School Foundation of Guadalajara, Mexico. She was recognized as an expert in school leadership, has served as a presenter at the Tri-Association and a panelist on the Ethical Leadership in Education Board, and is an authority in early childhood education, Mexican education, and international education. She has designed an effective six-step program to address and face low performance, conflict, problem solving, and hard conversations in work environments.

Alondra's knowledge, experience, and commitment to building healthy, strong communities at schools and in educational environments have placed her in leading positions for Mexican and American programs. She has created projects for the well-being of diverse private and public institutions.

Alondra earned bachelor's degrees in psychology and early childhood education and a master's degree in education focused on cognitive development from Tecnológico de Monterrey University, and earned a doctorate in education with a specialty on leadership from the UNIVES University.

To book Mike Ruyle, Libby Child, Nancy Dome, Jason Cummins, Brian Farragher, Crystal Green-Braswell, or Alondra Velasco Ledezma for professional development, contact pd@SolutionTree.com.

Foreword

By Robert J. Marzano

The School Wellness Wheel: A Framework Addressing Trauma, Culture, and Mastery to Raise Student Achievement by Mike Ruyle, Libby Child, Nancy Dome, and colleagues integrates powerful constructs into K–12 schooling that, to my knowledge, have never before been discussed together in the context of school leadership and instruction. The metaphor the authors use for this endeavor is the Native American medicine wheel, which is historically associated with harmony, connection, symmetry, and the sacred cycles of life—certainly fitting goals for educators. As applied to education, the school wellness wheel articulates the interrelationships between mastery-based learning, trauma-responsive schooling, and culturally responsive teaching. These interrelationships support positive outcomes relative to wellness, learning, and college and career literacy, ultimately resulting in healing- and resilience-centered education for students. Rather than focus independently on specific strategies for each element, the authors focus on developing cultural emphases within a school in the six following ways.

1. **A culture of adult ownership, expertise, and professionalism:** The adults in a school must first seek to transform themselves to accomplish this emphasis. These are not just idle words from the authors. They propose that all educators begin by examining their beliefs and the actions that stem from those beliefs; they should then seek to nourish a personal worldview that maximizes their effectiveness as educators working on a common goal. Additionally, they should examine their level of commitment to the mission of the school such that school leaders can count on all staff members to put their full professional energies into the success of the school's wellness wheel approach.

2. **A culture of mastery:** This involves establishing a system that provides clearly articulated learning goals in all subject areas. These goals should

be transparent to teachers, administrators, school staff, parents and guardians, and most importantly, students. Educators should articulate such goals as proficiency scales and address traditional academic content as well as cognitive and metacognitive skills.

3. **A culture of learning:** The way students think about themselves as learners and how they choose to process the content they are learning are both within their purview of influence if they are willing to develop mindfulness skills. A culture of learning makes students conscious of the fact that effective learning is an active process over which they have some control. To aid in this process, schools should develop ways of assessing students that let them know their precise level of competence at any given moment on any given topic and what they might do to increase their competence.

4. **A culture of connection:** Not surprisingly, this involves developing empathy and building community. It also involves addressing a very interesting construct the authors refer to as *co-regulation*.

5. **A culture of empowerment:** This culture involves offering voice and choice to students. However, this should be done using a gradual release model, where students obtain more control and autonomy as they develop the requisite skills in these areas. Empowerment also involves fostering high expectations for all students. Ultimately, these activities serve to promote student agency.

6. **A culture of humanity:** Strategies in this area are designed to draw students' attention to the common issues that affect all humankind through the use of trauma-responsive consequences. The basic purpose of this cultural focus is to heighten students' awareness of the human condition, including the frailties and travails all humans must face and address.

One of the more powerful aspects of the book is that the authors provide readers with a proficiency scale for each cultural focus. The scales allow schools to determine their current level of implementation with the constructs for each area of cultural emphasis and determine what they must do next to increase their level of implementation. Finally, the authors offer readers a variety of options for implementing the school wellness wheel.

This book is sure to offer educators perspectives and strategies they have never encountered before—perspectives and strategies that can foster a true paradigm shift in K–12 education.

Robert J. Marzano is the chief academic officer and cofounder of Marzano Resources.

Introduction

*This is how you spark a revolution. You shift
the frame, you change the lens, and all at once
the world is revealed, and nothing is the same.*

—Nadine Burke Harris

Trauma and long-term (toxic) stress can contribute to an array of mental health issues that pose a serious public health problem and exact a staggering cost on society (Rosenberg, 2012). Adverse childhood experiences (ACEs) are a major source of childhood trauma and toxic stress, and are defined as follows:

> potentially traumatic events that occur in childhood and adolescence, such as experiencing physical, emotional, or sexual abuse; witnessing violence in the home; having a family member attempt or die by suicide; and growing up in a household with substance use, mental health problems, or instability due to parental death, separation, divorce, or incarceration. (Jones, Merrick, & Houry, 2020, p. 25)

The California Surgeon General has identified that the annual health-related costs of ACEs and toxic stress to the state exceed $112.5 billion (Bhushan et al., 2020). On an even larger scale, a report issued from the World Economic Forum (2020) stated that psychological health disorders have a greater impact on economic output than heart disease, diabetes, or cancer. Untreated anxiety and depression alone place a cost burden on society of $1.15 trillion annually and the worldwide cost of psychological health issues is on pace to exceed $16 trillion by 2030 (Fleming, 2019).

The human costs of these issues on families and communities are even more severe than the economic ones. Research shows more than 60 percent of Americans experienced at least one traumatic event as children; conservative estimates are that nearly a quarter of adults have experienced three or more ACEs (Merrick et al., 2018). As the number of ACEs increase, so too does the risk for long-term negative effects on health, behavior, and learning. Seven of the ten leading causes of death are associated with a high number of ACEs, and these causes can shorten a person's life span by as many as nineteen years (Harris, 2018; Peterson, Florence, & Klevins, 2018).

As sobering as the statistics are, the full extent of psychological health issues is likely to be even greater than these data suggest due to the fact that mental and emotional health problems tend to be stigmatized, misdiagnosed, and under-recorded across both the developed and developing worlds. Moreover, even people who are properly diagnosed don't always receive effective treatment due to lack of access or professional expertise (Fleming, 2019; GBD 2017 Disease and Injury Incidence and Prevalence Collaborators, 2018; World Economic Forum, 2020). The need to aggressively address psychological health, trauma, and toxic stress is a critical component of all social service, health, and educational systems.

For schools, trauma and toxic stress constitute a domestic and global crisis that impacts every level of education. Between half and two-thirds of all school-aged children experience trauma in that they are exposed to one or more adverse experiences that can be trauma inducing (Finkelhor, Turner, Ormrod, & Hamby, 2010; Harris, 2019; Osher, Cantor, Berg, Steyer, & Rose, 2018; Listenbee, 2012; World Health Organization, 2020). California surgeon general Nadine Burke Harris (2019) asserted that these adverse childhood experiences are at the root of our public education crisis: "Toxic stress affects how we learn, how we parent, how we react at home and at work, and what we create in our communities" (p. 188).

What educators know all too well is that students bring their experiences of trauma into daily school life. Childhood adversity and toxic stress can significantly impact how a person's brain develops (Oh et al., 2018). Sadly, even when educators recognize the importance of responding to these issues—attempting to implement trauma-informed or culturally competent education—traditional school systems simply are not usually structured in a way that allows them to effectively address the "insidious ways in which the day-to-day onslaught of chronic adversity undermines learning" (Harris, 2019, p. 185). As an example, many common yet coercive disciplinary practices, including detention and suspension, can be retraumatizing for individual students, which can lead to their subsequent disengagement and failure (Bethell, Newacheck, Hawes, & Halfon, 2014).

The great challenge confronting schools is how to balance the expectation for educational excellence and academic success with a safe, supportive environment that can imbue students with the ability to heal their brains and also build their capacity for resilience. Fortunately, vast amounts of research indicate that the successful integration of emotional, cognitive, and social processes in the brain are vital to successful learning and motivation (Cantor, Osher, Berg, Steyer, & Rose, 2019; Osher et al., 2018). Research also indicates that this integration is best accomplished in a well-designed mastery-based educational framework in which students benefit from developmentally appropriate relationships with adults as well as high levels of teacher expertise in the areas of trauma, stress, and cultural responsiveness (Cantor et al., 2019; Osher at al., 2018).

The Insidious Impact of Trauma on the Brain and Learning

Since the early 1960s, a massive amount of research from diverse fields including education, psychology, epigenetics (investigating the interaction between genes and environment), pediatric medicine, and resilience theory has greatly contributed to our knowledge about how children develop physically and emotionally, how their brains operate, and how a number of factors can impact their learning and overall growth.

This network of research is increasingly vast, deep, and robust. For example, in 1966, John Coleman and his colleagues from Johns Hopkins University published their study titled *Equality of Educational Opportunity*. Widely known as the Coleman Report, it was the first large-scale academic study to focus on tangible differences in schooling resources available to White and minority students and to clearly document the impact of differing school resources on student growth. Although controversial in many ways, the Coleman Report brought to light important conclusions about the critical role of teacher quality and expertise in terms of student learning as well as recognized the tremendous impact of the home environment and other outside influences as powerful predictors of student academic success. The Coleman Report opened the door to considering how students' complicated, stressful lives can hinder their learning.

Later, on March 8, 1989, the United States Congress passed a joint resolution that was subsequently issued as a formal proclamation by President George H. W. Bush that declared the 1990s the "Decade of the Brain," purposefully allocating extensive government funding for neurological research (Bush, 1990). This massive infusion of capital resulted in creating and advancing such innovative devices as the PET-CT scanner (which can help doctors see disease in the body and was named by

Time magazine as the medical invention of the year in 2000), magnetic resonance imaging (MRI) that uses powerful magnets and radio waves to create pictures of the body, and functional magnetic resonance imaging, or fMRI, a technique used for charting and measuring brain activity. Some of these breakthroughs had a direct and substantial impact on schools. For example, researchers in the 1990s discovered how a child's early experiences can have a *physiological* impact on the brain. As a result, a number of states began a push for prekindergarten education, which is now commonplace in schools across the country (Aspen Institute, 2018; Cantor et al., 2019; Osher et al., 2018).

Toward the end of the decade, in 1998, a landmark report was presented by doctors Vincent Felitti, Robert Anda, and their colleagues that became widely known as the Adverse Childhood Experiences (ACEs) Study. A collaboration between Kaiser Permanente and the United States Centers for Disease Control (CDC), the study was one of the first and largest investigations ever conducted to assess connections between chronic stress caused by early adversity in children and corresponding long-term health outcomes in adults.

Since the publication of the original ACEs Study, a vast amount of additional research has validated the assertion that ACEs can directly correlate with increased risk for negative outcomes later in life, including a wide range of chronic diseases and leading causes of morbidity and mortality such as heart disease, diabetes, cancer, and suicide (Evans-Campbell, 2008; Fallot & Harris, 2008; Harris, 2018, Harris et al., 2017). Further studies indicate that ACEs are also associated with impaired educational achievement and future employment potential, and this risk is increased for people who experience multiple types of ACEs (CDC, 2019; Felitti et al., 1998; Harris, 2018; Merrick et al., 2019).

As powerful as the original ACEs study was, however, an important limitation to be recognized is that the sample group—over 17,500 participants—was comprised primarily of middle- to upper-middle-class subjects who were generally well educated and predominantly White. This fact left unanswered the question of whether various other subgroups could be impacted by ACEs differently. For example, is it possible that certain demographic groups could have unique situations or adversities that were not effectively measured by the original survey? The original ACEs Study restricted its focus to important in-home adversities such as physical abuse, parental violence, and substance use in the household. But subsequent research has led to the realization that a vast range of daily exposures outside the home can also shape children's lives, experiences, and behaviors (Philadelphia ACE Project, 2019). Simply stated, the original ACE measure apparently underreported the rates and types of childhood adversity and generational trauma in many historically disenfranchised communities.

Thus, researchers began to examine whether the traditional concept of ACEs needed to be expanded to assess the impact of community-level adversities such as living in an unsafe neighborhood, being bullied, and feeling discriminated against. As a result, in 2013 the Philadelphia Urban ACE Study took the findings from the original Kaiser Permanente sample and specifically studied additional toxic or traumatic elements that could result from living in an urban environment (Philadelphia ACE Project, 2019). The Philadelphia Urban ACE Study was immensely beneficial as one of the first research reports to examine ACEs with a racially and socioeconomically diverse urban population and found clear differences in ACE exposure based on demographic characteristics. The researchers asserted that marginalization due to gender, race, or class was associated with higher exposure to community-based ACEs that are unrelated to in-home ACEs. In doing so, the authors identified new urban ACE indicators and created a new overall ACE score, as shown in figure I.1.

Five urban ACE indicators identified in 2013 follow.

- Experiencing racism
- Witnessing intense violence of any kind
- Living in an unsafe neighborhood
- Living in foster care
- Experiencing bullying

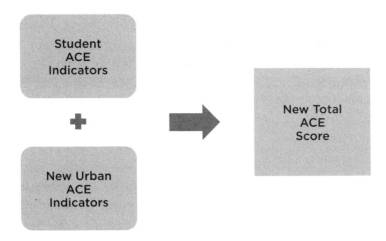

Figure I.1: ACE score.

As the research base continued to widen and deepen, the American Academy of Pediatrics (AAP, 2011), a professional organization representing sixty thousand physicians, issued a policy statement and a technical report that further detailed the impact of childhood trauma and toxic stress in shaping health outcomes across the entire life spectrum. This policy statement directly referenced the immense and expanding body of scientific evidence from molecular biology, genomics, immunology, and neuroscience to help clarify our understanding of how childhood stress can ultimately weaken brain architecture and, thus, affect learning capacities and adaptive behaviors. The report also addressed the historical and ongoing effects of racism and poverty—specifically how living in poverty, living in racially segregated environments, or experiencing housing or food insecurity can exacerbate the effects of ACEs, thus dramatically impacting adult productivity as well as a person's lifelong physical and mental health. This policy statement called for a seismic shift in pediatric medicine to expand outreach efforts to family and community groups that could help build strong foundations for children's lifelong health by preventing toxic stress and actively addressing ACEs early in the life cycle.

Even more contemporary medical and psychological research has further cemented the fact that childhood stress and trauma can have a tremendous impact on health outcomes throughout life. Leaders such as Nadine Burke Harris (2019) and Rachel Yehuda and colleagues (2016) have presented innovative research in the field of epigenetics, which seeks to explain how this toxic stress can alter the way in which our DNA is adapted biologically and can be passed on to subsequent generations. We now know, for example, that trauma and high-level stress are toxic and can have a dramatic impact on the body through the hormonal and immune systems. They also affect cognition, as evidenced by the fact that young people with four or more ACEs are 32 percent more likely to be diagnosed with learning and behavior problems (Harris, 2019). Chronic stress impacts the brain through, among other things, increased activation of the amygdala, the brain's fear center; the locus coeruleus, which regulates impulse control, arousal, and attention; and the prefrontal cortex, which is the seat of executive functioning, cognition, judgement, and mood. When children are exposed to complex, acute trauma, their brains shift their operations and functioning from normal growth and development to the stress response, which can have lasting repercussions over time.

On the bright side, contemporary research strongly indicates that we humans also have a profound ability to heal ourselves and each other. An exponential increase in research from cognitive neuroscience has revealed a remarkable period of rapid neural development as evidenced by a high level of *neurogenesis* (the brain's ability to produce new neurons and grow grey matter) and *neuroplasticity* (the brain's ability to continually form new synaptic connections whenever we learn something new) during adolescence that is second only to infancy. This can open a critical window in which schools can help heal traumatized brains, strengthen resilience in nontraumatized brains, and build the habits of mind and body that support a thriving adulthood

(Cantor et al., 2019; Harris, 2018). In fact, negative experiences can spur positive change, including the personal realization of strength and resilience, improved interpersonal relationships, being more open to the exploration of new possibilities, and a deeper passion for life and well-being. This phenomenon is often referred to as *post-traumatic growth* and can be demonstrated in people who have been survivors of war, disasters, bereavement, economic devastation, job loss, and serious illnesses or injuries (Tedeschi, 2020; Tedeschi, Shakespeare-Finch, Taku, & Calhoun, 2018). Thus, despite being subjected to trauma-inducing events and toxic stress, many people can grow and develop in beneficial ways. Educators, in particular, can help the students in their care to do just that. By bringing the science of toxic stress and trauma into mainstream school systems, we can help people learn a host of skills and strategies that could potentially boost synaptic plasticity in the brain, which can, ultimately, facilitate healing and help build resilience (Cantor et al., 2019; Harris, 2019; Yehuda, Daskalakis, et al., 2016; Yehuda, Spiegel, et al., 2016).

An Evolved Vision of Schooling

Unfortunately, the tremendous power of this diverse and robust research base to address personal learning and overall human development has not been realized in schools. Simply stated, vast amounts of research remains dramatically underutilized in schools and classrooms, which continues to directly contribute to persistent disparities and inadequacies in our educational systems. As Pamela Cantor and her colleagues (2019) stated, "there exists a great need to align and synthesize this increasingly vast, field-specific body of knowledge from biology, neuroscience, psychology, and the social sciences within a dynamic, holistic, contextualized framework" (p. 309).

Although the AAP policy statement called for doctors and medical agencies to expand their influence among the public, the reality is that our classrooms hold a special place in the pantheon of human services. Schools are uniquely positioned to impact every child, every family, and the overall community in ways unavailable to other social service organizations. Aside from the family unit, the school can provide the most proximal setting for cultivating and nurturing strong human relationships, which are a critical component of learning and development. In fact, when schools are organized in ways that provide a web of support and foster developmental relationships for students with their teachers and peers, they also cultivate key conditions for learning, such as engagement, agency, connectedness, challenge, respect, and physical, intellectual, and *emotional safety* (when one can recognize and accept feelings while trusting that someone will give them the benefit of the doubt; Berkowitz, Moore, Astor, & Benbenishty, 2016; Crosnoe & Benner, 2015; Osher & Kendziora,

2010). Plus, positive school climates can enhance students' social and emotional evolution, which will, ultimately, help them become more effective learners (Hamre & Pianta, 2010).

Schools are the bedrock of communities. They are social institutions that have the powerful capacity to touch every citizen. And schools can also have the immense potential to buffer the negative effects of stress and trauma, enhance the process of cognitive, social, and emotional growth, and promote resilience in the learners they serve on a daily basis. In sum, there needs to be much closer, bidirectional collaboration between education practitioners and researchers from outside fields in order to capitalize on the opportunities presented by translating the emerging developmental science into instructional and learning practice (Stafford-Brizard, Cantor, & Rose, 2017).

The Urgent Need to Adopt a Healing- and Resilience-Centered Model of Education

In their 2014 book *Awaken the Learner,* Darrell Scott and Robert J. Marzano asserted that K–12 schools primarily focus on knowledge and skills to the detriment of their students. Indeed, operating from a more humanistic, student-centered approach to thinking and teaching has taken a back seat during the academic standards–based accountability movement. Traditional schools still largely follow the *banking model* of education, which refers to the metaphor coined by Paulo Freire (1970a) in his seminal work, *Pedagogy of the Oppressed.* Freire argued that in traditional models, students are viewed as containers into which teachers must deposit knowledge through instruction and assignments that the students receive, memorize, and repeat. Thus, schools have been designed according to an industrial-age system in which learners are grouped into cohorts based on their chronological age and progress en masse through grade levels. This results in classrooms that are "fundamentally narrative in character" (Freire, 1970a, p. 57) in that the teacher serves as the active participant and the students as passive objects. This being the case, the focus for teachers in traditional school settings is usually external—curricula, instruction, assessment, and rules. Based on these practices, schools largely function under organizational cultures that relentlessly focus on standards, grades, and compliance. Poor behavior is seen as a willful violation of the clearly established rule structure.

By maintaining this focus, however, we are ignoring the key variable and asking the wrong questions. As a result, evolution in schools is glacial. A more immediate, updated, and compelling model is needed. *Personalized competency-based education, trauma-informed care,* and *culturally responsive pedagogy* are three distinct initiatives that many schools have adopted at some level (Bloom & Farragher, 2013; DeLorenzo,

Battino, Schreiber, & Carrio, 2009; Ladson-Billings, 1995; Noguera, 2008; Ruyle, 2019). Although they are powerful educational and psychological constructs in their own right, they are typically presented to teachers in an incomplete way with a narrow viewpoint that all too often results in simply tweaking existing educational models as opposed to helping facilitate a larger paradigm shift in which their true power may be realized. In other words, when powerful, innovative constructs such as these are simply adopted individually and implemented in traditional school settings as one of many new initiatives, they may prove helpful—but they are not usually transformational.

For example, Zaretta Hammond (2015) made the point that cultural competence training in schools can contribute to effective learning by doing two things.

1. Addressing factors that directly interfere with students' learning (factors like school discipline policies that exacerbate the impacts of implicit bias)

2. Deepening the knowledge base and internal capacity of the adults in a school, as well as creating supportive environments addressing cultural disconnects and disabling conditions (like anxiety or depression) that limit students' capacity for learning

Indeed, there has been a massive effort to include more social-emotional learning (SEL), along with cultural competency, in schools and classrooms. Many educators who are invested in SEL strive to ensure that those practices are enacted in equitable, culturally responsive ways. Schools implementing SEL often report improvements in school climate, as well as increases in student and adult satisfaction (Hammond, 2015).

Hammond (2015) critically asserted, however, that there is virtually no documented corresponding increase in subsequent student academic achievement to accompany the additional SEL or cultural professional development work. Thus, cultural competence training is not sufficient, in itself, to create conditions for deeper learning and domain-specific mastery in which students can internalize knowledge and apply it in real-world situations. Likewise, Harris (2018) stated that purposefully training teachers in utilizing trauma-informed care (TIC) strategies has had a generally positive effect in school culture, yet academic gains have proven to be virtually nonexistent unless metacognitive skills are explicitly taught and learned at a high level as well.

And finally, our research and informal studies suggest that implementing personalized, competency-based school protocols does indeed seem to result in higher levels of student engagement and teacher optimism (Ruyle, 2019). In spite of those exciting results, however, Russlyn Ali (2019), CEO and cofounder of the XQ Institute reported, "Low-income students and students of color in some of today's competency-based models are doing worse on traditional measures than their counterparts in more traditional schools—a challenge that many innovators are aware of and are actively seeking solutions." Providing teachers and school personnel with professional training in competency-based school models, trauma-informed care, and culturally responsive pedagogy—while asking them to continue operating in a traditional school mindset—is ineffective in bringing sustainable growth and lasting change. Putting more things on the plates of teachers and principals without evolving the existing educational construct is, ultimately, futile.

Educators are just beginning to grasp that trauma and toxic stress are detrimental to brain development and deeply understand their role in the origins of many diseases. Thus, there is a professional need for educators to continue to leverage the most current science to inform the creation of innovative school structures and classroom instructional strategies to reduce the impact of toxic stress on children and to mitigate its negative effects on development and health across the lifespan. As such, a teacher's role is to become an expert in learning and the brain, as well as in the factors that can either enhance or inhibit learning.

Becoming doctors of learning rather than purveyors of content is the ultimate challenge of every educator as the world and the profession continue to evolve into the future. When a school or district offers professional learning sessions in areas such as SEL or culturally responsive instruction, but doesn't revise or evolve the overarching system , it only adds more to teachers' already full plates. The school wellness wheel provides the framework in which schools can accomplish this new vision. This model for success focuses educators' cognitive energy. As the education research becomes more robust, schools and teachers can adopt it into the school model as appropriate.

If we encourage ourselves to approach the critical issues from a different perspective, it can open up a new world of unlimited possibilities. This is about the humans and the learning. It's not about the curriculum and the content. By understanding and responding to students' past and current experiences with trauma and stress, school administrators, teachers, and staff can break the cycle of trauma, help reduce its negative impact, prevent retraumatization, support critical learning, and create a more positive school environment.

Until we create schools that actively focus on the overall health of the brains, bodies, and psyches of the humans in the building, the quality of the curriculum, instruction, and assessments is irrelevant. Thus, the adults in the educational system have a critical responsibility to adjust their professional orientation away from simply delivering curriculum, providing instruction, and maintaining traditional grading systems, to adopting and growing within a humanized educational model that recognizes students' individuality and helps them grow to the greatest capacity possible.

A Powerful Solution

Ultimately, by educating educators on the diverse and complex pathways through which children develop, engage, and learn, the school wellness wheel can help align schools and instructional design with students' individual capacities and needs. This alignment can better facilitate the healthy development of the whole child, enhance culturally responsive approaches to academic mastery, and personalize high-level learning for every student.

We believe that the solution to educational inertia lies in integrating the school wellness wheel as the foundational layer in the educational evolution process. Humans adapt to stressful environments in ways that can undermine learning and can also foster their involvement in unhealthy or high-risk behaviors (Crick & Dodge, 1994; Martin & Liem, 2011). However, research on neurogenesis and neuroplasticity speaks to the power of developmentally robust environments that promote resilience and improve learning outcomes (Hunter, Gray, & McEwen, 2018; Masten & Coatsworth, 1998).

Education centered on healing and resilience allows teachers to focus first on internal factors, such as healing damaged brains and tired bodies, building resilience through validation and human connection, and actively responding to students' personal contexts. Based on these practices, healing- and resilience-centered schools relentlessly focus on learning, mastery, connection, and empowerment. Poor behavior is seen as a result of internal dysregulation that can be addressed in an effective manner. In healing- and resilience-centered schools, teachers start from the inside. They become experts in the learning process and understand the corrosive effects of personal and historical trauma on cognition. They know that helping students move toward mastery is, in itself, healing.

As such, it is important to reconfigure schools around a different perspective and to employ language specific to the new model. Thus, we assert that healing- and resilience-centered schooling happens best in the context of *mastery-based learning*, the effective use of *trauma-responsive schooling*, and *culturally responsive teaching*. These three evidence-based constructs have the immense power—when combined—to transform the entire educational model.

Once the school wellness wheel is effectively implemented, higher levels of wellness, learning, and mastery of college and career skills can be achieved through strong instruction and curriculum along with high-quality assessment protocols. If the educational structure is such that the adults in schools purposely attend to the brains, bodies, and psyches of students first and foremost, deeper academic engagement and learning will naturally follow, and greater expectations for student growth are finally realistic and attainable.

The differences between traditional education and healing- and resilience-centered schooling in terms of educational focus, school structure, and philosophical foundation are described in table I.1.

Table I.1: Traditional Versus Healing- and Resilience-Centered Schools

Traditional Schools	Healing- and Resilience-Centered Schools
Focus	
Curriculum	Literacy
Instruction	Wellness
Assessment	Learning
Rules	Connection
Structure	
Time-based schooling	Mastery-based learning
Teacher-driven and content-focused	Student-driven and learning-focused
Standardized testing-focused	Personalized and authentic high-level learning
Philosophy	
Content and curriculum	Mastery
Instruction	Connection
Assessment	Learning
Compliance	Empowerment
Standardized	Humanized

We assert that the *school wellness wheel*, described in greater detail in this book, provides the functional integration of educational, psychological, social, and medical research, and establishes a specific framework to help schools provide dynamic, rich contexts that can better facilitate and support the healthy development and high-level learning of all students.

About This Book

Change does not happen in schools unless someone leads it well. A massive paradigm shift like the one toward a healing- and resilience-centered model entails an array of leadership qualities and behaviors that are critically necessary for the vision to come to fruition. Thus, this book is fundamentally leader-centric. This shift, however, is a very heavy lift that requires the entire staff's commitment and combined cognitive energy. So, we assert that this book is for everyone in an educational organization to delve into and digest over time.

Students' brains are malleable and can be supported and healed through mastery learning principles, culturally responsive school practice, and developmentally designed settings that address the impact of trauma and stress (Cantor et al., 2019; Osher et al., 2019; Vander Ark, Liebtag, & McClennen, 2021). The purpose of this book is to help schools become healing- and resilience-centered organizations in which personal mastery, as well as trauma-competent and culturally responsive practices are the norm in the educational process. If we know that trauma can negatively impact and even damage the brain, we also know that there are actions educators can take to reverse those effects, heal the brain, and build resilience in nontraumatized brains. The research is clear: if people engage in these activities, they get better and stronger (Bath, 2008; Bloom & Farragher, 2013).

This being the case, we maintain that schooling's primary purpose is to help every student reach their fullest potential—as students, certainly, but also as human beings. Many educators are familiar with the hierarchy of needs by Abraham Maslow (1943), the prevalent model that researchers use to explain human motivation. Maslow's hierarchy of needs was heavily influenced by his work with Blackfeet people in 1938 (Michel, 2014; Bray, 2019). In fact, the familiar triangular shape of the hierarchy diagram was inspired by the Blackfeet tipi. Interestingly, Blackfeet philosophy recognizes self-actualization (fulfillment of the self) not as the topmost goal of human development, but rather as a critical foundational component for the more highly valued evolution of the community. Thus, *community* actualization sits at the pinnacle of the Blackfeet hierarchy (Kingston, 2020).

In any case, Maslow's (1943) construct involves the pursuit of specific needs and goals, and teachers must be cognizant of the physical and psychological needs of their students in order to capture attention and eventually move them to subsequently higher levels of engagement. Maslow (1943) asserted that motivation and inspiration occur when we believe that an activity or opportunity will help us meet a specific need or goal. Conversely, they do not occur when we believe we will be unable to accomplish a specific need or goal. Each level is generally not available without fulfilling the needs related to the prior levels. See figure I.2 (page 14).

Since we assert that a primary function of schools is to foster healthy and resilient people who have the skills and strength to be successful, we have purposefully aligned the chapters of the book with Maslow's famous hierarchy. Just as students

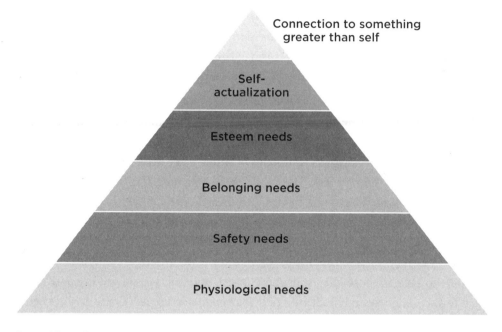

Source: *Adapted from Maslow, 1943.*

Figure I.2: Maslow's hierarchy of needs.

and teachers must have their lower-level needs met in order to work up to the higher-level drives, so too must a school or educational program focus on the needs at different levels from an organizational level to achieve their ultimate purpose. In addition, simply referencing research or employing strategies in the traditional model will not result in authentic, substantive, evolutionary shifts in schools. The paradigm shift only happens as a result of changes in the educators' hearts and minds. Thus, each chapter covers a critical cultural shift that *must* happen for healing- and resilience-centered education to take root.

- Chapters 1 and 2 provide the deep theoretical and philosophical underpinnings that form the foundation of the school wellness wheel. They also relate specifically to the first three levels of Maslow: (1) physiological, (2) safety, and (3) belonging needs. Teachers must recognize these needs and understand what happens to students who are stuck in these levels before they can address academic content. Thus, chapter 2 focuses on the changes that must take place in the hearts and minds of the adults in the school building, as well as the continued professional growth and understanding of mastery-based learning, trauma-competent principles, and culturally responsive teaching in order to bring the school wellness wheel to fruition.

- Chapters 3–7 explain how to implement and merge the three pivot points in a day-to-day school setting. Chapter 3 centers around cultivating a culture of mastery and presents a vehicle for addressing traditional standards and curriculum through the use of established learning goals and proficiency scales, and the impact such a model has on the engagement of students and optimism of teachers. Since mastery-based-learning schools typically see increased trust between students and teachers (as evidenced through higher levels of academic optimism), creating a culture of mastery is empowering and serves as the foundational academic component of the school wellness wheel. Along that same vein, since relationships are the antidote to trauma, chapter 3 also stresses the importance of developmentally appropriate adult relationships in terms of trauma-sensitive and culturally responsive teaching, and explains how those relationships can help lead to higher levels of student mastery.

- Chapter 4 focuses on the need for schools to exist in a continuous culture of high-level learning—for the students as well as the adults—and thus, presents a new vision for classroom assessment as a tool for providing feedback and driving instruction as opposed to students completing tasks or earning grades. Mindfulness and motivation, two hallmarks of trauma-responsive and culturally responsive teaching, form the foundation of preparing young brains for optimal learning. In addition, chapters 3 and 4 also relate to the hierarchy's fourth level—the need for esteem in a community.

- Chapter 5 focuses on building a culture of connection and presents research indicating that the ability of teachers to regulate their own emotions is critical to teaching students how to regulate theirs. The power of connection is inherent in mastery-based learning programs. This chapter then addresses how connection can lead to high-level implementation of personalized instructional strategies from *The New Art and Science of Teaching* (Marzano, 2017) that are based on student needs as opposed to teachers creating blanket lesson plans. The chapter also draws from the third level—the need for belonging—from Maslow's (1943) hierarchy of needs.

- Chapter 6 discusses creating a culture of empowerment for teachers and students, and how—specifically—encouraging student voice, choice, and agency, as well as trusting that every learner is held to high expectations, are necessary elements in all three pivot points of the school wellness wheel. This chapter relates to the hierarchy's fifth level—self-actualization.

- Chapter 7 looks at the school wellness wheel from the larger organizational structure perspective and presents ways to address subjects such as school discipline and effective implementation of the school wellness wheel model. This chapter also relates to the hierarchy's sixth level—the desire to connect to something greater than oneself.

All chapters contain vignettes, quotes, examples, and advice from educators who have been actively engaged in the work of transforming their schools into centers of healing and resilience. Also, since the shift to educational models that use the school wellness wheel is a heavy lift that will be very difficult to make happen without focused, strong leadership, each chapter ends with the leadership qualities that are critical to bring the transformation to fruition. Chapters 2–7 have reproducible proficiency scales for assessing your school's mastery level in creating each type of culture, and each scale includes components of all three pivot points.

A final, and important, word on the structure of the book entails the following three pivot points.

1. Mastery-based learning
2. Trauma-responsive schooling
3. Culturally responsive teaching

All the pivot points are equally important to the cultivating of a healing- and resilience-centered school model, but we assert that trauma-responsive schooling and culturally responsive teaching form the foundational level—the true bottom line—that must be sound before the academic excellence piece can be recognized and brought to full fruition. This is similar to the concept from Maslow's (1943) hierarchy of needs in that people must have their most basic needs met in order for them to progress to higher levels of self-actualization. Thus, we will begin each chapter discussing the trauma-responsive schooling and culturally responsive teaching components of the school wellness wheel in order to ultimately reach mastery-based learning and subsequent improved academic growth.

Chapter 1
The School Wellness Wheel

You never change things by fighting the existing reality. To change something, build a new model that makes the existing model obsolete.

—Buckminster Fuller

This chapter introduces the school wellness wheel in greater depth. At its core, the school wellness wheel revolves around the dual concept of healing- and resilience-centered education. Although traditional school models typically place standards and curriculum at the center of their mission, we assert that it is only in building human capacity through healing and resilience that it will be possible for every student to learn at their highest possible level. Fortunately, the same strategies that can heal traumatized brains can build resilience in nontraumatized brains.

The three critical pivot points that empower healing- and resilience-centered education are mastery-based learning, trauma-responsive schooling, and culturally responsive teaching. Although all three pivot points are critical and equally important in the context of a high-functioning healing- and resilience-centered school, we assert that trauma-responsive schooling and culturally responsive teaching form the foundation—the bottom line—for high-level mastery learning to happen for every student. Schools that effectively implement all three pivot points will witness a corresponding increase in the wellness, learning, and college and career readiness of the students they serve.

Explaining the School Wellness Wheel

The concept of sacred hoops runs deep in human history, and there are numerous models that have existed for thousands of years and in many cultures around the world. These circles can take a number of different forms, ranging from artworks made with paint, fiber, wood, or bone to large-scale physical constructions using stones or images carved into the land. For our purposes, we draw your attention to the *medicine wheel*—a circular symbol associated with many Native American tribal cultures representing harmony, connections, symmetry, and the sacred cycles of life. Medicine wheels have been seen as a path to wellness, healing, health, and balance (Waziyatawin & Yellow Bird, 2012). Ultimately, the medicine wheel (figure 1.1) is a sacred place to which people can travel to receive guidance, healing, or instruction. Schools would do well to offer guidance, healing, and instruction in much the same way.

Figure 1.1: Medicine wheel example.

The school wellness wheel, inspired by the medicine wheel, presents a framework to help traditional schools serve, first and foremost, as centers of wellness, healing, health, and balance in order to subsequently help elevate every student to high-level learning. Trying to bring more SEL and resilience into schools is nothing new. But simply adding SEL and resilience training to traditional curricula is largely ineffective in that it simply adds more content and stress to the lives of students and teachers—and rarely results in substantive growth and evolution.

We assert that a dramatic culture shift toward transforming our schools into healing- and resilience-centered academic organizations is the direction schools must focus on and actively pursue. Reconfiguring schools as healing- and resilience-centered organizations is best accomplished through the daily implementation of the three critical, innovative, and interrelated pivot points of mastery-based learning, trauma-responsive schooling, and culturally responsive teaching. It is from this solid foundational perspective that schools will see an increase in student wellness, and student and teacher learning focused around high-level academic objectives. It takes all three.

The school wellness wheel works for all students and adults. Trauma and toxic stress can damage the brain, but properly designed schools can create an environment that can help heal the brain and heal the person. And, in a critically important corollary, the educational practices that can serve to heal the damaged brain and biological systems of traumatized children can also serve to build resilience in the brains of healthy, nontraumatized learners, thus setting all students up for a greater possibility of success as they grow into adulthood.

Simply stated, mastery-based learning, trauma-responsive schooling, and culturally responsive teaching are solid initiatives that are insufficient by themselves to shift the existing educational paradigm. But their combined force in a comprehensive system can form a new model of schooling that is ultimately transformational.

The foundational components of the school wellness wheel are shown in figure 1.2 and introduced in the following sections, where we describe them in greater detail, outlining how they fit into evolving school structures, in subsequent chapters.

School Wellness Wheel

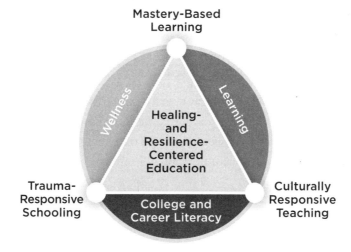

Figure 1.2: The school wellness wheel.

Preparing for College and Career

Ultimately, the job of schools is to prepare every student with the skillset to be successful in life beyond the school building. The outer ring of the school wellness wheel specifically addresses the critical qualities we would expect our teachers to focus on and our students to master once we have helped build healthy and resilient brains. First, the concept of wellness must be addressed in terms of brain, body, and psyche. It is critical in that we should strive to provide every student in our schools with the guidance to heal their brains, build their emotional and mental resilience, and practice the skills that will stand them in good stead for the rest of their lives. It's not enough that we cover some components of wellness in our existing curricula. Wellness speaks to physical and metacognitive skills that must be consistently addressed and practiced in order for students and teachers to be able to draw from them in the future.

Second, the act of learning in humans is a dynamic process that requires the coordination of a variety of complex intellective, physical, and social systems. Thanks to scientific breakthroughs, the internal and external factors that can profoundly impact students' school readiness, learning processes, and academic performance are known. Cognitive capacity—brain power—is physiologically grown through the cellular structures in the brain. Studies have demonstrated that the brain is able to grow virtually an unlimited amount of gray matter in response to our continuous learning (Greenberg, Domitrovich, Weissberg, & Durlak, 2017; Hammond, 2015; Immordino-Yang, Darling-Hammond, & Krone, 2018). Learning and thinking help contribute to the brain's physiological development, growth, and organization. In fact, the wrinkles and folds in a brain contribute to gray matter volume and provide evidence of neuroplasticity following extensive cognitive learning, which speaks to a person's capacity to continually evolve and engage in complex thinking and problem solving (Cantor et al., 2019; Hammond, 2015; Osher et al., 2018).

Finally, ensuring that every student is able to master the critical skills and knowledge to be successful in college or career is the foundational purpose of schools. Rather than plowing through curriculum based on pacing guides, mastery of identified skills and knowledge that can be applied in future settings must be the main focus for students and teachers.

Healing and Showing Resilience

Healing- and resilience-centered education sits at the core of the school wellness wheel (figure 1.2). While it is clear that the impact of trauma and toxic stress can, over time, damage the brain, the question facing the education system is, Are there things we can do to heal the brain and build resilience against future neurological attacks? The goal of the school wellness wheel is to address this question. The answer is elegant and profound: schools can help repair and strengthen neurophysiology.

Everyone faces challenges and hardships. Children and families representing all types of demographics and socioeconomic backgrounds will experience stress. It is simply a fact of life. The critical factor that determines whether or not a child (and family) can successfully move through stress and trauma is resilience. Resilience is the path by which the child navigates a traumatic event or periods of extreme stress, utilizing various protective factors for support and returning to baseline in terms of an emotional and physiologic response to the stressor (Garner & Shonkoff, 2012a). Resilience somewhat buffers the child from the traumatic event, lowering the negative effects. Stated most clearly, we define *resilience* as our ability to cope with stress and adversity, bend but not break, and hopefully bounce back from and even grow through the experience. Resilient people are more likely to do the following (Cornell Health, n.d.).

- Display a sense of purpose and have identified long-term goals for their future

- Successfully manage the challenges of their academic, work, and personal lives

- Navigate challenges, setbacks, and personal issues

- Seek assistance and guidance when necessary

- Understand when to stop, rest, and replenish

- Develop and cultivate appropriate relationships that are positive and mutually respectful

Most importantly, students (and adults) can learn, practice, and strengthen their resilience. Resilience is not a fixed state. Everyone is more or less resilient at different times in their lives. This notion of differential susceptibility speaks to the powerful opportunities that schools have to redirect the life journeys of students whose experiences of stress and adversity have disrupted and dysregulated their capacity for learning and relating to others (Bakermans-Kranenburg & van Ijzendoorn, 2007). The great news is that these students also may be more neurologically pliable and stand to benefit most—in the context of environments rich in support and interventions (Johnson, Riis, & Noble, 2016). Research clearly indicates that the effects of chronic, toxic stress on students can be offset by effective teaching practice, behavior support, and a positive classroom environment, which improve outcomes for students at high risk (Kellam et al., 2011). Thus, schools have the moral responsibility to facilitate healing and build resilience while also ensuring all students master critical academic content.

Healing- and resilience-centered education entails a vast array of attitudes, values, and skills that promote success in school and in life. It is a strength-based approach that supports the development of all students. It begins with the fundamental recognition that education is, at its foundation, an interpersonal endeavor in which knowledge and skills are developed through a series of trusting relationships between teachers and students as well as between students and their peers. It explicitly acknowledges the importance of qualities such as mindset and empathy, as well as skills such as managing emotions, setting and achieving goals, perseverance, and collaboration. It asks educators to consciously consider the experiences our students have encountered—and continue to encounter—while also empowering them to rise above those challenges and create a holistic identity that approaches the world from a place of power rather than victimization. Healing- and resilience-centered schooling recognizes the communal nature of trauma and culture and seeks to create healing and resilience through relationship and educational action.

Early experiences have a significant, enduring impact on development. Yet even if a child's early experiences are poor, cultivating relationally rich contexts at any point in a student's life can optimize development and may serve as a preventive buffer to negative outcomes (Saeri, Cruwys, Barlow, Stronge, & Sibley, 2018; Sege et al., 2017). Thus, teachers and school professionals have an incredible opportunity to impact the lives of their students and families to help increase protective factors and strengthen resilience.

Healing- and resilience-centered schools can become a sanctuary in which healing can safely occur and resilience can be built simply because the safety and well-being of everyone involved—including the adults—is valued and ensured. We assert that schools reaching this level of trauma-informed and culturally responsive care can become recognized as healing- and resilience-centered institutions. When trauma-informed and culturally responsive principles are applied rigorously in every encounter with students and families, schools can change lives for the better.

Mastery-Based Learning

Mastery-based learning is the first of the critical pivot points and sits at the pinnacle of the school wellness wheel. A crucial element of the healing- and resilience-centered approach is that the purpose of school is not to focus on the trauma in a student's life to the detriment of high academic standards. Our students must not be defined by their trauma or struggles. Schools must effectively address student trauma and cultural needs so that they are able to learn and achieve at high levels. Thus, demonstrated mastery of critical skills and knowledge is a nonnegotiable expectation that schools must embrace if our learners are to be successful in their future lives.

As stated earlier, simply implementing trauma-informed principles and culturally responsive teaching in traditional school systems does not empower students to reach their full potential. It is only in a mastery-based system that personalized education can be truly brought to fruition.

In his often-cited article "Learning for Mastery," educational researcher Benjamin Bloom (1968) spoke to the potential power of personalized schooling when he expressed the view that, with the right interventions, 95 percent of students "can learn a subject up to a high level of mastery" (p. 4). This assertion flies in the face of many established educational paradigms that rely on such statistical formulas as the bell curve to explain variations in student growth. Bloom was a leading proponent of mastery learning, which entails a shift in mindset away from what teachers teach to what students learn. It is also a shift away from requiring teachers to teach and assess all standards to one that ensures each student demonstrates knowledge of specific high-priority learning goals. In the best-case scenario, teachers are empowered to personalize the learning experience so that every learner can grasp and understand the critical material and content in ways that are personally relevant and challenging within their individualized time frame.

Conceptually, mastery-based learning is a general approach to education that is also commonly referred to in the literature as some variation of *standards-based grading, personalized schooling, personal mastery, performance-based schooling,* and *personalized competency-based education.* For the purposes of this book, we employ the term *mastery-based learning* to draw directly from the original work of Bloom (1954) as well as to constantly stress the importance of *learning* among adults and students.

Educational programs based on mastery-based learning concepts shift the focus of schooling from that of a teacher-centered, time-based instructional protocol to a model designed around meeting every student's individual needs. Largely through the effective use of clearly articulated learning goals, proficiency scales, and high-quality assessments, students are able to proceed through the system based on their own needs and abilities, and acceleration is possible. Research has indicated that schools with instructional and curricular designs to support mastery-based learning often witness increased student engagement and teacher academic optimism, where teachers feel empowered, appreciated, and trusted by students and parents (Ruyle, 2019). Furthermore, schools that also consciously foster learning environments to integrate affective, cognitive, social, and emotional processes with curricular content can serve to accelerate the developmental growth of students (Hammond, 2015).

Through our experience and research, we assert that successful mastery-based schools see higher levels of student engagement, teacher academic optimism, and skillful, direct leadership as a result of their core philosophy and structure. Thus, mastery-based learning programs are well positioned to specifically address protective factors which can provide students with specific tools and practices to improve their attention, engagement, stress levels, and ability to control their emotions and behaviors.

Trauma-Responsive Schooling

Trauma-responsive schooling is the second of the critical pivot points and is a foundational component of the school wellness wheel. A deep understanding of important factors that impact learning and the brain is critical for all school professionals to embrace if our students are to be able to reach their highest level of academic success.

Due to a wealth of research in various fields, we now have more advanced knowledge regarding how the brain works and how humans learn. We also have become more aware of the prevalence of the exposure to trauma among youth (Finkelhor, Shattuck, Turner, & Hamby, 2013), along with the corrosive effects that chronic exposure to trauma can have on human physical, psychological, and social systems (Hamoudi, Murray, Sorensen, & Fontaine, 2015). For example, approximately two out of every three school-aged children are likely to have experienced at least one traumatic event by the age of seventeen (Perfect, Turley, Carlson, Yohannan, & Gilles, 2016). Those same researchers analyzed eighty-three studies which point to the widespread impact of toxic stress on the cognitive, academic, and social-emotional behaviors of students. Michelle Porche, Darce Costello, and Myra Rosen-Reynoso (2016) interviewed 66,000 young people in a national study and identified similar results. The impact of trauma and toxic stress is profound and prevalent, crosses all ethnic, social, economic, and gender lines, and can manifest in a number of ways.

People are different; they learn and respond to stimuli differently. How people react to life's stressors is affected by such factors as genetics and life experiences. Strong stress reactions can also be traced to traumatic events. Traumatized students can be particularly vulnerable to stress, as are adults who have experienced war, displacement, extreme poverty, or violence, or who are military personnel, police officers, and emergency first-responders. Overactive or underactive stress responses may stem from slight differences in the genes that control the stress response (Bloom & Farragher, 2013; Cole, Eisner, Gregory, & Ristuccia, 2013; R. Macy, personal communication, April, 2018).

The good news is that we know what works to address children's exposure to trauma and stress. Doctors Roger D. Fallot and Maxine Harris (2008, 2011) summarize the foundation of trauma-informed care in the following ten core values. Those values should guide every agency that provides social services (Fallot & Harris, 2008, 2011).

I.   Ensuring safety

2.   Encouraging choice

3.   Modeling trustworthiness

4.   Building resilience

5.   Empowering with knowledge and skills

6.   Fostering collaboration

7.   Sharing information transparently

8.   Cultivating inclusivity

9.   Developing a support network

10. Promoting nonviolence

Proponents of trauma-informed care in schools have mainly focused their efforts on changing our classroom management and disciplinary responses to a more compassionate and understanding approach. However, schools can utilize what we know about the impact of trauma on youth in many additional, powerful ways, including altering the structure, pedagogy, and content of our academic instruction. We can adapt these to not only help youth with trauma histories succeed academically, but also to help them heal some of the neurophysiological impacts of trauma themselves. It is critical that this happen in the school setting—beyond the scope of mental health services—because school is the environment in which students find themselves for most of the day and because the neurophysiological effects of trauma impact behavior and learning. Our educational system needs broad, coordinated steps that address the impact of early adversity on health and development.

Just as medical professionals can provide treatment for germs and viruses, education professionals can provide treatment for the exposure to trauma and toxic stress. Evidence-based interventions, provided effectively and in a timely manner, can dramatically reduce the adverse impacts of physical and psychological trauma, put students back on a healthy developmental course, and provide them with a number of skills that allow them to engage in high-level academic and social connections that can help them move toward a healthier, more fulfilling life (Berkowitz et al., 2016; R. Macy, personal communication, May 2018).

Specific to education, Substance Abuse and Mental Health Services Administration (SAMHSA; 2014) identified four critical components for trauma-informed schools that include the following.

1.   Realizing the impact of trauma

2.   Recognizing the signs of trauma exposure

3. Responding with effective practices

4. Resisting retraumatizing students

When specific treatment protocols are implemented in schools, the positive impact on traumatic stress reactions is compelling. This has been reinforced via federal legislation through the reauthorization of the federal Every Student Succeeds Act (Pub. L. 114-95), which established provisions for trauma-informed school approaches that call for increased professional development for staff so as to better support student growth (Prewitt, 2016; Rolfsnes & Idsoe, 2011).

Culturally Responsive Teaching

Trauma-responsive schooling, although powerful in its own right, is incomplete without culturally informed schooling—a relevant education protocol that can help support the healing of generational trauma. When students feel silenced or undervalued, they can suffer from poor learning outcomes. In these cases, student academic success often comes at the expense of minority students' psychosocial well-being, as they are forced to assimilate into mainstream culture (Darling-Hammond, 2007). In other words, academic growth without cultural competency often results in students being marginalized from their culture of origin (Ladson-Billings, 1995). However, policies that support bilingual education and cultural competence can support students' self-determination and help them gain access to the *culture of power* (Delpit, 1993)—that majority people hold power and make unwritten and mostly unacknowledged rules—without harming their personal and cultural identities. Thus, culturally responsive teaching is the third critical pivot point and foundational component of the school wellness wheel.

It is critical that educators understand the profound, undeniable interplay between race (culture) and trauma, as well as its effects on students. A combination of cultural competence and responsiveness allows teachers to actually become culturally proficient—proficient being *what you do* and *how you do it*, as compared to competence being *what you know* (Lindsay & Lindsay, 2020).

Hammond (2015) divided culturally responsive teaching into three functional dimensions.

1. The **institutional dimension** includes the need to review school policies, procedures, and structures in terms of things such as funding and community involvement in order to address culturally responsive mindsets.

2. The **personal dimension** includes how teachers are effectively educated about and grow their capacity to become culturally responsive.

3. The **instructional dimension** includes the challenges and practices that occur while implementing classroom cultural responsiveness.

All of these dimensions require that we identify and overcome the barriers that maintain the status quo. Grasping the important role of cultural factors that impact learning and the brain is critical for all school professionals. According to Randall and Delores Lindsay (2020), the following are some barriers to cultural competency and responsiveness.

- Resistance to change
- Systemic oppression
- Unawareness of need to adapt
- A sense of entitlement

Many American educators were raised in a system that has indoctrinated them to assume that personal success comes simply as a result of hard work and great character. They often view cultural difference as something that the minority group should work to overcome and believe that people need to adapt to fit the needs of the organizations. Thus, resistance to change happens as a common result of an unawareness of the need to adapt and sometimes people do not recognize the need to make personal and organizational changes in response to the people with whom they interact. Systemic oppression is tied up in the concept of privilege and speaks to societal issues that impact people based on their inherent membership in distinct cultural groups. This privilege can sometimes make people blind to the barriers experienced by people who are different from them.

As a result, cultural proficiency entails a paradigm shift in their thinking. Cultural proficiency is a mindset, and when educators learn it, they typically tend to embrace it as a de facto way to interact with people who are different from them. Educators' work is to recognize how they might contribute to these barriers and repair the harm in their daily practice.

The connection between culture and resilience is profound, and we now have a solid base of research focused on the concept of cultural resilience that speaks to the important role culture can play as a resource for building resilience in people. Cultural resilience can be defined as possessing a sense of belonging to one's culture and community, and it is positively correlated to improved mental health functioning in that it can serve as one protective factor against psychological health issues (Fleming & Ledogar, 2008; Terry, Townley, Brusilovskiy, & Salzar, 2019). For example, in a study of Native American youth, Amy Bergstrom, Linda Miller Cleary, and Thomas D. Peacock (2003) asserted that the highest-achieving students were those who were actively connected to various cultural activities and who cultivated strong positive feelings of belonging to their Native communities. The researchers attributed this student success to the powerful impact of community and pointed to culture as a strong protective factor in their emotional and cognitive development.

Culturally responsive teaching is, specifically, a multipronged methodology that is about teaching students how to learn. It comprises cultural awareness, information processing, learning partnerships with students, and supportive learning environments (Hammond, 2015). Culturally responsive teaching is not simply an engagement strategy designed to motivate historically disenfranchised students, nor is it a way to make race-based connections to content so that it becomes relevant to minority students. At its core, culturally responsive teaching is based in brain research and is about connecting to students' cultural learning styles (Hammond, 2015). For example, many students come from diverse cultural traditions such as African American, Native American, Latino, Southeast Asian, and Pacific Islander communities, which historically have strong oral cultures. These communities have traditionally used verbal communication as a way of making meaning and facilitating knowledge transfer. In the learning research, we know that storytelling is a natural way to access the brain's memory systems and enhance people's ability for turning inert information into useable knowledge (Marzano, 2017; Marzano, Scott, et al., 2017). Thus, teachers should be adept at using an array of oral strategies and understand how it is be a more natural way for some students to learn new content. This just makes sense.

When done well, culturally responsive teaching can be powerful in helping students improve their learning. It results in improving instruction and can help students of color or other historically disenfranchised groups become better learners. It specifically addresses learners who have often been deprived of high-quality schooling due to structural inequities in an education system. Specifically, culturally responsive teaching supports the use of students' prior knowledge, drawing from their cultural background and experiences as a means to make connections between what they know and what they need to learn. These prior connections make the learning process easier and thus favorably supports the attainment of new information. It also encourages the teacher to become culturally competent as a way to tap into learning modalities that are most in alignment with how the student learns. Neuroscience research shows that culture drives how the brain processes information (Hammond, 2015). Therefore, it is crucial that the teacher understands the unique cultural experiences each student brings.

Conclusion

Trauma and resilience theory is on the verge of transforming schools and the science of learning. As we continue to grapple with and understand emerging educational paradigms, we must more deeply consider how we can possibly create a better, personalized experience for all students. Educators have the unprecedented opportunity to understand and positively impact students' lives in a way that can have a dramatic influence on the rest of their experience. This is the mission of schools.

This is especially true in light of the fact that schools, communities, and government agencies continue to debate over such issues as funding, graduation rates, and teacher quality while refusing to recognize and acknowledge the gaping hole that lies directly in front of them: it doesn't matter whether the funding, the quality of the school building, the academic programs utilized, or the innovation of the teachers is adequate if the students are unable to efficiently engage in the learning process as they struggle with non-school factors such as poverty, trauma, toxic stress, inequity, and other associated burdens. Trauma and stress are personal. Culture is personal. Inequity is personal. But our traditional school system continues to stress the value of standardization and relies on outdated notions about human brain development and how people learn. Thus, the urgent call for real, substantive evolution in schools remains a moral and economic imperative. We need to ensure a more effective system in which teachers and students can thrive as opposed to simply maintaining the status quo.

For so long, the focus of schools has been on curriculum, assessment, and instruction. We assert that it is the critical time to move toward a focus on high-level learning for all, and this will only happen with a shift of paradigm to healing- and resilience-centered education that allows educators to focus their energies on the brain, the body, and the overall wellness of the students in their schools. This is the only way in which skills and content can be effectively learned. It is an issue of social justice, and we owe it to all our students to create a better system that is designed to meet their individual needs and abilities rather than simply continue tweaking the existing model. The school wellness wheel reflects the convergence of research across multiple fields and lines of inquiry. It presents the opportunity to better align existing knowledge and to build new knowledge about how students learn and develop.

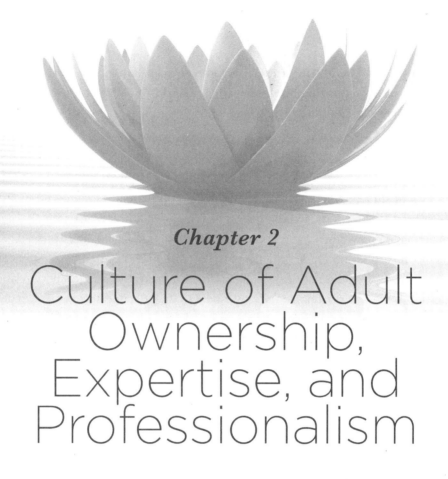

Chapter 2

Culture of Adult Ownership, Expertise, and Professionalism

In a time of drastic change, it is the learners who inherit the future. The learned usually find themselves equipped to live in a world that no longer exists.

—Eric Hoffer

The most critical assertion we present in this book is that schools will not evolve unless the adults in the building are able to transform themselves internally. Very simply, transformational growth in educational organizations all starts—first and foremost—with the grown-ups. We strongly suggest that deeply evolving schools into the future requires the successful implementation of the school wellness wheel, and this implementation requires a two-fold philosophical shift on the part of the adults in schools. First, educators must commit to a new belief system in which schools exist to provide every student with the best possible opportunities to learn and achieve at their greatest capacity—it's about the student learning more than about the adult teaching. Second, those same educators must also believe in building an enhanced, learning-focused educational platform and commit to a new level of continuous professional growth so that they can provide the conditions and expertise to make it all happen. It's about embracing a more current, relevant model of learning, under-standing critical factors that impact learning, and delving deeper into various cul-tural components that influence how and where learning takes place.

The move from a content-driven, time-based, teacher-focused system to a truly student-centered model focused on the specific needs of each learner being served is massive and profound. Transformation at this level happens as a direct result of a paradigm shift in which the adult stakeholders are able to create and nurture new cultures that form the foundation of the school—cultures of learning, mastery, connection, empowerment, and humanity. They are no longer simply purveyors of content who assess and grade students based on assignments, attendance, and com-pliance. As such, the most critical element is for administrators and teachers to study, understand, grow, and embrace the new model so that all educators become experts in the learning process and become adept in addressing the dramatic impact that trauma, stress, and culture can have on the brain.

Teachers' educational training, professional development, and instructional prac-tice often continue to focus primarily on delivering a state-approved curriculum *at* students as opposed to responding to individual students' educational needs. In fact, in our experience, many educators have openly stated their belief that school is not the appropriate place to address mental health care. We have heard the assertion that mental health care is not in a teacher's job description and that educators are not trained in the vastly technical fields of psychology, medicine, epigenetics, or neurol-ogy. Indeed, traditional paradigms and mindsets are exceedingly difficult to change. But although becoming knowledgeable in mental, physical, and neurological health to facilitate learning and growth is a heavy lift, it is the right work that teachers must embrace if they are to help ensure high-level learning opportunities for all students.

This chapter will provide an overview of how all educators must necessarily become fluent in the language of mastery-based schooling. They also must deepen their own understanding regarding how complex trauma, ACEs, and cultural com-ponents impact the brain's anatomy and functioning and other body systems, and how these effects manifest themselves in students in terms of learning, affect, behav-ior, and relationships. Thus, this chapter relates specifically to the bottom three levels of Maslow's (1943) hierarchy: (1) physiological, (2) safety, and (3) belonging needs. The chapter also focuses on the changes that must take place in the hearts and minds of the adults in the school building, as well as the continued professional growth and a deep grasp of the three pivot points of mastery-based learning, trau-ma-competent principles, and culturally responsive teaching in order to fully imple-ment the school wellness wheel. Finally, you can assess your school's efforts toward this change by using the "Culture of Ownership Proficiency Scale" (page 61).

Understanding Why New Initiatives Rarely Transform School Systems

Since the standards movement started in the early 1990s, tremendous legislative energy along with billions of dollars have been spent with the admirable goal of updating and transforming education, creating a common core curriculum that would result in more equitable schooling, and ensuring that more students would be successfully prepared to contribute to a rapidly changing world. These investments, however, have largely resulted in only incremental change rather than in systemic innovation and sustainable growth.

As stated earlier, we now clearly understand the profound power of combining knowledge from a variety of human disciplines such as education, medicine, psychology, and epigenetics—and teachers are required to regularly undergo mandatory professional development over the course of the school year. The pressing question, therefore, is, Why hasn't the assimilation of critical research from these fields happened in a way in which teachers could learn how to fully integrate it into their regular instructional practice? Why do powerful innovations so often fail to take hold in schools? What would keep educators from adopting the change that would create the necessary healing- and resilience-centered schools? There are a number of reasons for this phenomenon.

- Teacher resistance to change
- Difficulty imagining an alternative
- Lack of funding
- Small return on investment
- Educational inertia and initiative fatigue

Teacher Resistance to Change

First, based on our combined experience, when educational change or reform is presented to traditional teaching faculties, people tend to infer the message that they must have been doing things incorrectly in previous times. Although nothing could be further from the truth, there is a natural professional pushback to innovation based on this perception. Social scientists Carol Tavris and Elliot Aronson (2007) addressed this phenomenon when they made the point that the human brain is psychologically constructed to make us believe we are always right—even when directly confronted with overwhelming evidence to the contrary. Old habits die hard. Thus, in terms of new initiatives, many teachers are more apt to change the reform efforts to fit in their current teaching reality rather than to personally make changes that are necessary to alter the existing paradigm.

In addition, education researchers Gene E. Hall and Shirley M. Hord (2011) claimed that shifting a school's culture and traditional practices can actually result in a profound sense of loss and grief among teachers, which may be mistakenly perceived as resistance to change. Furthermore, Robert Macy, the president of the International Trauma Center, asserted that there is a physiological component to this resistance: when people feel fearful, challenged, or threatened, their brains shift into fight, flight, freeze, or fawn (acting helpless; Walker, 2013) mode; once that happens, rational thought and personal reflection shut down, and people tend to react emotionally rather than reflect using calm, reasoned thinking (R. Macy, personal communication, April, 2018). Simply stated, the cognitive energy to bring substantive change is immense, and asking teachers to fully participate and effectively change how they do things in their classrooms without time, support, regular guidance, resources, and feedback is unrealistic.

Difficulty Imagining an Alternative

Another reality is that educators have no true frame of reference for what their schools and classrooms can look like other than what school looked like for them both as students and as teachers. We all only know what we know, and the cognitive energy required for substantive growth and functional change is immense, difficult to harness, and uncomfortable to experience. Our brains are innately drawn to patterns and routines, and the confirmation bias—our powerful tendency to look for things we already believe to reinforce our existing mental models—often forces us to remain inside the box of conventional thinking. As a result, educators typically end up trying to reform new initiatives—to manipulate them to fit their current practice and perspective—as opposed to evolving their practice and mindset to fully implement the new innovation (Ruyle, 2019).

Lack of Funding

On a more practical level, schools, as a rule, rarely have the funding to allow for the consistent, focused professional learning required to take an initiative and bring it to fruition in real-life classrooms. Teachers are often presented with vast amounts of information in professional development training over the course of their careers, but are simply not provided with the corresponding time, resources, guidance, and opportunities for feedback from deliberate practice to learn new skills at a high level.

The consequences of this reality can be profound. As an example, the concept of *least restrictive environment* (LRE) has been federally mandated since the Education for All Handicapped Children Act of 1975 (P.L. 94-142), which stated as a foundational practice in schools that children with disabilities be educated to the maximum extent appropriate with students without disabilities. After numerous amendments and reauthorizations of the original act, known as Individuals With Disabilities Education Act (IDEA, 2004), the requirements for educating students with disabilities in the least restrictive environment is even more complex, yet remains a woefully underfunded mandate forty-six years later.

Thus, in spite of decades of legal requirements and professional training, LRE typically remains bound up within the concept of *proximity* in that students with disabilities are simply placed in the same physical space as their peers from the general population. Furthermore, according to the National Center for Learning Disabilities (2019), fifty years after implementing special education law in schools, teachers' perceptions lag behind current thinking.

- Only 17 percent of teachers who are not specifically trained to do so feel very well prepared to teach students with mild to moderate disabilities.

- Less than 40 percent believe Individualized Education Plans (IEPs) help them to be better teachers.

- One in three teachers attribute learning and attention issues to laziness.

- One in four educators believe attention deficit hyperactivity disorder (ADHD) is the outcome of poor parenting.

Although decades of research estimated that up to 90 percent of students with disabilities are capable of performing at grade level given the right supports (Bloom, 1968, 1977; Guskey, 2007), nationwide, just 20 percent score proficient on state mathematics and reading assessments. In 2017, the four-year graduation rate for students in special education was 67 percent, versus the overall rate of 85 percent (National Center for Education Statistics, n.d.). School funding has been and will continue to be a political conflict.

Small Return on Investment

The fourth reason school initiatives often fail to take hold focuses on John Hattie's (2009) point that although virtually every educational intervention can have a positive effect on learning, the impact is usually mediocre, and the costs are high. He asserts that unless an intervention has an effect size of at least 0.4 or greater (the average expected growth effect size for one year of progress in school, based on over 140,000 effects Hattie has studied), it is too ineffective to base decision and investments on it.

Hattie (2015a) refers to the myriad of initiatives and popular ideas regularly implemented in schools as the *politics of distraction*. He describes the following five typical distractions as techniques typically embraced by people in school systems that may, on the surface, seem to speak to real problems but ultimately are superficial and serve to distract everyone from the substantive issues.

1. Doing things to appease the parents

2. Doing things to fix the infrastructure

3. Doing things to fix the student

4. Doing things to fix the school

5. Doing things to fix the teachers

These five distractors are often eagerly adopted by various stakeholders in an educational system, but an overemphasis on these reform approaches creates a real distraction from other, more effective ways to improve education.

As Hattie (2015a) clearly points out, traditional approaches to school reform typically focus on merely tweaking existing models and rarely address the larger issue of substantive change and growth. Two examples are particularly relevant here. First, although millions of dollars were spent during the implementation of No Child Left Behind (NCLB; 2002) as the accepted model of school improvement, the achievement gap between majority White and majority Native American schools did not get smaller but actually grew larger, as the methods for improvement merely focused on superficial issues (National Center for Education Statistics, 2012). As a second example, there has been a vast amount of research and a huge push to change the traditional, antiquated A–F grading system that is commonly employed in schools across the world (Guskey, 2010, 2011; Marzano, 2000, 2006). However, there is minimal concrete evidence that shifting to a different model of assigning grades such as standards-based grading has resulted in helping schools evolve to a more contemporary model of education. Usually, schools and districts spend huge amounts of funding in discussing a transition in grading practice, yet the overall school experience for students remains largely unchanged. Simply altering the grading system is not the answer. Distractions such as these lead us to focus on the wrong things.

Educational Inertia and Initiative Fatigue

Based on our combined experience as teachers, administrators, and consultants, we posit that the dual concepts of educational inertia and initiative fatigue also cause initiatives to fail. Robert J. Marzano (personal communication, March, 2018) has stated that schools or districts typically add between four and seven new initiatives every year. School professionals can feel frustrated by this constant attempt to find the silver bullet in education and can easily adopt a *this too shall pass* mantra that is common among teachers.

It's important for leaders to understand that these challenging reactions are completely normal. Clearly, for leaders evolving their schools, the personal interaction involved with educational organizations and cultures is an important component to consider. Many teachers may initially resist the change needed to successfully implement innovative educational models and foster new cultures (Fullan, 2007; Murphy, 2016). This is especially true for those teachers who have experienced a multitude of new initiatives and reform efforts throughout their careers, only to bear witness to the initiative's subsequent failure.

Teachers' attitudes toward a proposed reform are crucial for its success. The vast majority of educators willingly accept that schools need to grow and evolve, but some may be averse to changing their own teaching practices; some may doubt they will receive support and commitment from administrators; and others simply may not know how to implement the changes in their daily work. Most teachers also have a limited frame of reference, knowing only the traditional Industrial Age model of schools. Leaders' transparency is crucial when addressing teachers' natural resistance to change; it is important to be clear about the purpose for the change and the expectations for teachers' roles and responsibilities (Fullan, 2008). Offer staff and stakeholders opportunities to build their knowledge and skills, hire people who have potential to enact the desired change, and ensure that leaders personally involve themselves in evaluating each teacher or principal's progress (Fullan, 2008). This is why it is so critical to begin implementing a healing and resilience-based school by starting with the healing and resilience of the adults.

Embracing Mastery-Based Learning

The following sections define mastery-based learning, present the research and science behind it, and reveal why this is important. Adopting a mastery-based approach to learning provides schools with the framework for delivering rigorous, high-quality instruction while addressing students' diverse experiences and empowering them to operate according to their unique strengths, interests, and needs. Mastery-based learning can, in itself, be trauma informed and culturally responsive.

Definition of Mastery-Based Learning

Various definitions of personalized learning and mastery-based schooling exist in K–12 education (Getting Smart, 2018; KnowledgeWorks, 2016; Patrick, Kennedy, & Powell, 2013; RAND Corporation, 2015; U.S. Department of Education, n.d.). Many tend to incorporate the concept of competency into personalized learning. For the purposes of this book, we employ the term *mastery-based learning* and use it synonymously with personalized, competency-based education as well as standards-based learning. We define mastery-based learning by utilizing the updated, revised definition of personalized competency-based education (PCBE) as presented by the Aurora Institute's Eliot Levine and Susan Patrick (2019, p. 3), as follows:

1. Students are empowered daily to make important decisions about their learning experiences, how they will create and apply knowledge, and how they will demonstrate their learning.

2. Assessment is a meaningful, positive, and empowering learning experience for students that yields timely, relevant, and actionable evidence.

3. Students receive timely, differentiated support based on their individual learning needs.

4. Students progress [through the curriculum] based on evidence of mastery, not seat time.

5. Students learn actively using different pathways and varied pacing.

6. Strategies to ensure equity for all students are embedded in the culture, structure, and pedagogy of schools and education systems.

7. Rigorous, common expectations for learning (knowledge, skills, and dispositions) are explicit, transparent, measurable, and transferable.

From another perspective, educational pioneer Richard DeLorenzo created the digital personal-proficiency system (DPPS), which provides an additional visual of what mastery-based learning looks like and asserts that the model has had excellent results when deployed with fidelity. Some critical elements of DPPS are displayed in table 2.1 (R. DeLorenzo, personal communication, June 2021).

Although mastery-based learning theory has evolved and a number of educational reformers—Bloom (1968, 1971, 1977), Dewey (1916, 1938), Tom Guskey (1997, 2007, 2008, 2010), Hattie (2009, 2015b), Marzano (2017), and Marzano, Warrick, and Simms (2014)—have endorsed it, mainstream schools have not yet fully embraced it. However, brain science not only supports evolving toward a mastery-based model of schooling, but this is also an issue of social justice that cannot be ignored. Equity authors Sonia Caus Gleason and Nancy Gerzon (2013) made the case that effectively implementing schoolwide personalized learning addresses each student's needs and is, therefore, essential to the pursuit of greater educational equity. Furthermore, mastery-based learning actually gives learners an advantage over students who have endured the traditional system, as authentic learning and increased student growth is a subsequent, inherent result of increased engagement (Hattie, 2015b).

Table 2.1: Digital Personal-Proficiency System

Traditional System	Digital Personal-Proficiency System	Benefit of a Digital Personal-Proficiency System
Student Role		
• Students sit and get. • Students are primarily passive, compliant learners who frequently try to game the system to get passing marks or a high GPA.	• Because of shared beliefs and agreed learning expectations, students are able to navigate their own learning. • Students are placed in their zone of proximal development (ZPD), or where they have the most success (Vygotsky, 1978). • Students' roadmaps provide individual learning trajectories.	• Student engagement increases by allowing more voice and choice in their learning. • Students can learn anywhere, anyplace, any time. • This approach prepares students for the global economy by accelerating their learning especially with 21st century skills.
Teacher Role		
• Teachers instruct to the middle of the class through whole-group instruction (common to nearly all classes in the U.S.).	• The teacher's role changes from a traditional one to that of a facilitator. • Teachers become very agile in their approach and constantly adjust their strategies to meet the needs of every child (through, for example, whole-group, small-group, or individual instruction).	• Teachers begin to understand the art and science of their profession by allowing students to partner with them. • In this new learning environment, teachers are learners together with students about how to meet students' needs.
Grading		
• A–F scoring is based on arbitrary criteria. For example: final quarter grades may be based on various combinations of participation, attendance, and test scores.	• Grading is based on mastering individual standards. • "A, B, or try again" is the scoring approach. Students have multiple opportunities to achieve and improve their grades. • Minimum grade point average for graduation is 3.0.	• Creates transparent and consistent expectations across classrooms so that students, parents, teachers, and administrators know expectations. • Reliability and validity of this system dramatically increases.

continued →

Traditional System	Digital Personal-Proficiency System	Benefit of a Digital Personal-Proficiency System
Curriculum and Assessments		
• Students have traditional core subjects plus some electives. • Rigor rarely goes beyond students' recalling information. • Classes are mostly textbook driven with paper-and-pencil testing.	• Reprioritization of what students need for their future. In addition to core traditional subjects, there is a stronger emphasis on embedding 21st century skills. • Performance tasks and projects are driven by clear rubrics.	• Students create multidisciplinary projects that solve real-world problems, thus increasing student engagement and better preparing them for their future.
Instruction		
• A one-size-fits-all approach is taken. • Students move on even if they are not ready for next steps. • Whole-group instruction dominates the delivery system. • Prescribed programs and textbooks drive instruction.	• Instruction is balanced. (Students must first understand then apply in real-life situations whenever possible.) • Instruction is differentiated, thus meeting individual students at the point of their needs and interests.	• All students' needs are met, resulting in more efficient and effective learning. • There is a natural increase in equity. • Instruction is not just about learning the skills but applying them in a meaningful way, thereby increasing student engagement.

Source: Adapted from R. DeLorenzo, personal communication, June 2021.

Research and Science

Mastery-based learning is linked to a vast and robust pedagogical research base (Bloom, 1968, 1971; DeLorenzo et al., 2009; Dewey, 1916, 1938; Guskey, 1997, 2007, 2008, 2010; Hattie, 2009, 2015b; Marzano, 2017; Ruyle, 2019). Beyond the education field, however, mastery-based schooling finds a foundational footing in the science of individuality, which recognizes that individuals vary in how they develop, grow, and learn. From the spread of disease to how people respond to different stimuli to the evolution of literacy to the developmental impact of adversity, research grounded in the science of individuality allows us to think beyond traditional structures and examine personal differences across a variety of domains, such as medicine, genetics, psychology, and education (Cantor et al., 2019).

A critical assertion of the science of individuality as it applies specifically to education is that there is no single developmental pathway for everyone. Rather, there are multiple pathways to personal evolution and there are patterns that can be discerned within that variability. For example, effective instructional design is grounded in an understanding of the differing ways in which novice and more advanced students learn. Novice learners require factual knowledge and explicit guidance, whereas more advanced or expert learners benefit from the increased engagement engendered by applying factual knowledge in a more realistic setting or using foundational information to create solutions to real-world problems. As such, effective designs are best started by identifying clear learning goals aligned with learning progressions and, ultimately, engaging in high-level, complex tasks. Collectively, the mastery-based learning approach can strengthen our ability to understand variation in students and their individual developmental pathways toward mastery learning (Cantor et al., 2019; Fischer & Bidell, 2006; Hammond, 2015; Marzano, Scott, Boogren, & Newcomb, 2017).

What is becoming crystal clear in the research literature across various fields is that it is impossible to separate trauma, stress, and personal culture from the learning experience. Our understanding of how early environmental influences and genetic factors affect the way children learn and adapt, with lifelong effects on their physical and mental health and adult productivity, has been greatly expanded by advances in biology, social sciences, and behavioral sciences. Schools are thus faced with the question of how to change the way education is delivered so that students and families facing these long-lasting, complex threats to health and development have their needs addressed (Garner & Shonkoff, 2012b; Harris, 2018; Immordino-Yang et al., 2018).

There is great hope for positive results and empowering all learners through shifting to a healing- and resilience-centered model of education. Albert Bandura's (1993, 1997) work on the concept of self-efficacy, which refers to an individual's belief that he or she possesses the abilities to control one's own life, has had a profound effect on learners. In addition, research over subsequent decades expanded the concept of self-efficacy by addressing the critical need to personalize the educational experience by differentiating instructional strategies based on individual needs (Martin, 2012; Martin & Liem, 2010, 2011; Schenck, 2011). Ronald F. Ferguson (2015) redefined the concept of self-efficacy in learners as *student agency*, which he identifies as "the capacity and propensity to take purposeful initiative—the opposite of helplessness" (p. 1). Ferguson (2015) declared, "The development of agency may be as important an outcome of schooling as the skills we measure with standardized testing" (p. 1).

The Importance of Mastery-Based Learning

In traditional school settings, students endure typical instructional practices that consist of organizing curricular content into units. They then respond to teacher direction, submit assignments required of their coursework, and have their knowledge assessed at the conclusion of each unit or chapter of a textbook. In a content- and task-centered system, learners are usually graded largely on their compliance as well as their ability to follow teacher direction and complete tasks. This commonly results in a passive learning environment in which students often take little ownership of their own education.

In many contemporary organizations, however, we are witnessing a transformation from bureaucratic to participatory styles of interaction. For example, Google uses a business model that encourages employees to share responsibility for the management of the company. They have found that the model allows for teams to self-organize and make decisions and also provides more opportunities for learning and growth. This has also fostered a culture of shared leadership that has proven to be empowering to employees and has led to massive profits for the company (Schwantes, 2016). In schools, the Wallace Foundation (2007, 2009, 2013) has conducted a number of research studies focused on what leads to the highest level of student growth. They have concluded that students learn to their utmost potential—and that teachers operate at their best—when school leaders cultivate a cooperative spirit among staff and actively share leadership so that teachers and other adults assume increased roles in realizing the school vision. They assert that teacher voice and shared ownership for professional learning are the two critical features of a highly functioning educational environment (Wallace Foundation, 2013).

Likewise, educational programs based on mastery-based learning shift the focus of schooling from a teacher-centered, time-based instructional protocol to a model designed around meeting the individual needs of every learner. Students proceed through the system based on their own needs and abilities, and acceleration is possible and encouraged. Student voice and shared ownership for learning are the two critical features of a highly functioning mastery-based learning environment. The model is designed to ensure students master required content regardless of the time constraints common in the more traditional school model, and learners cannot simply get by each year with very little academic knowledge and low-level skills (DeLorenzo et al., 2009). The system is effective because it is a profoundly student-centered approach that provides a path for individual growth toward mastery of a clearly identified set of skills and content knowledge.

Evolving from teacher-centered to student-centered, mastery-based classrooms means moving from perceiving schooling as a system in which one teacher provides information to many students toward a system where all students can access many information resources, only one of which is the teacher. This paradigm shift can accurately be characterized as transitioning from an emphasis on *instruction* to a laser-like focus on *learning*. A teacher's job is not to teach students; a teacher's job is to *help students learn*. This distinction is subtle, yet massive in that it shifts the power paradigm in the teacher-student relationship and is the fundamental concept behind personalized competency-based education.

Empowering student agency and elevating student voice in the model means placing young people at the center of their own education by actively involving them in educational decisions and treating them as equal stakeholders. When done well, the benefits for students and teachers alike can be enormous: students are more invested in their education, teachers are more engaged personally with their students and happier in their jobs, and schools are more successful in creating programs and policies that motivate students and put them on a path to success (Ruyle, 2019).

Tapping Into Trauma-Responsive Schooling

Just as teachers must actively strive to increase their knowledge in the area of mastery-based education principles, it is equally important that they understand the factors that can either enhance or inhibit a student's learning—trauma and toxic stress, for example. Hence, the understanding of trauma-responsive schooling strategies form a foundational pivot point of the wellness wheel. The following sections define trauma and toxic stress, explore applicable research and science, and explain why this topic is important.

Definition of Trauma-Responsive Schooling

Trauma is a construct whose universally accepted definition is a challenge to identify. The *Diagnostic and Statistical Manual of Mental Disorders* (*DSM-5*; American Psychiatric Association [APA], 2013) defines trauma as instances when a person is exposed "to actual or threatened death, serious injury, or sexual violence" (p. 271). Stated differently, the Substance Abuse and Mental Health Services Administration (SAMHSA, 2014) asserts that trauma is a result of an "event, series of events, or set of circumstances that is experienced by an individual as physically or emotionally harmful or life threatening and that has lasting adverse effects on the individual's functioning and mental, physical, social, emotional, or spiritual well-being" (p. 7). Typically, trauma is the result of a personal experience with violence, abuse, neglect, loss, or a host of other harmful events.

Toxic stress, on the other hand, refers to the emotional, psychological, or physiological response to those traumatic experiences (APA, 2013). Robert Macy, president of the International Trauma Center, differentiates between three types of stress (R. Macy, personal communication, May 2018).

1. *Positive stress* relates to mild, transient elevations in stress hormones, heart rate, and blood pressure. In adults, driving a car or falling in love are examples of positive stress. Positive stress is also an important part of healthy child development.

2. *Tolerable stress* involves greater activation of the body's alert systems in response to longer-lasting or more severe threats. In adults, driving a car in heavy traffic or being overbooked are examples of tolerable stress. In children, these stress spikes quickly return to baseline when the child has supportive relationships with adults or when conducting healthy practices such as mindfulness.

3. *Toxic stress* occurs when stress is prolonged and intense. This level of stress can often result in sleep deprivation, isolation, and ongoing headaches or other physical ailments. In children, toxic stress response occurs when they are exposed to stress that is overstimulating, frequent, and unmitigated by adequate adult support. In these cases, toxic stress response often results in a chronic elevation of stress hormones, which can disrupt how the brain and physiological systems develop, and it can also potentially have serious effects on health, learning, and well-being later in life.

Simply stated, toxic stress is persistent and systemic. Although it can result from a single incident, it typically happens when a person has no control and is powerless to change a situation. Furthermore, toxic stress response can manifest itself in a number of ways, such as impaired brain and neurological development, risk taking (World Health Organization, 2020), substance use disorder (Khoury, Tang, Bradley, Cubells, & Ressler, 2010), and chronic health issues such as exhaustion, anxiety, depression, confusion, physical arousal, numbness, and disability (Harris, 2018; Oral et al., 2016). Toxic stress is also associated with chronic mental health conditions such as mood syndromes, posttraumatic stress disorder (PTSD), and attention deficit hyperactivity disorder (ADHD), which have replaced chronic physical illness in the top five most significant pediatric health issues affecting learning (Johnson, Riley, Granger, & Riis, 2013).

Trauma crosses all boundaries with no regard to age, gender, ethnicity, socioeconomic status, geography, or sexual orientation. Some groups, however, are more prone to experiencing the instances and effects of continued trauma. Specifically, historical or generational trauma is a powerful construct that can be defined as the cumulative emotional and psychological harm of an individual or generation caused by a traumatic experience or event such as genocide, slavery, poverty, discrimination, and the loss of vital aspects of culture. Historical trauma can have a devastating effect on individuals as well as entire communities. The enslavement of African Americans, the forced relocation and attempted eradication of Native Americans, and the genocide of Jews during the Holocaust provide some obvious, graphic examples of historically traumatic events that can be transferred to subsequent generations and can deeply affect individual members of those targeted communities (Duran, 2019;

Yehuda, Daskalakis, et al., 2016). Historical Trauma Response (HTR) refers to the manifestation of emotions and actions that stem from this perceived trauma and is often associated with racial and ethnic population groups who have suffered overwhelming intergenerational assaults on their culture and overall well-being (Duran, 2019: SAMHSA, 2017; Yehuda, Daskalakis, et al., 2016).

The effects of collective injuries can linger for generations. The plight of Native American communities provides a stark example. The colonization of North and South America partly depended on controlling populations of Native peoples; one method used on Native people in the United States and Canada during the mid-nineteenth century was to forcibly isolate them within a reservation system. But even before the removal of Native peoples to reservations, the U.S. and Canadian authorities advocated policies designed to assimilate tribes to the White Eurocentric ways of life (Pember, 2019). In the United States, the Civilization Fund Act of 1819 ushered in an era of assimilation policies that culminated in the Indian boarding-school era from 1860 to 1978 (Northern Plains Reservation Aid, n.d.), in which Native children were taken from their families and placed in federally funded boarding schools (often run by Christian missionaries). The children commonly faced physical and emotional abuse and were forced to speak only English, slowly dismantling their traditions, languages, and cultures. Similar policies—with similar results—were enacted in Canada at about the same time. Simply stated, young, Indigenous children were torn from their families (traumatic enough) and taught to be ashamed of being Native American (retraumatizing already traumatized children).

University of New Mexico researcher Maria Yellow Horse Brave Heart and her colleagues (2000, 2012) have asserted that even though these traumas happened long ago in history, they are lived out and experienced again and again in each subsequent generation. Unresolved, these wounds can manifest in communities through serious difficulties such as poverty, violence, poor health, suicide, unemployment, addiction, hopelessness, and overall family destruction. Early exposure to traumatic events and losses can translate to a lower quality of life and a wide variety of poor health outcomes. Native Americans suffer severe psychological distress at a rate 2.5 times the general population, and they experience PTSD more than twice as often as the general population (Heron, 2019). In addition, rates of death due to unintentional injuries, infant mortality, and chronic diseases such as diabetes, cancer, and cardiovascular disease are consistently higher among Native Americans than the general U.S. population. Statistics indicate that between 2010 and 2014, the average age at death for Native Americans was 56.8 years compared to 76.6 years for the White population (Bauer et al., 2019; Belcourt, 2018b; Northern Plains Reservation Aid, n.d.; Wong et al., 2014).

The critical point to make here is that the impact of trauma via violence, racism, and exclusion is not only about what has happened in the past, but also about *what is still happening in the present* to a person or a group of people (Duran, 2019; Evans-Campbell, 2008; Harris, 2018; Yehuda, Daskalakis, et al., 2016).

For the purposes of this book, we refer to *trauma* as an event or series of experiences that overwhelms a person's ability to respond and effectively cope with life and *toxic stress* as the psychological or biological response to trauma or continued stress. In addition, we will focus specifically on childhood as well as historical trauma. Because critical brain development occurs during a child's early months and years, traumatic experiences such as abuse, neglect, exposure to violence and discrimination, as well as poverty and inequity during that critical time period can profoundly impact the brain's developing architecture, and result in such things as cognitive loss, learning problems, and physical, emotional, and social delays. In addition, exposure to violence in the first years of childhood deprives children of as much as 10 percent of their potential intelligence quotient (IQ), leaving them vulnerable to serious emotional, learning, and behavior problems by the time they reach school age (Center on the Developing Child, 2007; Harris; 2018; R. Macy, personal communication, April 2018; Osher et al., 2018).

Research and Science

Before the French chemist Louis Pasteur discovered that microbes caused infection at a cellular level, the prevailing thought was that the source of disease and infection came from within people—that they were somehow corrupt, lacking in virtue, victims of demon possession, or subject to the wrath of God. Pasteur was able to scientifically establish a cause-effect relationship between pathogens and disease. Germ science eventually became medicine's fundamental tenet, identifying how infectious agents could enter a person's physiology and, if that person were vulnerable, an infection would ensue.

Today, trauma science is the psychological version of germ science. Whereas germ science provided an understanding of the impact of external pathogenic forces on a person's internal pathology, trauma science provides a much greater understanding of the impact of external stress on the internal biology of people and communities. Just as bacteria and viruses are infectious agents, trauma and toxic stress are carriers of an infection that impacts child development, inhibits learning, affects behavior, and can cause chronic, infectious, multigenerational, and often lethal disease. The more intense the level of contact, the greater the likelihood that victims will suffer long-term consequences. Thus, we have the same moral responsibility to focus our efforts on helping people heal from these factors.

Advances in a wide range of biological, behavioral, and social sciences are expanding our understanding of how early environmental influences (ecology) and genetic predispositions (biology) impact students' learning capacities, adaptive behaviors, and lifelong physical and mental health. Thus, we will focus on research regarding risk factors for trauma, the biological components of the stress response, and how that response specifically impacts brain development, cognition, and learning.

ACEs are probably the most common framework for categorizing and assessing cumulative risk in children's exposure to chronic stressors (Felitti et al., 1998). In addition to the original ACE categories of physical, emotional, and sexual abuse, physical and emotional neglect, parental separation or divorce, domestic violence, substance abuse, psychological health issues in a parent, or incarceration of a family member, researchers have added new categories. Some are specific to the individual: hunger, familial dysfunction, loss of a parent, being the victim of bullying or harassment, poor health, and challenging peer relationships. Others are community focused, including ecological risk factors such as "community violence, economic hardship, racial and other forms of discrimination, overemphasis on achievement, and stressful experiences within the school, child welfare, and juvenile justice systems" (Cantor et al., 2019).

National Council for Adoption researchers Casey Call, Karyn Purvis, Sheri R. Parris, and David Cross (2014) have provided another framework, which asserts that trauma in children can be attributed to six primary risk factors: (1) prenatal stress, (2) birth trauma, (3) medical trauma or hospitalization in the early years of development, (4) abuse, (5) neglect, and (6) psychological trauma. Furthermore, a critically important report published by the United States Attorney General's National Task Force on Children Exposed to Violence revealed that exposure to violence in any form harms children. The report identified four main forms of violence—(1) sexual abuse, (2) physical abuse, (3) domestic or intimate partner violence, and (4) community violence—and asserted that the different forms of violence can have different negative impacts (Listenbee et al., 2012).

Severe, chronic stress and significant adversity—poverty, racism, abuse, neglect, neighborhood violence, or a caregiver's substance abuse or psychological health issues—can become toxic to developing brains as well as to the rest of a developing human body. The cumulative toll increases the likelihood of developmental delays, learning disabilities, and childhood behavior problems, as well as diabetes, heart disease, depression, drug abuse, alcoholism, and other major health problems in adults.

An important point to make is that risk factors for trauma and toxic stress are not confined to poverty, neglect, and violence alone. Anxiety has surpassed depression, alcoholism, drug use, and other disorders as the leading mental health problem around the world (Fleming, 2019; World Economic Forum, 2020). An estimated 275 million people suffer from anxiety disorders, of whom 62 percent are female. In addition, many of the most highly functioning and innovative personalities can also suffer from the profound impact of adversity and stress. For example, a study from the American College Health Association (2018) asserts that 63 percent of college students in the United States regularly feel overwhelming anxiety, and those numbers have remained consistent for the past decade. A 2020 survey of over 33,000 college students from Boston University revealed that 83 percent of students reported their mental health had negatively impacted their academic performance, and that two-thirds of college students were struggling with loneliness and isolation—an all-time high in college mental health research (Eisenberg, Lipson, Heinze, & Zhou, 2020).

Additional research indicated that these issues persist long after the college years for many people. Michael Freeman and his colleagues (2015) from the University of California in San Francisco conducted a study that focused on the mental health crisis plaguing innovators and thought leaders from the entrepreneurial community of business professionals. Researchers discovered that these entrepreneurs show the following (Freeman et al., 2015).

- Twice as likely to suffer from depression than the general population
- Twice as likely to have suicidal thoughts or be admitted for psychiatric hospitalization
- Three times more likely to suffer from substance abuse
- Ten times more likely to suffer from bipolar disorder

In a critical corollary, the researchers further asserted that these highly motivated entrepreneurs are often trained to ignore many of the critical needs of their own health and well-being, such as meaningful and authentic relationships, overall life satisfaction, and happiness (Freeman et al., 2015).

Educators must understand that many high performers in our schools learn or ascribe to an infectious message that success is purely measured in quantitative returns such as grades, esteem, or money. Ultimately, Freeman and colleagues' (2015) research indicates that many high-performing entrepreneurs crumble as they struggle to calibrate how their physical and emotional distress compromise their professional performance. Simply stated, the risk factors for trauma and toxic stress are pervasive in our society and in our schools.

Human Stress Response

One of the most debilitating factors that can negatively impact learning is how students respond to stress and trauma. A stressful situation or perceived threat—being bullied or socially isolated, persistent worry about grades, or a deep-level concern about the future—can trigger a cascade of neurological events that releases stress hormones and produces well-orchestrated physiological changes. Stress response is one of the few body systems that directly impacts brain architecture as well as immune system efficiency, which can directly affect the development and integration of all four brain structures—(1) brainstem, (2) diencephalon, (3) limbic system, and (4) cortex (Bucci, Marques, Oh, & Harris, 2016; Harris, Marques, Oh, Bucci, & Cloutier, 2017; Siegel, 2012).

The stress response begins in the brain. When someone is confronted by a threat, the eyes or ears send a message to the amygdala, the brain's fear center, which instantly sends a distress signal to the hypothalamus (Bezdek & Telzer, 2017). The hypothalamus activates the sympathetic nervous system, which functions like a gas pedal in a car and prompts your adrenal glands. The adrenal glands, located atop your kidneys, respond by pumping the hormone epinephrine (also known as *adrenaline*) into the bloodstream (Bezdek & Telzer, 2017). Epinephrine increases heart rate and raises blood pressure, which boosts energy. Breathing quickens, allowing extra oxygen to the brain, which results in increased alertness and sharper sight and hearing. Muscles tense and beads of sweat appear. At this point, the fight, flight, freeze, or fawn response is triggered, providing the body with a burst of energy so that it can respond to perceived and real dangers (Barlow, 2002; Cannon, 1927; Walker, 2013). As the body remains on high alert, cortisol—another primary stress hormone—is released, curbing nonessential functions and those that are detrimental in the situation: the immune system, digestive system, reproductive system, and growth processes (Mayo Clinic Staff, 2021). Figure 2.1 (page 50) represents the human stress response.

All of these changes happen so quickly that people aren't aware of them. In fact, our biology is so efficient that the amygdala and hypothalamus start this hormone cascade even before the brain's visual centers have a chance to fully process what is happening. That's why people jump away from a threat when startled, even before they think about what they are doing.

The body's stress-response system is usually self-limiting. When the threat passes, adrenaline and cortisol levels drop, and the heart rate and blood pressure return to baseline levels promoting the "rest and digest" response that calms the body so that other systems resume their regular activities (Harvard Health Publishing, n.d.). However, when a person regularly feels stressed, anxious, or fearful, the fight, flight, freeze, or fawn response remains activated. Although this system is lifesaving in the face of acute danger, long-term activation takes a toll on the body and can have a massive impact on the developing limbic and immune systems as well as future health (Harvard Health Publishing, n.d.).

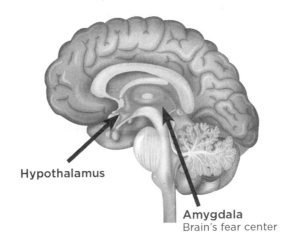

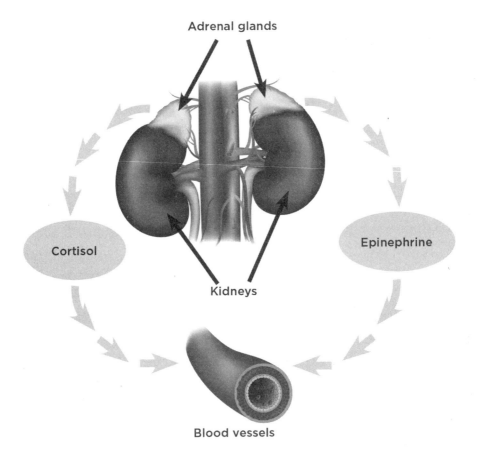

Source: Adapted from Bezdek & Telzer, 2017.

Figure 2.1: Stress response in the brain.

There is a direct link between exposure to childhood adversity and risk of negative health, social, and emotional outcomes; the emotional and physical reactions triggered by chronic stress can make us more prone to a host of ailments such as the following (Felitti et al., 1998; Harris, 2018; Kerr, Sacchet, Lazar, Moore, & Jones, 2013; Lazar et al., 2005).

- Anxiety
- Asthma
- Autoimmune disease
- Depression
- Diabetes
- Digestive problems
- Headaches
- Heart disease
- Hypertension
- Lung cancer
- Memory and concentration impairment
- Sleep problems
- Weight gain

Furthermore, a person can show increases in risk-taking behaviors, such as substance abuse, smoking, and suicidal behavior (Brenhouse, Lukkes, & Andersen, 2013). Together, these data help explain why people with ACEs are at higher risk of dying prematurely and why people who have no ACEs live twenty years longer than people who have more than five ACEs (Felitti et al., 1998; Harris, 2018).

The Impact of Adversity on the Brain

When functioning in a healthy manner, the human brain remains an evolutionary marvel—the world's greatest supercomputer with a vast network of one-hundred billion neurons capable of processing and organizing information, designing and creating art and music, and regulating our psychological world, all while keeping us alive and functioning. But when the neurological system is shocked by trauma or sustained levels of toxic stress, those traumatic experiences can linger in the brain and body, impacting health for years or a lifetime.

Trauma or chronic, unbuffered stress in children often triggers disrupted brain development and functioning, which can result in impairments in critical neurological structures (Harris, 2018; Teicher & Samson, 2016; Teicher, Samson, Anderson,

& Ohashi, 2016). As a result, trauma is highly associated with cognitive difficulties, which can impact social and academic learning, emotional regulation, and attention. For example, research has indicated that students with maltreatment histories have higher rates of cognitive difficulties, with 30 percent of abused children demonstrating language or cognitive impairment and 22 percent having learning disabilities (Call et al., 2014; Harris, 2018; Harris et al., 2017; Teicher et al., 2016).

The Importance of Trauma-Responsive Schooling

The science is clear: severe childhood trauma or toxic stress can be detrimental to the architecture of the brain and can cause lifetime damage. Furthermore, research clearly indicates a broad trend of declining mental health in adolescents and young adults (American College Health Association, 2018; Eisenberg et al., 2020; Harris, 2018). It is critical that educators are mindful that the burden of mental health is not the same across all student demographics. Students of color and low-income students are more likely to face additional challenges due to stressors in the home and larger community.

The manifestation of this trauma can be profound. Young children who suffer from toxic stress often lack self-regulation and are, therefore, less likely to develop supportive relationships, engage in school, pay attention in class, and they are more likely to withdraw and develop antisocial behavior as they grow older (Cole et al., 2013). In adolescence, these children often continue to be seriously disadvantaged, and are more prone to academic, behavioral, and relational challenges with peers and teachers. They often become labeled as troublemakers or lacking motivation in that they may monopolize attention and take significant time from instruction for behavioral management. Sadly, these students are often isolated from the academic setting due to their behaviors and can commonly drop out of school or end up in alternative educational settings, eventually developing serious problems such as addiction, impulsive or reckless behavior, depression and suicidality, or delinquency (Feinstein, 2007; Hammond, 2015; Harris, 2018; Harris et al., 2017; R. Macy, personal communication, June 2019).

What is critical to understand is that traumatized children's brains are not *broken*; they simply remain stuck in a state of perpetual readiness to react. They need healing- and resilience-centered school settings that adjust to the students. They need adults who will stop, engage, and, instead of asking "What's wrong with you?" ask the question that is essential to healing and resilience: "What is triggering this behavior?" We can create systems to foster wellness in response to this reality. Providing solid, effective social supports combined with academic press or rigorous learning goals and high expectations will support the student to overcome challenges (Bloom & Farragher, 2013; Delpit, 2013; Hammond, 2015).

Trauma-responsive schools provide a crucial setting where the focus is on providing students with strategies and guidance that emphasize coping and resilience. Effective interventions that foster self-regulation and executive function can prepare students who have experienced adversities to successfully engage in learning and succeed in school (Center on the Developing Child, n.d.; Hammond, 2015). In this way, trauma-responsive schooling merges with culturally responsive teaching to form the bottom line of the school wellness wheel and can provide the foundation for higher-level learning for every student. The major elements of culturally responsive teaching are discussed in the next section.

Practicing Culturally Responsive Teaching

Emotions, social relationships, and the contexts from which people come are inextricably linked to cognition, which drives learning and academic development. Hence, the practice of a culturally responsive teaching mindset forms the other foundational pivot point of the school wellness wheel. The following sections define culturally responsive teaching, present the research and science behind it, and reveal why this is important.

Definition of Culturally Responsive Teaching

Gloria Ladson-Billings (1995) introduced the concept of culturally relevant pedagogy as "a theoretical model that not only addresses student growth but also helps students accept and affirm their cultural identity while developing critical perspectives that challenge inequities that schools (and other institutions) perpetuate" (p. 469). It is the instructional practice of recognizing, exploring, and responding to students' cultural contexts, references, and experiences. Cultural responsiveness builds on the following eight principles (Ladson-Billings, 1995).

1. Communication of high expectations
2. Active teaching methods
3. Practitioner as facilitator
4. Inclusion of culturally and linguistically diverse students
5. Cultural sensitivity
6. Reshaping the curriculum or delivery of services
7. Student-controlled discourse
8. Small-group instruction

This theory has become a common and important component to teacher preparation programs. Tyrone C. Howard (2003) has asserted that the most important goal of culturally relevant teaching is to increase the academic growth of historically underserved students. Yet, as schools continue to become increasingly diverse, English-language texts and curricular materials that reflect mainstream cultural values often remain the norm. Thus, teachers and school leaders must continue to evolve current educational practices that move beyond the simple tolerance of historically marginalized groups.

Research and Science

The concept of learning in regard to biology and culture has a long history of debate in human history. In 1874, Sir Francis Galton coined the terms *nature* and *nurture* to describe his theory on intelligence and asserted that personality was impacted most by heredity (Rushton, 1990). Since that time, a vast research base has examined how children and adults across different cultural groups and geographical contexts perform on various cognitive tasks. Since the 1990s, numerous studies on genetics and neuroscience illustrated the critical role of environment.

We understand that both nature and nurture are equally important in human development (Plomin, 1994, 2018). For example, in 1974, Michael Cole and Sylvia Scribner attempted to assess whether certain developmental milestones on problem-solving tasks were universal or if they varied across cultures. The researchers also were interested in identifying cognitive processes that could account for differences in the rate of academic development or in the highest level of intellectual development obtained by participants (Cole & Scribner, 1974). Their work strongly suggested that culture plays a large role in basic cognitive processes such as memory and perception that help students learn and understand.

Additional cross-cultural studies have confirmed that the environment in which a person lives impacts how they think "and that people construct their perceptions by drawing on their prior learning experiences, including cultural ones" (National Academies of Sciences, Engineering, and Medicine, 2018, p. 25). For example, Marshall Segall and colleagues conducted a study in 1966 using the Müller-Lyer illusion (shown in figure 2.2) to determine the impact of culture on basic developmental processes. The illusion examines the misperception that a set of lines of equal length—flanked by angles pointing inward or outward—are actually different lengths.

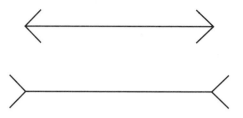

Source: Müller-Lyer, 1889.

Figure 2.2: Müller-Lyer illusion.

The researchers asserted that people living in urban, industrialized environments were more susceptible to the Müller-Lyer illusion than people who live in physical environments in which straight lines and right angles are not often seen. This work challenged the assumption that people everywhere, regardless of their backgrounds, see the world in the same way because they share the same perceptual system. Furthermore, researchers have continued to identify other examples of cultural differences in cognition and learning that were previously believed to be universal, such as cultural differences in attention, and variation in eye movements while perceiving a scene (Chua, Boland, & Nisbett, 2005; Nisbett, 2003).

Finally, professors Douglas Medin and Megan Bang (2014b) argued that despite the widely held view that education is objective, teachers do not shed their own cultures at the classroom door. Rather, their daily instructional practices reflect their values, belief systems, and worldviews. The researchers compared Native American and European American orientations toward the natural world and asserted that traditional European American philosophies view humans as separated from nature while Native American cultures commonly view humans as part of a natural ecosystem (Medin & Bang, 2014b). They then spoke to the importance of incorporating cultural, Indigenous, and community perspectives in science teaching by developing ecologically oriented, community-based science education programs on the Menominee reservation in Wisconsin and at the American Indian Center of Chicago.

Researchers Mary-Helen Immordino-Yang, Linda Darling-Hammond, and Christine Krone (2018) spoke to the importance of changing how we teach academic content because we have a greater appreciation of the dynamic interdependencies of students' social-emotional experiences and how tapping into a person's identity can lead to greater engagement and deeper learning. Furthermore, Medin and Bang (2014b) assert that diversity—in terms of students and educators with different cultural orientations—has important implications for questions of minority underrepresentation in science, but that diversity can empower teachers to think more deeply and effectively about cultural variations, which can provide new perspectives and can lead to more effective education.

The Importance of Culturally Responsive Teaching

Human learning, behavior, and growth occur in complex systems that entail a variety of interactions, cultures, and societal structures. A person's environment impacts cognition and learning, which includes the family and other social relationships, as well as the larger contexts in which their families and communities are. Factors that affect learning—such as the amount of stress hormones in the learner's blood, or the quality of their nutrition—begin at the biological level and move up to the macro level, which entails larger social components.

In doing this work, we have heard statements and questions such as, "Why do we still talk about this old history? Slavery is a remnant of a different era . . . the Indian Wars are long over . . . the Holocaust was an isolated event eighty years ago . . . segregation and apartheid have been discredited. . . . It does us no good to dwell on the past. Isn't it finally time to just move on?" We assert that the appropriate response to these statements is that we talk about this history because we need to understand how this history of genocide, slavery, inequity, erasure, and trauma is still impacting historically disenfranchised communities today. When we grow in awareness of our behavior patterns, our community relationships, and our mental models and where they come from, we have the chance to evolve and to help others grow as well.

It is important to recognize that even inequity is unequal. For example, African American, Latinx, and Native American children experience poverty at a rate of roughly three times that of their White and Asian American peers (Belcourt, 2018a; Boser, Wilhelm, & Hanna, 2014; Native Hope, 2021). Asian American children are more likely, compared to White children, to be affected by violence as a result of racism or generational trauma, as their parents or grandparents may have fled war, violence, or poverty in their region of origin before emigrating to the United States (Beers at al., 2021; Macy et al., 2004; Wycoff, Tinagon, & Dickson, 2011). Even White children, though usually spared the damaging physical and emotional violence of racism, can be discriminated against based on economic or social class and geographic factors; being "from the other side of the tracks" or "from the trailer park" carries a stigma (including the perception of lacking education or intelligence) that may lead to marginalization. As we delve deeper into these issues, it is imperative that we continually expand the conversation to remain inclusive of those most marginalized, acknowledging the disparities between races while remaining open to supporting all people.

The further away a group or one's identity is removed from what has been normalized, the more difficulties are laid in the path. Our challenge is to expand our definitions of what has been considered normal and acceptable to become more inclusive and allow for differences. To achieve this, educators must step into discomfort, acknowledging that they may not actually know how to make these connections. L. S. Vygotsky (1978) referred to this as the *zone of proximal development* (**ZPD**) and said that it was "the distance between the actual developmental level as determined by independent problem solving and the level of potential development as determined through problem-solving under adult guidance, or in collaboration with more capable peers" (p. 86). That is to say, educators must first recognize that there is information to be learned and then create the circumstances through engaging with other peers to expand their thinking and, thus, their practice.

Although this is very complex work, implementing the school wellness wheel allows educators to learn about these issues at the beginning of the implementation process and helps propel them into a deeper level of awareness and competence over time. The effort to implement the three pivot points does not end after one year. Rather, efforts continue and evolve based on the school's and community's needs. For example, Maria Yellow Horse Brave Heart and her colleagues (2012) present a four-step process that can help people to move from generational grief.

1. Confront the historical trauma.

2. Understand the trauma.

3. Release the pain of historical trauma.

4. Transcend the trauma.

Brave Heart and colleagues (as cited in Native Hope, 2021) advocate making a conscious choice to confront trauma and recognize negative patterns of behavior to help release and resolve the pain of traumatic events. Although the process she developed was specifically intended for Native Americans, there are deeply valuable lessons to glean for others who are negotiating traumatic pasts, whether multigenerational or personal, and many of these strategies benefit any person or group seeking ways to cope.

Historically marginalized communities are often full of joy and resilience and need not be defined by their trauma. Traumatized children, specifically, are survivors and can exhibit great strength and resourcefulness. This is where culturally responsive teaching comes in. This concept goes beyond most anti-racist educational constructs in that it entails more than simply adding diversity to curriculum—which does not result in creating higher levels of equity. Culturally responsive teaching is a powerful educational framework that is of critical importance anywhere where there is colonization and communities need repair.

Culturally responsive teaching differs from other culturally responsive constructs, so a brief definition is important as language is critical. Hammond (2015) differentiates between multicultural education, social justice education, and culturally responsive education. *Multicultural education* is a movement that stresses diversity, equity, and inclusion in curriculum and has the capacity to enhance social harmony. *Social justice education* speaks to critical consciousness and is where most anti-racist efforts in schools exist. Multicultural and social justice education, although important and powerful, have not been proven individually to have a great impact on the learning process or to accelerate learning (Hammond, 2015). Culturally responsive education, on the other hand, does accelerate learning in that it is based in the science of learning and is built on the foundation of creating independent learners and increasing student agency in that the students are expected and empowered to carry the bulk of the cognitive load. Culturally responsive teaching is not about activities and professional development, nor is it simply about lesson plans, strategies, and grades. It's about design principles that help students wrestle with content and skills at a deeper level, and it's about preparing teachers to better facilitate learning and cognition in every student.

Culturally responsive teaching is often equated with engagement, relationships, and trauma-informed care. But it is a powerful construct in its own right and is different from trauma-informed care, which is why both constructs are necessary to form the foundation of the school wellness wheel.

Making It Happen: Extreme Ownership

Cultivating a culture of ownership in a healing- and resilience-centered school is a massive undertaking that necessarily starts, first and foremost, with the adults in the building. It entails teachers and students operating in an evolved system for which they previously had little or no frame of reference or knowledge. For the philosophical and structural shift to occur successfully, it must be led from the top. Thus, leaders learn it, consciously focus on it, and model what it looks, feels, and sounds like. Successfully evolving our schools into the future demands strong leaders with vision, skill, and unwavering conviction.

The only way this shift can happen is through intense focus on improving classroom practice and a personal commitment by all stakeholders to take the action necessary to make that transformation a reality. In too many schools, teaching remains a private activity—teachers go into their rooms, close their doors, and do their thing. Thus, it is critical for leaders to model, coach, and demonstrate an evolved way of operating in classrooms. Business leaders and former Navy SEALs Jocko Willink and Leif Babin (2015) assert that excellent leadership is contagious and absolutely critical in transforming organizational models. Leaders must personally own the change and be actively committed to their schools' continued evolution or it simply will never happen.

Extreme ownership in this case speaks to leaders who continually build their own internal capacity in terms of staying at the forefront of what healing- and resilience-centered education is all about, constantly keeping up to date in terms of trauma-responsive and culturally responsive theory, and be engaged in the discussion about mastery-based instructional and assessment practices. Organizations like the following could be especially useful for leaders as they continue honing their skills and clarifying their message.

- Epoch Education at https://epocheducation.com
- Getting Smart at www.gettingsmart.com
- KnowledgeWorks at https://knowledgeworks.org
- XQ Foundation at https://xqsuperschool.org

Extreme ownership entails leaders monitoring current trends so they can speak to the school mission effectively and with confidence. All stakeholders will look to the principal to truly lead the initiative. Principals and superintendents cannot simply ask people to do new things—they must lead and demonstrate. And if the results are not what is desired, the principal must own the responsibility that they didn't lead well enough.

In terms of what practical actions leaders can take to strengthen their internal capacity and assume extreme ownership, it is crucial to acknowledge the great personal commitment and energy necessary to lead the evolution of traditional schools into a more contemporary design. Extreme ownership entails cultivating the internal choice to move ahead boldly and assume personal responsibility for the success or failure of the mission. Leaders of healing- and resilience-centered programs model extreme ownership every day by asking the right questions and maintaining a laser focus on the ultimate goal. For example, these leaders do not ask, "Why aren't the students more successful?" Rather, they own the problem and ask, "What will I do to help our students enjoy greater success throughout the school and community, and engage all students at a higher level?" Effective school leaders understand and embrace the reality that demonstrating higher levels of healing and resilience begins with the leaders, then moves to teachers, and then moves to students.

Conclusion

It is essential that all students are presented with the best possible educational opportunities available to them, and our commitment as leaders must be to ensure that each can find and fulfill his or her greatest potential. Thus, the urgent call for real, substantive evolution in schools remains a moral and economic imperative. It is an issue of social justice, and we owe it to all our students to not simply continue tweaking the existing model, but rather to create a better system that is designed to meet their individual needs and abilities. The only way in which the system can be effectively reformed so that it can remain current in the ever-changing global construct is by recognizing the new reality and constantly adapting on a structural level. In other words, the system must move as an entire entity and simultaneously on all levels.

Shifting paradigms can be painful and difficult for people and organizations, so helping people see the failures of current paradigms and imagine new possibilities requires powerful leadership, moral courage, and a commitment to social justice. Personalized competency-based education, trauma-informed care, and culturally responsive pedagogy are not, by themselves, enough to shift the entire education paradigm in a way that is sustainable. Until educators address the fundamental issues, continued discussion centered on such topics as instructional strategies, assessments, grading practice, and other traditional measures is completely inconsequential. We believe that—as a solution to this problem of educational inequity—integrating the school wellness wheel simultaneously tackles the issues of pedagogy, therapeutics, and social relevance, and moves the discussion of true reform to a whole new level that entails a new conceptual construct.

Culture of Ownership Proficiency Scale

As a team, rate your school on the following skills.

		Sample Evidence
Score 4.0	*In addition to score 3.0, in-depth inferences and applications that go beyond what was taught.* School becomes a center of wellness and learning for the community in which teachers and staff can speak to the power of healing and resilience for all segments of the larger society.	School presents opportunities for facilitating healing and building resilience via social media, websites, and in-person educational presentations.
3.5	In addition to score 3.0 performance, in-depth inferences and applications with partial success	
Score 3.0	The educators will: • Exhibit the changes of hearts and minds to adopt a healing- and resilience-centered school model. • Demonstrate wellness practices personally. • Explain the three pivot points of the school wellness wheel and how they are interrelated. *The educator exhibits no major errors or omissions.*	• Staff meetings begin with mindfulness and other wellness practices • Mission or vision statements have healing and resilience at the center as the way to reach high-level learning.
2.5	No major errors or omissions regarding 2.0 content and partial knowledge of the 3.0 content	
Score 2.0	There are no major errors or omissions regarding the simpler details and processes as the educators: • Recognize or recall specific terminology, such as *professionalism, mastery-based learning, trauma, toxic stress, ACEs, culturally responsive teaching, extreme ownership,* and *brain research.* • Perform basic processes, such as: + Understanding the critical components of mastery-based learning + Understanding the critical components of trauma-responsive schooling + Understanding the critical components of culturally responsive teaching + Engaging professionally with the need to evolve educational practices *The educator exhibits major errors or omissions regarding the more complex ideas and processes.*	• Research in the areas of mastery, trauma, and culture are provided and considered in collaborative team and staff meetings. • Professional development in the areas of evolving school structures are presented.
1.5	Partial knowledge of the 2.0 content, but major errors or omissions regarding the 3.0 content	
Score 1.0	With help, a partial understanding of some of the simpler details and processes and some of the more complex ideas and processes	
0.5	With help, a partial understanding of the 2.0 content, but not the 3.0 content	
Score 0.0	Even with help, no understanding or skill demonstrated	

Chapter 3

Culture of Mastery

I am entirely certain that twenty years from now, we will look back at education as it is practiced in most schools today and wonder that we could have tolerated anything so primitive.

—John W. Gardner

In mastery-based-learning schools, students work with teachers to choose tasks they feel let them display their proficiency with standards or learning goals based on learning progressions expressed as proficiency scales. They no longer simply complete assignments to plow through curriculum. Rather, learners are able to tap into their personal experience, knowledge, and cultural context to create learning plans or personal projects that empower them. This equates to students taking control of their own learning by expanding on their learning and applying previously mastered material to new learning objectives. It is this way that mastery-based learning is closely aligned with trauma-responsive schooling and culturally responsive teaching.

This chapter centers around cultivating a culture of mastery, which empowers students to demonstrate proficiency on high-level learning goals. The chapter also presents a vehicle for addressing traditional curriculum and standards through the effective use of proficiency scales, which results in higher engagement of students and teachers. In addition, nurturing a robust culture of mastery also helps build relationships through learning partnerships that are inherent in mastery-based-learning models. Furthermore, creating a culture of mastery aligns with the belonging and esteem levels on Maslow's (1943) hierarchy. You can assess your school's efforts toward this change by using the "Culture of Mastery Proficiency Scale" (page 81).

Cultivating Relationship and Engagement

Relationships and engagement are critical components of trauma-responsive schooling. In our examination of numerous schools and districts that have implemented mastery-based educational practices, students strongly express that their level of engagement is far greater due to the fact that instructors in the [mastery-based learning] model teach differently and respect their individual styles of learning more effectively than they had experienced in their traditional classes (Heflebower, Hoegh, Warrick, & Flygare, 2019; Ruyle, 2019).

All students, to some extent, attempt to master skills and understand content, and they all yearn for positive interpersonal relationships (Ryan & Deci, 2020; Strong, Silver, & Robinson, 1995). Students want and need work that empowers them to practice and demonstrate skills independently and at a high level, which helps improve their sense of themselves as competent and successful human beings. This is the drive toward autonomy, mastery, and purpose that Daniel Pink (2011) asserted are the hallmarks of motivation. As students notice their progress and feel autonomous, masterful, and purposeful, they are likely to believe they are capable of further learning (Pink, 2011).

Traditional schools, however, often create classroom cultures that make truly personalized approaches to learning and instruction difficult to implement. Students in industrialized educational systems are part of a typically passive learning environment. They often take little ownership of their own learning in that they are grouped based on their chronological age, respond to teacher direction, and submit required assignments to earn enough credits to move through school and, eventually, graduate. Accordingly, the core practice of teachers often tends to reflect an antiquated system of beliefs in which the classroom remains teacher centered or curriculum centered. Far too often, as UCLA distinguished professor of education Pedro A. Noguera (2008) stated, students find discrepancies between their beliefs, values, and effort and the support they receive from their teachers and the broader traditional school culture and structure.

That these models tend to facilitate deeper individual teacher-students relationships is one of the most exciting benefits; they also increase engagement and motivation (DeLorenzo et al., 2009; Priest, Rudenstine, & Weisstein, 2012; Ruyle, 2019). Designed for flexibility and personalization, mastery-based learning practices encourage teachers to adapt to the unique needs of their individual learners, which leads to higher levels of student engagement and deeper trust in relationships between students and teachers.

As one high school student in California stated:

> In mastery-based [learning], kids have more of a chance to get
> motivated because they can follow their own interests. It's liberat-
> ing to be able to think differently and do what I want. I'm encour-
> aged to do better because I'm able to. I already know if the work I
> do is good enough or not. I really don't need for the teachers to tell
> me, because the learning goals and proficiency scales have already
> spelled it out. (R. Franz, personal communication, May 9, 2018)

A middle school learner in Vermont reinforced the difference between educational models:

> In my last school, I was just in the middle of a big herd of people, and
> we were moved along like cows. In mastery-based [learning], I get to
> choose my own path and move that way. It's so much more interest-
> ing and motivating. And now I'm doing better in school and am get-
> ting better grades! (A. Flynn, personal communication, May 30, 2019)`

Students and teachers in successful mastery-based-learning schools continually speak to the deeper level of connection, relationship, and engagement in the model. Teachers in mastery-based-learning classrooms haven't necessarily changed their strategies, but they have altered how they implement and execute their strategies, as well as review the frequency with which they use a particular strategy. In any group of students, individuals will be at different points in the learning sequence, so it makes sense for teachers to focus whole-group instruction on cognitive and metacognitive skills but use small-group instruction regularly to meet students where they are any given moment. It is for this reason that we assert the argument that mastery-based learning, when effectively practiced is, in itself, trauma responsive as well as culturally responsive.

Our continued research and conversations with students in mastery-based-learning K–12 models reveal the following commonalities that are especially important to learners' increased academic engagement (Dyer, 2015).

- **Increased pride in their school:** Students in mastery-based school systems demonstrate and report higher engagement than when learning in more traditional models, and they demonstrate higher engagement than peers who are in traditional schools (Guskey, 2008, 2010; Ruyle, 2019). Students and teachers in mastery-based-learning schools also consistently report greater motivation and believe all learners can achieve at high levels, leading to increased pride in themselves and their schools (Guskey, 2008; Marzano, Norford, et al., 2017; Ruyle, 2019). Motivation is a critical element in the learning process, and it is molded by foundational skills and elements of the learning environment (Cantor et al., 2019). Empowering learners to tap into their own motivation is also a foundational piece of trauma-competent systems.

- **Personal connection and mentoring:** Students consistently rate the individual attention they receive in mastery-based learning systems the most important factor in their engagement and ultimate success (Ruyle, 2019). The personalized guidance students access to reach more advanced levels of skill and knowledge is foundational in mastery-based learning systems. This connection and mentoring lead to a conscious creation of learning partnerships that are a fundamental component of culturally responsive teaching.

Developing Learning Partnerships

To truly develop learning partnerships in the classroom, it is necessary to know who you are as a teacher and who your students are personally. This attention is foundational to creating culturally responsive teaching practices. The knowledge of oneself and one's students is the building block to deepening relationships and ultimately creating a climate and culture that engender motivation, shared risk taking, and accountability in the learning process. Consider the fact that "identities play a powerful role; students are motivated to think and act in ways that are congruent with their identities, which, in turn, are contextually situated" (Oyserman, 2009). If we ignore the importance of understanding how specific identities are portrayed and how that portrayal can impact student success, we can unintentionally marginalize and undermine students' success.

All students begin school as dependent learners by virtue of their age and development, but a disproportionate number of students from historically disenfranchised groups typically remain dependent indefinitely because of inequitable educational practices that result in less effective instruction and a less robust curriculum (Medin & Bang, 2014b; Vander Ark & Liebtag, 2020). In other words, many students of color continue to receive the pedagogy of poverty. This approach suggests that the students are the ones who are broken and need to be fixed. This deficit thinking limits opportunities given to students of color and reduces their interactions with the teacher to one of compliance or silence, because in traditional systems it is viewed as the only way to reach the desired outcomes. To develop independent learners, use mastery-based learning to organize curriculum and instruction and engage students actively in authentic, challenging work. Students achieve more academically when they feel competent and become confident and in charge of their own learning (Deci & Ryan, 2012). The goal for teachers, therefore, is partnering with students to increase their competence.

Supporting students' capacity for independence and responsibility offers benefits for the teachers in that it shares the cognitive workload between them, rather than putting the entire burden on educators who are already processing a great many inputs as they teach. Yet the benefits for the student are clear, too: students gain a positive sense of their abilities and greater engagement when they feel part of a community of learners that can develop strategies on their own for finding answers to an inquiry they've helped develop. A positive learning environment isn't one where the teachers always lead and the students always follow; rather, it's one where students have opportunities to develop routines and techniques to effectively process information and direct their own learning.

Implementing Learning Goals and Proficiency Scales

You can view educational paradigms as existing along a continuum. At one end is the traditional, teacher-centric, curriculum-driven model in which all students are expected to progress through the same content, in the same way, in the same amount of time (Ruyle, 2019). Teachers covering a specified amount of content by certain dates via pacing guides is the structural norm, and all students move through the curriculum at the same pace regardless of whether they have mastered the learning goals or standards. In this traditional system, time is the constant, and learning is the variable (Bramante & Colby, 2012).

Mastery-based learning systems occupy the other end of the continuum; they are human-centric and driven by learners' needs. They are also a necessary part of healing- and resilience-centered schools. The differences between the traditional and mastery-based learning systems are profound, and only in the mastery-based model can trauma and culturally responsive education be powerfully addressed. Two specific differences put the models in stark contrast.

1. Flexible use of time is a hallmark of mastery-based learning and ensures that learning is the constant and time is the variable (Bramante & Colby, 2012).

2. Mastery-based learning systems acknowledge that the instructional strategies that work for one student may not work for another and that tailoring instruction to individuals or groups of student interests can be a powerful engagement tool.

The same learning goals or standards to cover apply in both systems, but in the mastery-based system, students move through the curriculum only when they have demonstrated mastery of the priority standard or learning goal, not according to a strictly enforced, arbitrary pacing calendar. A guaranteed and viable curriculum forms the structural core of mastery-based learning systems in that it clearly communicates what learners will be expected to master in the instructional time available. It is *guaranteed* in the sense that every student will have the opportunity to learn the critical core curriculum, and it is *viable* in that there is enough time available for students to demonstrate mastery (Marzano, Norford, Finn, & Finn, 2017).

The key to determining the guaranteed and viable curriculum lies in prioritizing and unpacking standards, which, ultimately, results in the expression of curriculum through *learning goals.* We have heard learning goals commonly referred to by a host of terms such as *prioritized standards, power standards, core competencies, essential understandings, educational learner outcomes,* or *measurement topics* that entail the academic knowledge and skills, thinking skills, social and personal skills, work habits, dispositions, and other domains that the school and community believe are important for students to master. Prioritizing standards—or establishing learning goals—is necessary because most standards documents (whether Common Core State Standards or other individual state or provincial standards documents) simply contain too much content to teach and assess. Teachers are placed in the situation in which they are forced to plow through content, as opposed to helping students understand and master critical skills and knowledge.

Teacher teams who are content experts usually are responsible for prioritizing identified standards or establishing learning goals. In our experience, the vast majority of schools have gone through some sort of prioritizing process since 2000. It is important, therefore, that content teams do not get bogged down in this process. This is especially true in light of our continued observations that having priority standards or learning goals established is not the issue holding back schools from becoming mastery based. The major sticking point is communicating those learning goals to students and parents in a way that ensures two things: (1) that students have a clear understanding of what the goal entails and (2) what mastery of the goal looks, sounds, and feels like. Until that critical step is grasped, schools commonly revert to old habits of simply moving through curriculum. It's easy for teachers to explain that their standards documents have been streamlined and priorities established, but until students are able to clearly understand and explain how daily activities lead them to proficiency on the overarching goal, and until teachers are able to alter their practice around helping every learner master the identified goal, schooling tends to look the same it always has.

A powerful tool that teachers, schools, and districts can use to understand priority standards in a way that simplifies a larger standard as a clear learning goal is the Critical Concepts (www.marzanoresources.com/educational-services/critical-concepts) from Marzano Resources. The product of a multiyear project, the Critical

Concepts reconfigures the overwhelming weight of Common Core State Standards in English language arts, mathematics, science, social studies, technology, and meta-cognitive skills into a much more learner-friendly version that students have a much easier time understanding.

After establishing learning goals, the knowledge and skills that students will master are presented via clear steps or learning progressions as expressed in proficiency scales. Marzano has addressed these concepts at an even deeper level in *The New Art and Science of Teaching* (Marzano, 2017) and has asserted that providing and communicating clear learning goals and tracking student progress with proficiency scales are essential elements of effective instruction.

Proficiency scales are the critical element—the game changer in mastery-based learning—that provides teachers, students, and parents with a clear picture of what knowledge and skills students must demonstrate, while establishing a measurable definition of mastery (Marzano, 2017; Ruyle, 2019). For the purposes of this book, and to maintain a common language with the school wellness wheel, we also employ the term *mastery scales* to refer to proficiency scales. In its simplest form, a proficiency scale is a statement of progressively more complex expectations regarding the knowledge and skills within a measurement topic. Well-designed proficiency scales provide a blueprint for students to follow to achieve mastery and display a clear focus for instruction. The effect on the learners can be powerful in that, if used correctly, all instructional activities will have a purpose that makes sense to them. A proficiency scale brings often esoteric standards to life.

Proficiency scales are directly aligned with identified learning goals or prioritized standards and display a learning progression that provides students with the roadmap to mastering the skills and knowledge their teachers have identified as essential. Scales organize standards into manageable learning progressions and allow students to work toward goals sequentially on a continuum and provide a transparent way to communicate a learning goal. Once the majority of teachers have agreed on what mastering identified learning goals looks like, they plan and then provide learning opportunities. In these projects, activities, and tasks, students apply their knowledge and skills, practicing a skill to work toward mastery of learning goals (Priest et al., 2012).

A simplified example of a generic proficiency scale is presented in figure 3.1 (page 70). An array of more content-specific examples are presented in the following sections. For more detailed descriptions of how to construct and use proficiency scales, we suggest *Formative Assessment and Standards-Based Grading* (Marzano, 2010) and *A Handbook for Developing and Using Proficiency Scales in the Classroom* (Hoegh, 2020).

4.0	Going above and beyond the expectations listed at the score 3.0 level. Often, this requires students to make inferences and applications not addressed in class.
3.5	In addition to score 3.0 performance, partial success at score 4.0 content
3.0	**The ultimate learning goal that clearly expresses what mastery looks like in terms of what learners must know or be able to do**
2.5	No major errors or omissions regarding score 2.0 content, and partial success at score 3.0 content
2.0	Simpler content that is necessary for students to master the learning target (score 3.0) and that will be directly taught. Includes key vocabulary, basic processes, basic details, and the cognitive skills or knowledge at a more basic level than that of level 3.0.
1.5	Partial success at score 2.0 content, and major errors or omissions regarding score 3.0 content
1.0	With help, partial success at score 2.0 content and score 3.0 content
0.5	With help, partial success at score 2.0 content but not at score 3.0 content
0.0	Even with help, no success

Source: © 2016 by Marzano Resources. Adapted with permission.

Visit **MarzanoResources.com/reproducibles** for a free reproducible version of this figure.

Figure 3.1: Simplified, generic proficiency scale.

Many teachers have difficulty understanding the difference between proficiency scales and rubrics. We assert that mastery scales serve as *learning tools*, while rubrics serve as *grading tools*. Thus, in a mastery-based learning model, the most important element in the use of proficiency scales is for teachers to get them into the hands of students and parents from the first day of the new school year and use them constantly as the roadmap to mastery. Often, we see teachers spend a great amount of time and effort in building proficiency scales and trying to align them to their assessments—but very little time using them as their intended purpose. It is critical that students see proficiency scales as their learning blueprint and for them to serve as their curriculum design and the learning goals to which they will be held to proficiency.

Effective mastery-based-learning schools often include three general categories of knowledge as part of the content that students are expected to master.

1. Traditional academic content

2. Cognitive skills

3. Metacognitive skills

Traditional Academic Content

A school or district can establish the learning goals for a content area through their own prioritization process, or they can start with a set of standards or learning goals that are already unpacked and professionally developed at different grade levels, such as the Critical Concepts (Simms, 2016).

The best way to create a proficiency scale is to start with score 3.0, which is the target content (that is, learning target) of the scale and represents the statement of expectations for each measurement topic. Score 4.0 content goes beyond the expectations listed at score 3.0. Often, this requires students to make inferences and applications beyond what was addressed in class. For example, the Characteristics of Civilization scale in figure 3.2 suggests that advanced students could "compare the relationships among the cultural, social, economic, political, and technological features of early civilizations" (Marzano Resources, 2019).

4.0	The student will: • Compare the relationships among the cultural, social, economic, political, and technological features of early civilizations (for example, explain how the confluence of religion and political power influenced the character of major structures in Mesoamerica and Egypt, while the large public works of the Indus Valley Civilization reflect primarily societal and economic purposes).
3.5	In addition to score 3.0 performance, partial success at score 4.0 content
3.0	The student will: **CC1—Explain the relationship among the cultural, social, economic, political, and technological features of early civilizations** (for example, explain the connections between monumental cultural achievements, such as the Great Pyramids, and the development of state authority, aristocratic power, technological sophistication, taxation systems, and institutions of coerced labor).
2.5	No major errors or omissions regarding score 2.0 content, and partial success at score 3.0 content
2.0	**CC1—**The student will recognize or recall specific vocabulary (for example, *aristocracy*, *Bronze Age*, *civilization*, *Iron Age*, *kingdom*, *militarization*, *patriarchy*, *peasantry*, *social stratification*, *urban*) and perform basic processes such as: • Identify locations where civilization emerged around the world (Mesopotamia, Nile River Valley, Indus River Valley, Huang He River Valley, Mesoamerica, Central Andes Mountains). • Describe environmental conditions that influenced the development of early civilizations (for example, the prevailing wind, current, and flooding patterns in the Tigris-Euphrates, Nile, Indus, and Huang He river valleys). • Explain the concept of a patriarchal society and the ways in which the legal and customary positions of aristocratic, urban, or peasant women may have changed in early civilizations. • Describe significant technological developments of the Bronze Age and Iron Age (for example, invention of the wheel, plow, and sail; development of pottery, weaving, and metallurgical techniques).
1.5	Partial success at score 2.0 content, and major errors or omissions regarding score 3.0 content
1.0	With help, partial success at score 2.0 content and score 3.0 content
0.5	With help, partial success at score 2.0 content but not at score 3.0 content
0.0	Even with help, no success

Source: © 2019 by Marzano Resources. Adapted with permission.

Figure 3.2: Proficiency scale for characteristics of civilization (grades 6–12 world history).

In this example, *compare* is usually perceived as higher-order cognition than is *explain*, the mastery learning goal at level 3.0. In figure 3.2, the 6–12 grade social studies measurement topic Characteristics of Civilization is broken out into a proficiency scale. The learning goal is expressed in level 3.0. It requires that students *explain* the concept—which is traditionally viewed as a higher-level–thinking skill. The score 2.0 content is simpler but necessary for students to master the learning target (3.0) and that will be directly taught. Score 2.0 content typically includes key vocabulary, basic processes, basic details, and the cognitive skills or knowledge is at a more basic level than that of level 3.0.

Cognitive Skills

A foundational assumption and goal of mastery-based learning is to ensure that all students can think and are able to *learn how to learn*. Essentially, cognition entails brain-based skills that humans use to function effectively in the world and typically includes such things as thinking, memory, speech, the ability to learn new information, pay attention, understand written text, and engage.

The following cognitive skills can help students reach deeper learning outcomes (Marzano, Yanoski, Hoegh, & Simms, 2013; National Council on Measurement in Education, n.d.).

- Sustained attention
- Response inhibition
- Processing speed
- Cognitive flexibility and control
- Multiple simultaneous attention
- Presenting and supporting claims
- Pattern recognition
- Generating conclusions
- Problem solving
- Decision making
- Experimenting
- Identifying basic relationships between ideas

Mastery-based learning practices, in terms of helping students master cognitive skills, can result in deeper learning for students in that they engage in academic content while learning and continually practice how to think critically and creatively, collaborate, communicate, adapt to challenges, persevere through complex problems, and be accountable for demonstrating high-level mastery (Marzano, Scott, et al., 2017; Ruyle, 2019). We assert that in mastery-based-learning schools, cognitive skills like the ones listed in the preceding list should be taught directly and practiced—just like academic knowledge and skills.

Furthermore, schools should make clear plans to consistently reinforce these skills throughout the curriculum over the entire school year. For example, the cognitive skill *generating conclusions* is commonly expected to be mastered in English language arts (ELA) classes in that producing a well-constructed and logical conclusion is a necessary part of presenting an argument or opinion (either in oral or written communication). In this case, *generating conclusions* would typically be included at level 3.0 of many ELA proficiency scales. In the same vein, *generating conclusions* could and should be clearly articulated in many proficiency scales for content in social studies, science, and mathematics. Teacher teams should regularly look at the content they commit to helping their students master and ensure that cognitive skills are embedded in the corresponding proficiency scales.

In analyzing a proficiency scale for cognitive skills, consider the grades 11–12 Critical Concept, presenting and supporting claims, and the proficiency scale in figure 3.3. In this example, *analyze* is usually perceived as higher-order thinking as related to *consider* or *reflect*, the learning goals at level 3.0.

4.0	The student will: • Choose the strongest claim for an argument and an appropriate counterclaim by evaluating the available evidence. • Evaluate the argument and counterclaim by analyzing the available evidence from a Supreme Court case such as Brown v. Board of Education of Topeka.
3.5	In addition to score 3.0 performance, partial success at score 4.0 content
3.0	The student will: **PSC1—Present precise claims and counterclaims by distinguishing them from alternatives** (for example, clearly articulate a stance about how social media do or do not cause young adults to feel isolated as well as a counterclaim that can be disproven through the use of well-chosen evidence). **PSC2—Support claims and counterclaims using relevant, sufficient, and logical evidence** (for example, defend the claim that Jane Austen satirizes societal expectations in *Pride and Prejudice* using textual evidence, such as quotations, paraphrasing, and inferences, to support the claim). **PSC3—Strengthen claims using valid reasoning** (for example, plan the reasoning for an analytical text by mapping the premises that support the conclusion and the evidence that leads to the premises and conclusion).
2.5	No major errors or omissions regarding score 2.0 content, and partial success at score 3.0 content

Figure 3.3: Proficiency scale for presenting and supporting claims (grades 11–12 ELA). continued →

2.0	**PSC1**—The student will recognize or recall specific vocabulary (for example, *alternative, claim, counterclaim, credible, grounds, precise, reasonable, relevant, valid*) and perform basic processes such as: • Identify reasons from a text or other sources that support a claim. • Describe the grounds and backing that support a claim. • Describe any qualifiers for a claim. • Describe how closely several counterclaims mirror a claim's purpose. • Annotate passages of a text or source which support either a claim or counterclaim. • Describe how the evidence for a claim could refute a counterclaim. **PSC2**—The student will recognize or recall specific vocabulary (for example, *context, evidence, inference, sufficient, textual evidence*) and perform basic processes such as: • List main ideas in a text or other sources that support a claim. • Explain how a text's context can inform inferences about the text. • Rank evidence according to relevance for the claims in a text. • Explain what the evidence for a claim specifically illustrates or proves. • Identify any subtopics, ideas, or conflicts the evidence collected for a claim does not address. **PSC3**—The student will recognize or recall specific vocabulary (for example, *appeal to authority, deductive, fallacy, premise, reasoning, red herring*) and perform basic processes such as: • Describe how reasons and evidence support a claim. • Describe what conclusions the reasons and evidence for a claim suggest. • Explain what makes an argument valid or invalid. • Describe the relationship between a premise and a conclusion. • Provide examples of valid and invalid arguments. • Rewrite the argument of a text as a set of premises and a conclusion.
1.5	Partial success at score 2.0 content, and major errors or omissions regarding score 3.0 content
1.0	With help, partial success at score 2.0 content and score 3.0 content
0.5	With help, partial success at score 2.0 content but not at score 3.0 content
0.0	Even with help, no success

Source: © 2016 by Marzano Resources. Adapted with permission.

Metacognitive Skills

Metacognition is the awareness of one's own thinking and learning. Metacognitive skills entail a person reflecting on and improving his or her thinking. Metacognitive skills are directly related to self-regulation and executive function (Hammond, 2015; Marzano, 2010, 2017; Osher et al., 2018). Students can learn, practice, and improve their metacognitive habits in order to improve their learning, studying, and thinking skills. When learners think about their thinking, they are more capable of self-improvement. Metacognition helps people perform mental and physical actions more effectively and efficiently, become more self-aware, and self-assess their current status and progress (Hammond, 2015; Marzano, 2010, 2017; Osher et al., 2018). When students apply metacognitive strategies, they become better learners in that they can provide executive control over their thoughts and actions much more effectively. In fact, well-developed metacognition gives learners tools to adapt their learning strategies to the situation, discipline, or learning task (Conley & French, 2013), and ongoing metacognitive processes help students develop neural connections necessary to learn from errors, enabling them to design their own learning methodology and evolve their strategies to meet a variety of learning challenges (Marcovitch & Zelazo, 2009).

The following metacognitive skills can support students as they reach deeper learning outcomes (Kaplan, Silver, Lavaque-Mantry, & Meizlish, 2013; Norford & Marzano, 2016; Tanner, 2012).

- "Staying focused when answers and solutions are not immediately apparent" (Norford & Marzano, 2016, p. 5)

- "Pushing the limits of one's knowledge and skills" (Norford & Marzano, 2016, p. 6)

- "Generating and pursuing one's own standards of excellence" (Norford & Marzano, 2016, p. 6)

- "Seeking incremental steps" (Norford & Marzano, 2016, p. 6)

- Seeking clarity and accuracy (Norford & Marzano, 2016)

- Resisting impulses (Norford & Marzano, 2016)

- Self-questioning

- Active listening

- Reflecting and meditating

- Being aware of one's own strengths and weaknesses

- Thinking aloud

- Planning ahead

As necessary as these skills are for quality of life, we see them rarely, if ever, taught and practiced as skills that are just as or even more important than content standards. However, metacognitive skills must be given the commitment and focused attention to ensure every student has the time and resources to master them. Teachers should define *metacognition*, talk about metacognitive skills with learners and explain why developing the skills is important for school and for life. These skills provide yet another example of how mastery-based learning should align with trauma-responsive schooling and culturally responsive teaching in a healing- and resilience-centered educational setting—these skills are critical to nurturing healing and enhancing resilience.

For example, the metacognitive skill *staying focused when answers and solutions are not immediately apparent* (Norford & Marzano, 2016, p. 5) is one that many students struggle to master in school. Often, students are eager to rush through a project or an assignment to finish rather than understand how a specific task is intended to deepen knowledge and understanding. Students are typically more interested in grades, compliance, and work completion as opposed to in-depth learning. Thus, helping students understand and consciously practice *staying focused when answers and solutions are not immediately apparent* will help them in later academic years, as well as in their lives outside school. Likewise, *reflecting and meditating* are powerful strategies that are especially pertinent and necessary in trauma-responsive schooling to help regulate emotions and soothe the human stress response so that a person can train their mind to remain calm, focused, and in the best possible place to enhance cognition and learning.

Just as mastery-based-learning schools address academic and cognitive skills directly, they also hold students to mastery in terms of their metacognitive skills. Teachers can accomplish this by using direct instruction and being mindful of grade level. For example, elementary school teachers can instruct and reinforce some metacognitive skills like *planning ahead* and *thinking aloud*. Others, like *generating and pursuing one's own standards of* excellence, are better left for direct instruction at higher grade levels. Yet other metacognitive skills, such as *resisting impulses* and *reflecting and meditating* should be learned, practiced, reinforced, and assessed across all grade levels.

In analyzing a proficiency scale for metacognition, consider the grades 5–12 measurement topic *Reflection* (figure 3.4). In this example, *analyze* is usually perceived as higher-order cognition as related to *consider* or *reflect*, the learning goals at level 3.

4.0	The student will:
	• Analyze the positive effect on his or her reflection when he or she participates and the negative effect on his or her learning when he or she does not.
	• Reflect *while* doing a task so that he or she can make adjustments to thinking processes along the way. This is called *reflection in action*.
3.5	In addition to score 3.0 performance, partial success at score 4.0 content

continued →

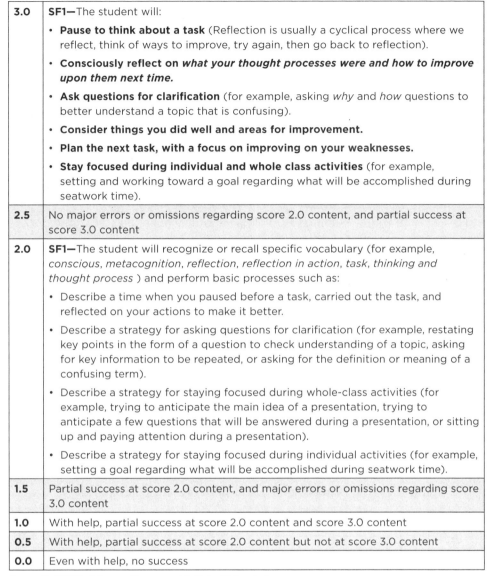

3.0	**SF1**—The student will:
	• **Pause to think about a task** (Reflection is usually a cyclical process where we reflect, think of ways to improve, try again, then go back to reflection).
	• **Consciously reflect on *what your thought processes were and how to improve upon them next time.***
	• **Ask questions for clarification** (for example, asking *why* and *how* questions to better understand a topic that is confusing).
	• **Consider things you did well and areas for improvement.**
	• **Plan the next task, with a focus on improving on your weaknesses.**
	• **Stay focused during individual and whole class activities** (for example, setting and working toward a goal regarding what will be accomplished during seatwork time).
2.5	No major errors or omissions regarding score 2.0 content, and partial success at score 3.0 content
2.0	**SF1**—The student will recognize or recall specific vocabulary (for example, *conscious, metacognition, reflection, reflection in action, task, thinking and thought process*) and perform basic processes such as:
	• Describe a time when you paused before a task, carried out the task, and reflected on your actions to make it better.
	• Describe a strategy for asking questions for clarification (for example, restating key points in the form of a question to check understanding of a topic, asking for key information to be repeated, or asking for the definition or meaning of a confusing term).
	• Describe a strategy for staying focused during whole-class activities (for example, trying to anticipate the main idea of a presentation, trying to anticipate a few questions that will be answered during a presentation, or sitting up and paying attention during a presentation).
	• Describe a strategy for staying focused during individual activities (for example, setting a goal regarding what will be accomplished during seatwork time).
1.5	Partial success at score 2.0 content, and major errors or omissions regarding score 3.0 content
1.0	With help, partial success at score 2.0 content and score 3.0 content
0.5	With help, partial success at score 2.0 content but not at score 3.0 content
0.0	Even with help, no success

Source: © 2017 by Marzano Resources. Adapted with permission.

Figure 3.4: Reflection (grades 5–12 metacognitive skills).

Making It Happen: Instructional Leadership

Historically, the role of school leader was that of principal teacher. They were recognized experts in pedagogy and models who their peers could strive to learn from and emulate. Their responsibility as a manager and bureaucratic leader came secondary to being a teacher. Over time, however, principals have assumed a vast array of new responsibilities that often take them further away from the learning and teaching that happens in classrooms.

As stated earlier, the job of teachers in healing- and resilience-centered education is not simply to teach students, but rather to help them learn. This asks teachers to learn new skills, to assume the role of doctors of learning, to help students navigate the road to mastery, to look at assessments from a different perspective, to implement trauma-responsive and culturally responsive protocols, and to model constant learning. If teachers are ever going to be able to do their jobs at a high level, they require professional expertise, feedback, time, and resources to make it happen. Thus, the principal's role of *instructor of the instructors* has become paramount.

This concept is now common in the educational leadership research base. For example, thought leader Phillip Hallinger (2012) has asserted that instructional leadership has taken on a new urgency across the world under the title of *leadership for learning* and is a powerful construct that aspiring new principals must embrace. In addition, Hattie (2015b) has asserted seven major mindsets, behaviors, or personal commitments that epitomize an instructional leader.

1. They focus on the learning first and how teachers impact it.

2. They believe their main job is to consider how everyone in a school impacts student learning.

3. They believe all learning is a direct response to the leaders' and teachers' actions in a school.

4. They understand assessment is not a means of assigning a grade, but rather provides feedback about the leaders' and teachers' effectiveness.

5. They understand and protect the integrity of student and teacher voice.

6. They understand how to set challenging targets for leaders and teachers to maximize student learning.

7. They embrace the concept of learning as a result of recognizing mistakes, and they create environments where taking risks and making mistakes are seen as critical component of learning.

Principals in healing- and resilience-centered schools must serve as instructional leaders, with these mindsets, who provide expertise and guidance to teachers. Growing healthy, resilient students starts by building healthy, resilient adults. This starts by principals modeling health and resilience and teaching educators how to continually stretch, grow, and learn so that the same things can happen with their students. And just as students require exceptional teachers to guide them on their journey of learning, teachers require the same from their building leaders.

Leaders must provide the following instructional leadership for teachers.

- Substantive direction

- Coaching with feedback

- Time to practice new skills

- A process to reflect on their growth based on feedback

- Evidence of their progress

In other words, university training, professional development, and collaborative teams should model for teachers what we would expect to see in their classrooms—clear learning goals and proficiency scales that are utilized in trauma- and culturally responsive ways, and aligned assessments that help drive continued professional growth.

A successful instructional leader's work begins with the principal serving as a model of continuous learning and maintaining focus on the critical elements of communication—understanding learning goals, effectively using proficiency scales for staff, and understanding trauma- and culturally responsive teaching principles. In defining effective instructional leadership, research consistently emphasizes a leader's ability to clearly discern what is happening and what should be happening in the classroom (Petrides, Jimes, & Karaglani, 2014). The main elements of learning goals and proficiency scales must be present and practiced across the building. In many schools, learning goals and scales are not new concepts, but the *intentionality* of using them consistently is often not evident in classrooms.

Principals can facilitate teachers' learning in an array of ways, such as by implementing effective professional learning community (PLC) practices, empowering instructional coaches to have substantive impact in the classroom, and offering demonstration classrooms. Furthermore, principals must be physically present in teacher meetings when they are considering critical components, so they can contribute their own expertise regarding how trauma- and culturally responsive practices are embedded in the goals and scales. In collaborative meetings, the instructional leader should also serve as the voice of students, challenging assumptions and increasing clarity. The leader can speak with the expertise of someone who has been in an array of classes and knows what works and what doesn't.

Collaboration is a powerful way for principals to increase their own learning capacity and instructional expertise. This can happen very effectively through some version of administrative collaborative teams or some other model in which leadership teams learn to be more focused, disciplined, and accountable. Effective administrative PLCs—or instructional leadership teams (ILTs), which typically include the principal, assistant principals, instructional coaches, and other school leaders—supply guidance for systematically implementing and executing mastery-based learning elements, which in turn become a powerful change-making force (DuFour, DuFour, Eaker, Many, & Mattos, 2016). In addition, we have seen regular, focused collaboration with other schools be a powerful way to increase ILT capacity.

The intention of instructional leadership is to focus on staff behaviors and choices that affect the quality of teaching and learning and includes action both on organizational matters, such as scheduling and curriculum, as well as on promoting and developing schools as collaborative organizations with adults who are lead learners. The bottom line is that building leaders must partner with teachers in the educational process so that everyone learns and grows together.

Conclusion

Cultivating a culture of mastery is one of the four foundational paradigm shifts that are necessary in moving schools toward a healing- and resilience-centered model of education. Moving from traditional school practices that produce the well-known bell curve focused on a "normal" distribution curve to a competence-based classroom approach that moves all students toward proficiency is a heavy lift. Mastery learning can be implemented in classrooms in a variety of ways such as via peer teaching or cooperative learning. But the main component of mastery learning entails the effective, regular use of proficiency scales by teachers and students to provide a pathway for students to follow on their journey to competence and a way to monitor their progress. Putting the power for learning in the hands of the students and providing them with opportunities for their own voice and choice is empowering, healing, and helps them build resilience.

Cultivating a culture of learning, as opposed to one of compliance, is a critical piece in the shift toward new, innovative schooling. As such, it is important that all educators become fluent in the language of learning and effectively address cognition, metacognition, and instructional expertise.

Culture of Mastery Proficiency Scale

As a team, rate your school on the following skills.

		Sample Evidence
Score 4.0	*In addition to score 3.0, in-depth inferences and applications that go beyond what was taught.* Students can provide evidence of learning that directly align with their growth and progress toward mastery of specified learning goals. Students explain how progress toward mastery provides a culture that demands higher levels of expectation than submitting assignments and following direction that is common in more traditional educational settings.	High Reliability Schools (HRS) level 1 certification (Marzano, Warrick, & Simms, 2014)
3.5	In addition to score 3.0 performance, in-depth inferences and applications with partial success	
Score 3.0	The educators will: • Effectively implement learning goals and proficiency scales as the model of education rather than relying on lesson plans to simply deliver content. • Monitor how the use of learning goals and proficiency scales allows teachers and students to deepen relationships and connections based on learning as opposed to compliance. • Explain how helping students master learning goals results in a more collaborative school environment between teachers and students. *The educator exhibits no major errors or omissions.*	• Proficiency scales or Critical Concepts
2.5	No major errors or omissions regarding 2.0 content and partial knowledge of the 3.0 content	

Score 2.0	There are no major errors or omissions regarding the simpler details and processes as the educators:
	• Recognize or recall specific terminology, such as *academic optimism, cognitive skills, engagement, learning goals, mastery, metacognitive skills, proficiency scales,* and *relationship.*
	• Perform basic processes, such as:
	  + Discuss and engage in collaborative efforts to understand how leaning goals and proficiency scales form the foundation of mastery-based learning.
	  + Understand how proficiency scales provide a learning progression and a roadmap for student mastery of identified skills and knowledge.
	  + Consider how proficiency scales can be utilized in a manner that encourages culturally responsive teaching strategies.
	The educator exhibits major errors or omissions regarding the more complex ideas and processes.
		• HRS level 1 survey data (Marzano et al., 2014)

1.5	Partial knowledge of the 2.0 content, but major errors or omissions regarding the 3.0 content.	
Score 1.0	With help, a partial understanding of some of the simpler details and processes and some of the more complex ideas and processes	
0.5	With help, a partial understanding of the 2.0 content, but not the 3.0 content	
Score 0.0	Even with help, no understanding or skill demonstrated	

Chapter 4
Culture of Learning

For the sole true end of education is simply this: to teach [people] how to learn for themselves; and whatever instruction fails to do this is effort spent in vain.

—Dorothy L. Sayers

Schools are centers of learning. Learning, by definition, is an act processed in the brain. Human behavior is also driven by the brain. As such, a healthy functioning brain is the most critical factor in the acts of thinking, understanding, and learning. Although we all share the same basic physiological brain structures and we proceed through similar developmental stages in life based on age, an individual's brain evolves and is shaped by the specific set of experiences and influences that are unique to him or her. From before birth and throughout life, the brain's physiology and structure continually develop and are impacted by a person's environment as well as their cultural, social, emotional, and physiological experiences (Cantor et al., 2019; Harris, 2018; National Academies of Sciences, Engineering, and Medicine, 2018; Osher et al., 2018). Human development is not fixed, linear, or predetermined by genetics—it is individual and unique, and it responds and adapts to inputs from environment, culture, and personal relationships in an ongoing organization and reorganization throughout one's lifetime.

The critical point to make is that learning does not happen in the same way for all people because different physiological, biological, and cultural influences pervade human development from before the beginning of life. The variety of stimuli and mental demands that children are exposed to from infancy through adolescence and into young adulthood results in continuous reconfigurations to neural connections that affect the growing brain (National Academies of Sciences, Engineering, and Medicine, 2018; Yehuda, Daskalakis et al., 2016; Yehuda, Spiegel et al., 2016). Recognizing these principles is essential to understanding the forces that help shape learning for all students, and thus has profound implications for schools.

This chapter focuses on the need to exist in a continuous culture of high-level learning—for the students as well as the adults—and thus, presents a new vision for classroom assessment as a tool for providing feedback as opposed to students completing tasks or earning grades. Two crucial parts of of trauma- and culturally responsive schooling, (1) mindfulness and (2) motivation, help prepare students for optimal learning. In addition, chapter 4 aligns to the fourth level of Maslow's (1943) hierarchy—the need for esteem. In a community, that culture of learning can enhance students' sense of competence, significance, and recognition. You can assess your school's efforts toward this change by using the "Culture of Learning Proficiency Scale" (page 97).

Bringing Mindfulness to the Classroom

One of the most powerful discoveries to emerge from the vast amount of research on trauma and toxic stress is about the therapeutic potential of many contemplative practices such as mindfulness, meditation, prayer, and reflection. For the purposes of this book, we will refer to the general collection of contemplative strategies as *mindfulness*. *Mindfulness*, the intentional cultivation of moment-by-moment, nonjudgmental focused attention and awareness (Kabat-Zinn, 1990), has spread to education. Table 4.1 provides an easy-to-understand visual explaining mindfulness.

Table 4.1: Mindfulness

Mindfulness Is	Mindfulness Is Not
• Historically based in Buddhist and Hindu practices • Supported by psychological research and evidence (Bauer et al., 2019; Black & Fernando, 2014) • The habit of being aware of one's thinking and emotions in a nonjudgmental way • Focused on attention to the present moment instead of dwelling on the past or future • A way to strengthen one's attention and focus • Effective for managing stress (American Academy of Pediatrics, 2011; Iberlin & Ruyle, 2017) • Helpful for increasing positive feelings toward oneself and others (Catalino, Algoe, & Fredrickson, 2014; Immordino-Yang et al., 2018) • Inclusive of many strategies and activities	• A religious practice • Associated with any particular set of beliefs • A spiritual or supernatural activity • The same as or limited to meditation • Time consuming or expensive

As stated in chapter 2 (page 31), teachers deal with a vast array of stressors. Not only do educators have their own cultures, experiences, stressors, and trauma to address, but they are confronted by the variety of issues their students present on a daily basis. As such, teachers are at very high risk for secondary traumatic stress, which can also be known as vicarious trauma, secondary trauma, and compassion fatigue (Walker, 2019). By working with those in pain, educators may experience emotional, physical, and relational symptoms that can feel a lot like emotional exhaustion or burnout, and can also manifest as physical symptoms such as headaches, stomachaches, constipation, and decreased energy; some affected teachers note a depression rooted in a reduced sense of personal accomplishment (Clay, 2020). Left untreated, emotional symptoms can also affect personal and workplace relationships the following ways (R. Macy, personal communication, March 2019).

- May become more irritable

- May isolate self from friends and colleagues

- May react more negatively to students

It is imperative that teachers, like people in other demanding professions prone to secondary trauma, be provided with healing, cost-effective methods to cultivate their own resilience. Often, teachers operate under the auspice that schools are about prioritizing students. While we understand and agree that schools exist for the education and growth of the children they are built to serve, continuing to espouse the concept of "students first" can have the de facto effect that teachers are, at best, second. If teachers are not taking care of themselves and nurturing their own mental and physical health, they are bringing their damaged selves to their classrooms. In a healing- and resilience-centered school, the health and resilience of the teachers and staff must happen first so that they can bring their best to their students. Extensive neuroscientific, medical, and psychological research with adults provides a mountain of evidence that teachers can benefit personally and professionally from contemplative practices. These findings have indicated strong correlations between mindfulness practice with and the qualities of a healthy, resilient brain, such as increased thickness of gray matter in neurological areas associated with learning, cognition, attention, memory, self-reflection, empathy, and emotional regulation (Greenberg et al., 2019; Hölzel et al., 2011; Lazar et al., 2005).

In addition, although much of the early research on contemplative practices focused on the effects of mindfulness and meditation on adults, a growing body of research points to the same benefits in children. For example, two studies demonstrated that sixth graders who received focused mindfulness training for as few as eight weeks reported lower stress levels; less frequent negative emotions including sadness, anger, and anxiety; and higher levels of well-being. Furthermore, scans revealed less activation in the amygdala, the brain area that processes fear and other emotions (Bauer et al., 2019). In an important second study, the researchers used a questionnaire to evaluate mindfulness in more than two thousand students in grades 5–8. Students who showed more mindfulness tended to have better grades and test scores, as well as fewer absences and discipline issues (Caballero et al., 2019).

Making mindful strategies part of the daily routine for everyone in a healing- and resilience-centered school is important in that mindfulness is like going to the gym. Going for a short time brings some benefit, but the effect will not last without regular practice. Mindfulness is a form of mental exercise that needs to be sustained. In our experience, working with the staff to implement mindful practices is an effective way in which to introduce the practice into the school community. Schools that begin every staff meeting with a moment of mindfulness have been especially effective. A vignette of such a practice can be found in chapter 7 (page 123).

A few easily implemented strategies follow: focus on the breath, the five senses, gratitude, and listening. These exercises work for any grade level. For a full explanation of an array of bringing mindfulness to schools, we suggest *Cultivating Mindfulness in the Classroom* (Iberlin & Ruyle, 2017).

- **Focus on the breath:** An easy and common way in which to bring attention to the present moment is by focusing on our breathing. Taking five deep , or belly, breaths and focusing attention on your inhaling and exhaling can help focus the mind.

- **Focus on the five senses:** One common way to bring attention to the present moment is to observe what is happening in one's immediate surroundings. For example, ask students to consider what noises they hear and what the air feels or smells like. Encouraging students to observe a moment through their five senses can be very soothing.

- **Focus on gratitude:** Asking students to consider something positive in their lives can help them to create more positive thoughts, which impacts mood. A positive mood increases our attention, ability to problem solve, and interest in socializing with others. Positive emotions also can contribute to our creativity, physical health, relationships, the ability to acquire new knowledge, and psychological resilience (Catalino et al., 2014).

- **Focus on listening:** Usually when we are involved in conversation, we tend to think about our response instead of what the other person is saying. Encourage students to try active listening, putting all their attention on the other person's message. Model for them. Practicing mindful listening can often lead to improved conversation and connection almost immediately.

Strengthening Motivation

There are many factors to consider when discussing motivation. In education, motivation is often seen as immeasurable and therefore difficult to pin down. For example, qualitative research studies often focus on students' emotions to help gain clarity on what motivation looks like (Hammond, 2015; Ladson-Billings, 2009). Furthermore, although we recognize the necessity of motivation for student growth, there is a tendency to view motivation as something that is extrinsic or given, like a reward for completion or a grade, rather than intrinsic to the learner and the learning process.

Empowering learners to tap into their own motivational capacities, however, is a foundational piece of trauma- and culturally responsive systems. Motivation is a key component in the learning process, and it shapes and is shaped by foundational skills and elements in learning environments. High levels of student engagement and motivation are also a hallmark in schools that have successfully implemented mastery-based learning. Students in mastery-based school systems demonstrate and report more engagement than they did when they were in more traditional models, and they demonstrate more engagement than their peers in traditional schools (Guskey, 2008, 2010; Ruyle, 2019).

We assert that engagement is changeable and can be learned. It is crucial that teachers understand and embrace this so that they can partner with students to guide them toward increased motivation and engagement. Thus, teachers should continuously strive to create and enhance four motivational conditions that are necessary to support students' intrinsic development (Csikszentmihalyi, 1997; Deci & Ryan, 2012):

1. Every student feels respected by and connected to others.
2. Every student understands the relevance of her or his learning experiences.
3. Every student experiences challenges that are in his or her reach.
4. Every student is able to authentically identify academic growth in personally and socially valued ways.

Teaching and learning have a symbiotic relationship and for both to be present and effective, educators must acknowledge the responsibility of lifelong learning in their own lives. Thus, teachers cannot forget that they are a massive element of the motivation equation. It is not enough to create the conditions in which students can learn and feel motivated. Teachers must also create the conditions for their own personal growth and development:

> As educators, one of our most important [responsibilities] is to stay motivated ourselves—to advocate for the conditions for our own learning that we seek to create for students and to experience a

sense of deep purpose in our own learning that prevails against shifting policy agendas, fiscal constraints, and daily challenges. (Ginsberg, 2015)

The teacher's role cannot be underestimated. Teachers are responsible for creating an environment that inspires a desire for everyone to learn. They create the conditions that influence and inspire student motivation (Ginsberg, 2015). While the conditions are very straightforward, creating an environment that accomplishes these things is trickier. It requires the teacher to be explicit about what students are learning and, more importantly, why they are learning it. It forces the teacher to make connections to students' lived experiences, which means knowing and understanding those experiences. It also requires that rigor be combined with social supports that provide scaffolds that ensure students stretch without getting discouraged. Creating these conditions in the classroom will go a long way in supporting diverse learners, and schools that have used the framework to plan and improve teaching consistently demonstrated impressive learning outcomes (Ginsberg, 2015).

Teachers can enhance motivation by following through on these four actions (Wlodowski & Ginsberg, 1995):

1. *Establishing inclusion*—creating a learning atmosphere in which students and teachers feel respected by and connected to one another

2. *Developing attitude*—creating a favorable disposition toward the learning experience through personal relevance and choice

3. *Enhancing meaning*—creating challenging, thoughtful learning experiences that include student perspectives and values

4. *Engendering competence*—creating an understanding that students are effective in learning something they value

Motivation and culture are inseparable, and motivation is essential to learning. Supporting an environment where students are able to see and make connections between what they are learning and their life experiences adds value and meaning to the curriculum, and when students are motivated, teachers become more motivated to teach (Ginsberg, 2015).

Getting a New View of Classroom Assessment

As schools continue to evolve in order to meet the needs of contemporary learners in the modern world, the new mantra of instruction for teachers is no longer *I taught it*, but rather *they've got it*. As such, it is necessary for teachers and school leaders to shift away from being presenters of content to being facilitators of learning. On a systemwide scale, this presents a transformative move for educators on all levels from classroom teachers, to building and district leaders, to the colleges that conduct preparation programs. This is the most difficult, yet critical, work we do and is the essence of substantive educational reform.

The importance of high-quality classroom assessments as a tool for deep learning goes far beyond simply figuring out how to monitor assignments and calculate grades. Brain research clearly indicates that educational practices that utilize positive communication and interaction in order to increase engagement correlate with students developing emotional regulation, executive functions, and academic skills (Zelazo, Blair, & Willoughby, 2016). For example, learners must consciously and reflectively process new information and connect it to prior knowledge and experience in order to develop executive functions and to reduce cognitive load (Zelazo, 2015).

A teacher may ask, "Why should we be experts on formal assessments?" The answer is compelling: we cannot prove that students are learning in our classes without valid, reliable assessments. Education is about development, and our assessment and feedback strategies must evolve to meet this purpose if we are to move our schools forward into the future. A 49-percentile-point increase in teacher skill in assessment practice could predict a 28-percentile increase in student achievement (Marzano, Norford, & Ruyle, 2019). Therefore, providing actionable feedback from sound assessment practice is a skill in which teachers simply must be better trained and their expertise enhanced. Better teacher assessment expertise equals more student growth.

What's especially new and innovative in the formative assessment research base is the importance of including students as decision makers in their own education. In order to ensure that this practice of student involvement may be effectively implemented, it is critical for educators to provide learners with specific information in a timely manner so that they may make appropriate decisions about their own learning.

Susan Brookhart made the point that successful student involvement in assessment flows from their understanding of classroom learning targets. As a result, Brookhart (2011) also created a codified skillset of assessment that should serve as a model for all teachers based on current theory and research. This represents a dramatic shift, however, in how teachers have typically defined their work and the manner in which they are prepared by the majority of teacher education programs. Brookhart (2011) asserts that, among others, teachers need to be adept at the following skills.

1. All assessment starts with specifying exactly what is to be assessed. Formative assessment, especially, requires clear learning targets for students to aim for. In addition, mastery scales are a necessary component as they allow teachers to focus their feedback and determine subsequent steps in terms of instruction and additional assessment.

2. Teachers must understand matching targets to methods to be adept at identifying how test items and performance assessments can draw out the knowledge and skills they intend to assess.

3. Teachers should also understand how to create or choose appropriate, high-quality assessments for selected response, essay, performance assessment, and personal communication methods. Thus, teachers need to understand and be better trained in the concepts of validity, reliability, fairness, and accessibility.

4. Teachers should provide useful feedback on student work. Effective teacher feedback gives students information about their work in relation to the articulated learning goals. Brookhart (2011) stated that for many teachers, providing sound feedback is equivalent to communicating in an unfamiliar language. As with any complex skill, writing clear and effective feedback requires much practice.

Assessing for Mastery

High-quality assessments are an essential element of any curriculum, but even more so in mastery-based learning systems. Teachers cannot prove that students are learning classes without reliable assessments. Thus, high-quality assessments serve as the primary means of providing feedback and therefore, must be designed to inform teaching and improve learning rather than sort students or justify grades. It is in this sense that assessments are a foundational feature of helping cultivate a culture of learning.

In a traditional system, there is more room for educators to assess student mastery incorrectly, as the goal in such a system is accumulating points as opposed to demonstrating mastery. Traditionally, formal measures of student growth have been left to benchmark assessments, final exams, and state tests. Yet we all know that benchmark and end-of-year assessments are more standardized and broader in scope—so they aren't designed to tell us much about what our individual students know or are able to do.

The importance of using learning goals and mastery scales in healing- and resilience-centered schools, as explained in chapter 3, cannot be overstated. In that vein, high-quality assessments to help students monitor their own growth and advancement toward mastery of those established learning goals are equally important. The consistency, reliability, predictability, availability, honesty, and transparency of assessments are all fundamental components of mastery-based learning that are related to the creation of safe, connected environments for students.

Actively engaging students in decision making as well as providing knowledge about their current academic situation is also important (Marzano et al., 2019).

The purpose of classroom assessment in a mastery-based learning system must not be simply to sort and select students or to justify a grade but rather to inform teaching and improve learning. Thus, classroom assessments must be effective and efficient in order to accurately monitor student growth. In order to make precise, reliable decisions about actual student skill and knowledge, our classroom assessments must be of high quality. They must be valid and reliable, reflect appropriate levels of thinking, and be free of bias (Marzano et al., 2019).

Valid and reliable classroom assessments should be the most effective and frequently used tool in our assessment toolkit in that they provide evidence of growth and progress toward specific learning goals. Teachers should be able to really *see* the student and *see* the evidence, and that knowledge of the student from the evidence gathered should be reflected in the gradebook. As part of a learning partnership, assessment must help provide teachers with information about who their students are, what they learn, how they learn best, what they are able to do, what they know, and what they understand (Brookhart, 2011). Most important for a healing- and resilience-centered school model, assessment provides students with the same information and empowers them with steps to move toward mastery and a vast array of choices to demonstrate that they have earned the distinction.

Validity

Validity refers to the extent to which a test measures what it is supposed to measure. The point of validity is discussed in the context of the form of the test, the test purpose, and for whom it is intended. Foundational questions as to validity are, How valid is this test for the decisions that I need to make? or How valid is the interpretation I propose for the test?

A common example to explain validity involves the use of a bathroom scale. If a person steps onto the scale to measure their weight, the scale will provide a valid measure. If they try to use the scale to measure their height or blood pressure, they will be using an invalid tool for that purpose. In a mastery-based-learning system, directly aligning assessments to mastery scales is a critical necessity as it improves the validity of the assessment. In this sense, the assessment will provide a valid measure to a degree of mastery.

Additional ways to improve validity follow (Marzano et al., 2019).

- Align assessments to identified learning goals and proficiency scales.

- Ensure that assessments are reviewed by colleagues or teams of experts in order to obtain feedback from an outside party who is less invested in the instrument.

- Involve students and solicit their feedback in terms of clarity, troublesome wording, or other difficulties.

- If possible, compare the assessment with other measures, or other data that may be available.

Reliability

Reliability refers to the level of precision or consistency in an assessment (Marzano, 2018). Expanding on the bathroom scale example, if a person steps on the scale five times and records five very different readings (150, 170, 195, 135, and 140 pounds) the reliability of the tool is in question. In other words, the scale will provide a valid score, but not one that's reliable.

All assessments are imprecise to some degree. Nothing is perfect. Political polls or survey data, for example, always acknowledge some sort of measurement error (margin of error) in their results to account for this variability. They may assert that a particular candidate has a 10-percent lead in polling data, but if they report that the survey has a plus-or-minus 5-percent margin of error, the candidate's true lead can be anywhere between 5 and 15 percent.

In the school setting, reliability is important in that teachers must understand that no single assessment can be reliable as an absolute indicator of student status in terms of skills or knowledge. In addition, a lack of reliability could lead to errors as to what steps to take next in the learning process.

Ways to improve reliability follow (Marzano et al., 2019).

- **Provide multiple parallel assessments:** This practice can provide patterns of data or information that give a much stronger indicator of student skill and knowledge. In other words, if more assessments are administered to a student on the same topic, a teacher will have more evidence about the student's true score.

- **Track students' growth over time:** Using this approach, a pattern of scores for an individual student can be analyzed mathematically to compile the best estimates of the student's true scores on each of the tests in the set.

As an example, if an eighth-grade mathematics student is to be held to mastery of the critical concept of volume, the teacher could use an array of assessment data to report his or her progress on the example proficiency scale in figure 4.1.

4.0	The student will: • Find the volume of compound three-dimensional figures (for example, calculate the volume of a rectangular house with a pyramidal roof when given the length and width of the house, the height of the walls, and the height of the roof).
3.5	In addition to score 3.0 performance, partial success at score 4.0 content
3.0	**The student will:** **V1—Find the volume of cones** (for example, calculate the volume of an ice cream cone when given the radius of its top and its height). **V2—Find the volume of cylinders** (for example, calculate how much soda is contained within a soda can when given the radius of its base and its height). **V3—Find the volume of spheres** (for example, calculate how much water a snow globe will hold when given the radius of the snow globe). **V4—Find the volume of pyramids** (for example, calculate the attic space of a house with a pyramidal roof when given the length, width, and height of the roof).
2.5	No major errors or omissions regarding score 2.0 content, and partial success at score 3.0 content
2.0	**V1—**The student will recognize or recall specific vocabulary (for example, *area, base, circle, cone, cubic, face, pi, point, radius, squared, three-dimensional, unit, volume*) and perform basic processes such as: • Identify cones. • State that the area of a circle is equal to pi times the radius squared ($A = \pi r^2$). • State that the volume of a cone is equal to one-third the area of the base (circular region of the cone) times the height, in which X is the area of the base. **V2—**The student will recognize or recall specific vocabulary (for example, *cubic, cylinder*) and perform basic processes such as: • Identify cylinders. • State that the area of a circle is equal to pi times the radius squared. • State that the volume of a cylinder is equal to the area of the base times the height ($V = B \times h$, in which B is the area of the base). **V3—**The student will recognize or recall specific vocabulary (for example, *point, radius, sphere*) and perform basic processes such as: • Identify spheres. • Explain that the volume of a sphere is calculated as four-thirds pi times the radius cubed ($V = \frac{4}{3}\pi r^2$). **V4—**The student will recognize or recall specific vocabulary (for example, *polygon, pyramid, two-dimensional, vertex*) and perform basic processes such as: • Identify pyramids. • State that the volume of a pyramid is equal to one-third the area of the base times the height ($V = \frac{1}{3}Bh$, in which B is the area of the base).

Source: © 2016 by Marzano Resources. Adapted with permission.

Figure 4.1: Proficiency scale for volume (grade 8 mathematics).

In this example, if the student were to present information through assessment data that included tests, quizzes, and discussions indicating level of knowledge, a teacher may record the following scores.

- Three quizzes: scores of 2, 3, and 3

- One test: score of 2.75

- Three instances of probing discussions with a teacher: scores of 3, 3, and 3.5

The combined scores of 2, 2.75, 3, 3, 3, 3, 3.5 would provide the teacher with solid evidence that the student is operating at mastery as five of the seven scores displayed increasing knowledge and examples of mastery on the concept. Simply stated, the student's assessment data provide a much more precise, or reliable, picture of his or her true level of knowledge or skill.

Fairness

The teacher must provide activities that expose students to the assessed content and allow them to practice the work before the assessment: a fair and just assessment task provides all students with an equal opportunity to demonstrate the extent of their learning (Marzano et al., 2019).

Improving fairness means making an assessment free from bias in terms of the following.

- **Stereotyping:** Avoid confirming negative stereotypes about a person's racial, ethnic, gender, or cultural group. What is called *stereotype threat* has been shown to disrupt working memory and overall executive function, increase self-consciousness about performance, and result in those who feel stereotyped thinking negative thoughts and feeling negative emotions (Steinke & Fitch, 2017).

- **Unfamiliar or offensive cultural phenomena:** This type of bias occurs when a test is comparatively more difficult for one group of students than for another group, or upholds a stereotype. It can occur when, for example, minority groups have not been given the same opportunity to learn the assessed material or when questions are worded in ways that are unfamiliar to certain students because of linguistic or cultural differences.

- **Poorly written items or directions:** This type of bias is closely related to the issue of *test fairness* and results in an assessment lacking validity in that the items are not able to measure intended outcomes.

At the very least, schools should consider the principles for quality assessment practice to ensure all teachers are best able to determine student progress toward mastery. For more detail descriptions of how to improve assessment literacy, *Making Classroom Assessments Reliable and Valid* (Marzano, 2018) and *The New Art and Science of Classroom Assessment* (Marzano et al., 2019) can prove especially helpful for teachers in deepening their assessment literacy.

Making It Happen: Mindful Leadership

Educators and students in schools evolving to healing- and resilience-centered systems need leaders who can model mindfulness during and following the change process. Mindful principles are fundamental to this model in that when practiced in a purposeful, consistent manner, mindfulness can improve brain health. This fact, obviously, can lead directly to higher-level learning. If bringing more mindfulness to the classroom is good for students, it is equally good for teachers. Thus, it is important that leaders are able to effectively help teachers improve their own mindfulness skills so that mindfulness becomes the school's cultural norm.

Since they wear many hats, school leaders often become adept at multitasking and can seem efficient by simultaneously writing an email during a meeting while completing a district-level task. When leaders are in this mode, it's good for them to ask themselves if they really heard what teachers were discussing or if they shared their best work in the email. Recall the effort to have students listen mindfully in the classroom as a way to engage in the present. When leaders are present and engaged, the effect is very different from when they are operating on autopilot or between several tasks at once. For the shift to happen, leaders must be willing to exert the cognitive energy to train their minds in a new way of thinking. This work of enhancing their leadership begins by becoming aware of how much time they currently spend in a state of partial attention.

Mindful leaders also exhibit two specific behaviors that embody the strength necessary to shift paradigms.

1. **Ability to connect to themselves, to teachers and students, and to the larger community:** Connecting to themselves is how leaders stay connected to their own health, feelings, values, and passion. Connecting deeply with other people is the difference between a school environment that values everybody and builds capacity as opposed to one that is traditional and where people operate in silos. Connecting to the community enables leaders to continually focus on the bigger picture and not get caught up in the minutiae of principal responsibilities.

2. **Ability to guide change:** It's also this capacity that fuels a leader's willingness to take a courageous stand, lead the school into a new

paradigm, and accept failures as opportunities from which to learn. Mindful leaders who embody connection are how healing- and resilience-centered schools communicate their vision and mission and inspire all stakeholders to shift to a new educational paradigm.

We recommend the following resources.

- *101 Mindful Ways to Build Resilience: Cultivate Calm, Clarity, Optimism and Happiness Each Day* (Altman, 2016)

- *Breathe: The New Science of a Lost Art* (Nestor, 2020)

- *The Mindful Brain: Reflection and Attunement in the Cultivation of Well-Being* (Siegel, 2007)

- *Teach, Breathe, Learn: Mindfulness In and Out of the Classroom* (Srinivasan, 2014)

Conclusion

As schools focus on creating and cultivating a culture of learning as opposed to a culture of grades or work completion, it is important for educators to come to a deeper understanding of the factors—internal and external—that combine to create context that impacts learning readiness and performance. Whole-child development requires looking at motivation, mindfulness strategies, and revised assessment to provide a continual feedback loop. These actions are critical in building healing- and resilience-centered models of schooling. These strategies facilitate brain health and ultimately can help align instruction and school design with students' individual capacities and needs, thereby facilitating deeper learning.

Culture of Learning Proficiency Scale

As a team, rate your school on the following skills.

		Sample Evidence
Score 4.0	*In addition to score 3.0, in-depth inferences and applications that go beyond what was taught.* Present how mindful practices have shifted the culture of your school at conferences, professional development sessions, or in books or articles.	• High Reliability Schools (HRS) level 4 certification (Marzano et al., 2014) • Articles, books, or presentations
3.5	In addition to score 3.0 performance, in-depth inferences and applications with partial success	
Score 3.0	The educators will: • Utilize norms to practice mindfulness with learners in classrooms. • Respond to stress in students and teachers. • Align assessment with proficiency scales to enhance validity. • Use classroom assessment data to drive instructional practices based on student progress rather than primarily for a grade. • Monitor student engagement and motivation as a natural product of personalized learning. *The educator exhibits no major errors or omissions.*	• Common assessments aligned to learning goals and proficiency scales • Classroom assessments aligned to learning goals and proficiency scales • Student engagement data • Teacher engagement data from tools such as the School Academic Optimism Survey (Hoy, 2005b) at www.waynekhoy.com/pdfs/saos.pdf
2.5	No major errors or omissions regarding 2.0 content and partial knowledge of the 3.0 content	
Score 2.0	There are no major errors or omissions regarding the simpler details and processes as the educators: • Recognize or recall specific terminology, such as *assessment, gratitude, meditation, mindful leadership, mindfulness, motivation, reliable,* and *valid.* • Perform basic processes, such as: + Recognize the impact of stress and trauma on the brain and body. + Explain the impact of mindfulness on healing and resilience in human brains. + Align assessments to learning goals and proficiency scales. + Utilize an instructional framework that provides teachers with a multitude of strategies to address student progress toward goals. • Students can explain how assessments provide evidence of learning rather than serve as a basis for grading. *The educator exhibits major errors or omissions regarding the more complex ideas and processes.*	• HRS level 4 survey data (Marzano et al., 2014) • Professional learning plans to enhance practice in mindfulness, motivation, and valid, reliable assessment protocols
1.5	Partial knowledge of the 2.0 content, but major errors or omissions regarding the 3.0 content	
Score 1.0	With help, a partial understanding of some of the simpler details and processes and some of the more complex ideas and processes	
0.5	With help, a partial understanding of the 2.0 content, but not the 3.0 content	
Score 0.0	Even with help, no understanding or skill demonstrated	

Hoy, W. K. (2005). *SAOS.* Accessed at www.waynekhoy.com/pdfs/saos.pdf on September 9, 2021.
Marzano, R. J., Warrick, P., & Simms, J. A. (2014). *A handbook for high reliability schools: The next step in school reform.* Bloomington, IN: Marzano Resources.

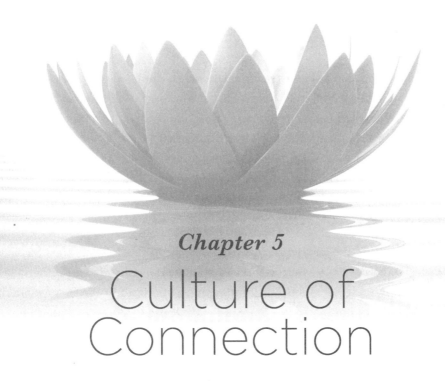

Chapter 5

Culture of Connection

One looks back with appreciation to the brilliant teachers, but with gratitude to those who touched our human feelings. The curriculum is so much necessary raw material, but warmth is a vital element for the growing plant and for the soul of the child.

—Carl Jung

A culture of connection is a foundational element in healing- and resilience-centered schools. In fact, the teacher-student relationships, as structured in this model, can contribute to an increase in student motivation that cannot be overstated. Trauma and toxic stress can disrupt human development, correlating with a host of negative outcomes such as behavioral, emotional, social, cognitive, and physical health issues (Harris, 2018). On the other hand, positive and responsive relationships paired with cognitive and social enrichment buffer the effects of adversity (Bloom & Farragher, 2013; Masten & Coatsworth, 1998; Osher et al., 2018).

Connection is the antidote to trauma, and building a teacher's capacity to regulate his or her own emotions is critical to teaching students how to regulate their own. In addition, the ability to authentically understand students is a nonnegotiable element of culturally responsive teaching. By truly connecting with students, teachers are better able to discern their educational needs. This chapter addresses how connection can lead to implementing solid instructional strategies based on student needs, as opposed to teachers creating a single lesson plan for all students. The chapter will also draw from the third level—the need for belonging—from Maslow's (1943) hierarchy of needs. Connection requires empathizing, co-regulating, and building community, which are powerful trauma- and culturally responsive ways that teachers can help cultivate a healing- and resilience-centered school. You can assess your school's efforts toward this change by using the "Culture of Connection Proficiency Scale" (page 108).

Nurturing Empathy

In their book *Born for Love: Why Empathy Is Essential—and Endangered*, Maia Szalavitz and Bruce D. Perry (2010) assert that relational poverty, defined as a profound lack of connectedness with others that is fundamental to our ability to survive and be healthy, is a form of poverty that is more destructive and debilitating than economic poverty. Relational poverty impacts all groups of people regardless of race, gender, or socioeconomic status. We assert that many students are showing up to school more dysregulated and suffering from relational poverty than in previous generations. There are a number of reasons for this.

Many modern societies are more focused on economics and financial status, often with broken social structures that prove challenging for young people's ability to relate to each other. In addition, innovative technology means young people spend more time in front of phones, computers, game systems, or television sets rather than interacting with significant adults. Screen time is a major factor in relational poverty. Perry (2008) noted that people from older generations experienced more significant face-to-face time with adults by age six than students in so-called Generation Z will encounter by the time they're eighteen. Finally, Szalavitz and Perry (2010) claim that that only 32 percent of Americans believe that most people can be trusted—a trend that has only seemed to deepen over recent years with the onslaught of a global pandemic as well as the fissures in society resulting from serious political division. Our schools provide environments in which students experience hundreds of daily interactions with peers and teachers—yet these interactions are often profoundly lacking in relational connections such as touch, rich conversation, or intergenerational mentoring. Relational poverty alienates us from one another.

We assert that the cure to relational poverty is empathy. Empathy is an action word that describes vicariously experiencing someone else's reality . It also means understanding, and sensitivity to, the feelings, thoughts, and experiences of another person. The presence of empathy can lead to trust, deeper personal connection, generosity of spirit, and love (Lesley University, n.d.). The lack of empathy can be the root cause of racism, crime, violence, war, abuse, and social inequity. The psychological benefits of empathy can be profound. Personal connection is an antidote to trauma in that it can reduce stress hormones and result in many of the same neurological benefits mindfulness offers, including calming the amygdala and increasing brain *neuroplasticity*, or pliability (Caballero et al., 2019; Hammond, 2015).

Our successful evolution as a species is due to our ability to empathize and connect (Bloom & Farragher, 2013; Lesley University, n.d.). Although empathy is deeply part of the human condition, it is usually pushed aside to make way for academics. We assert that empathy must be nurtured in order for people to properly develop and for children to learn at their highest capacity. Three critical pieces form the foundational structure of trauma-informed work: (1) safety, (2) connection, and (3) emotional regulation (Bath, 2008; Bloom & Farragher, 2013; R. Macy, personal communication, April 2019). Connection serves as the central element and is critical to education in that if students feel connected to their teachers, they will be better able to learn.

Teachers can cultivate connection and empathy in the following ways that epitomize healing- and resilience-centered education.

- **Provide purposeful attention:** Greet students and, if appropriate (you know the student doesn't have a problem with eye contact culturally or in terms of emotional needs), make soft eye contact as they enter the room. Using smiles and a warm, welcoming voice when speaking with students can be beneficial. This strategy may be counterproductive with students whose cultures discourage such eye contact, so teachers must be prepared to adjust their connection strategy based on each student's response or by being culturally sensitive.

- **Nurture relationships with students and between students:** Grouping strategies that are common in mastery-based classes can be practiced in a purposeful way to increase student interaction. Building opportunities for students to interact can increase empathy and reduce bullying. Also, encouraging healthy, positive touch can be a powerful way to build connection and empathy. Teachers can celebrate and greet students with methods the students are comfortable with, such as fist bumps, high fives, or gentle pats on the arm.

- **Take an interest in students' lives:** Ask questions. Listen. Remember. Take notes. Call home when students do things well as opposed to only when they make mistakes or make poor choices. If students are involved with sports or extracurricular activities, go watch them in action and check in with them in school later to comment on their performance.

- **Write and share:** Incorporate a journaling activity in class. Read and respond to entries.

Nurturing Co-Regulation

Co-regulation refers to our ability to regulate another person's brain. Just as an angry child can lash out and create responsive anger in an adult, we can help students who are in the stress response state and help bring them back to regulation. It takes a calm brain to regulate another brain. If students are dysregulated, teachers need to be more regulated to grapple with that, set a tone, and model the skills. Many students are showing up in school not having enough significant early contact with adults. We learn to regulate ourselves in relationships. For example, consider a small child who is upset because a toy breaks. A caring adult picks up and rocks the child, showing reassurance. Over time, children learn to do this for themselves. Many students have disrupted attachment and they do not have the skills needed to attach, or be close to, others. As a result, they do not have the skills they need to soothe themselves. All that needs to be taught. That work is a prerequisite for learning.

What happens far too often is that teachers end up being driven by their students' dysregulation rather than the students being influenced by their teachers' solid self-regulation. Many of the students whose behavior we struggle with are dysregulated and need well-regulated adults in their lives to help them manage their emotional world. You cannot help a young student whose heart is beating at one hundred beats per minute if your heart is beating at one hundred beats per minute as well. Mindfulness is a good strategy for working on your own ability to regulate your feelings. Feelings are contagious.

Co-regulation is a critical strategy that teachers can learn and hone over time. It typically involves warmth: a soothing tone of voice, communication that acknowledges the person's distress, supportive silence, and an invitation to reflective problem solving. As with a mother tending her young infant, the defining characteristic of effective co-regulation is that it is calming and designed to help the young person manage overwhelming emotional arousal.

There are a number of tools that teachers can use to help them better regulate their emotions (R. Macy, personal communication, September 2019).

- Hydrate
- Sleep
- Exercise
- Take breaks
- Practice mindfulness (page 84)
- Eat a healthy diet
- Learn something new

- Train professionally and keep learning
- Laugh

Building Community

It is difficult to discuss student growth without taking into account the impact families and communities have on the learning process. Historically, communities of color have been disenfranchised in the American education system and unable to realize their full potential due to long-standing barriers that restrict full participation:

> In response to widespread civil unrest, President Lyndon Johnson appointed the National Advisory Commission on Civil Disorders (also known as the Kerner Commission) to examine racial division and disparities in the United States. In 1968, the Kerner Commission issued a report concluding that the nation was "moving toward two societies, one black, one white—separate and unequal." Without major social changes, the Commission warned, the U.S. faced a "system of apartheid" in its major cities. [In 2018], 50 years after the report was issued, that prediction characterizes most of our large urban areas, where intensifying segregation and concentrated poverty have collided with disparities in school funding to reinforce educational inequality, locking millions of students of color from low-income families out of today's knowledge-based economy. (Immordino-Yang et al., 2018)

Poverty and institutionalized racism are identified as key factors to the deepening disparities:

> "White society," the presidentially appointed panel reported, "is deeply implicated in the ghetto. White institutions created it, white institutions maintain it, and white society condones it." (George, 2018)

As a consequence of these divisions, the resources available to White communities are scarce in many predominantly Black and Brown communities—not simply in relation to education, but also in relation to access to health care, housing, clean water, and food. Many of the same factors identified in the 1968 report are present and continuing to negatively impact communities of color. Lack of economic opportunity in communities of color, police brutality, and overt racism remain at the top of the list and remind us that we still have a lot of work to do. These ongoing issues manifest as unequal opportunities and unequal outcomes for students. Focusing our efforts on supporting these marginalized communities, along with using culturally responsive practices in the classroom can go a long way in bridging the academic and social gaps.

In order for the necessary changes to occur we must start investing in the education of our students of color and the communities they live in. Our spending must get on par with those states and districts that spend more than ten times that which is spent in marginalized communities. There was a small window during the 1960s and 1970s where we saw significant desegregation and financial reform, yet the efforts were short lived. New strategies to resegregate communities emerged and moved substantial tax bases out to the suburbs, which were composed largely of White people (Darling-Hammond, Goldhaber, Strunk, & Sutcher, 2018).

Latin American countries are not exempt from having groups that are marginalized or deprived of their basic rights and services. During the discussion "Marginalization in Mexico, a Decade in Retrospection" (Morales, 2018) in 2018 (the most recent year in which the problem was addressed with statistics at a national level), the issue of poverty was discussed as one of the main causes of marginalization in society. Ricardo Aparicio Jiménez, a teacher, a participant in the discussion, and the general director of the analysis of poverty of the National Council for the Evaluation of Social Development Policy defined poverty as the "inability to exercise social rights, which are: the right to have an income, access to education, health, social security, food, basic housing services and basic standards of living conditions" (as cited in Morales, 2018, p. 6). Senator Marlon Berlanga Sánchez, considering the data provided by the Ministry of Welfare in Mexico, explained that the poverty and vulnerability of more than 95 million Mexicans are caused internally by an imbalance in the distribution of wealth and externally as a result of the exploitation of the nation's natural resources, which causes slow economic growth: low wages, unemployment, corruption, and public policies with little or no impact (as cited in Morales, 2018).

In addition to living in poverty, marginalized groups who suffer from a lack of opportunities, discrimination, and educational backwardness have been identified in the report "Inequalities in Mexico 2018" (El Colegio de México, 2018), the main ones being Indigenous people, women, and people born into poor communities. According to the report (El Colegio de México, 2018), Indigenous people, especially those in southwestern Mexico, receive significantly lower labor income and have little access to school courses, which greatly hinders their social mobility. In respect to women, the percentage of those who work in paid employment has stagnated at a rate of around 45 percent, this percentage being one of the lowest in the world. This is in addition to women receiving a lower salary than men. On the other hand, people who come from a poor household are likely to not improve their living conditions in their adulthood. Only 2.1 percent of children with poor parents end up earning a higher income as adults.

Building strong communities is paramount to building strong schools within those communities. It is difficult to have one without the other. While this book does not address how to invest and rebuild communities specifically, it is crucial that schools figure out how to nourish the surrounding community as part of the commitment to improve student growth. Utilizing parents and parent organizations as collaborators rather than relegating them to funding sources is one way to begin to bridge the gap, while sharing the responsibility and empowering families to actively participate in the problem solving. Education does not occur in a vacuum. Strong communities affect student academic motivation in students (Nesbit & Graham, 2020).

Four pillars support community building that creates camaraderie, engagement, and a sense of belonging (Nesbit & Graham, 2020).

- **Help people feel connected:** Create opportunities to be social and build relationships outside of school between school staff and parents.

- **Step up communications:** Create systems to enhance communication to keep staff and families in the loop and allow opportunities for input and increased participation. This should be done in a number of ways, because not every family has access to technology.

- **Recognize different cultures:** Seek to understand the multiple cultures represented in the school community and authentically engage them by creating opportunities for them to share who they are beyond the ethnic contributions approach (Banks, 1988).

- **Focus on working together:** Identify common goals, create opportunities to collaborate between home and school, and increase community partnerships by utilizing local organizations to expand the classroom beyond the school's four walls. Frequently express appreciation and celebrate accomplishments to bring the communities together.

Building these four pillars can have a remarkable impact on strengthening the school climate and culture. Research shows that strong communities build strong schools: "Sure, the curriculum matters. Sure, funding for high-quality professional development matters. Sure, technology matters. But at the end of the day, it's the people who make the big changes happen" (Responsive Classroom, 2015). Focusing on the people, providing scaffolds and supports, and being open to multiple perspectives enriches the school culture and removes barriers to learning through connection.

Making It Happen: Transformational Leadership

The ability to transform everyone in a building is critical in helping to create a culture of connection in a healing- and resilience-centered school. No substantive transformation happens until the hearts and minds of the adults in a school shift first. Thus, the concept of transformational leadership is an important construct to cultivate. Transformational leadership strategies employed by leaders during the process of creating a healing- and resilience-centered school greatly increase the likelihood of that new system becoming the norm.

A seminal proponent for this style of leadership in schools, Bernard Bass (1985) stated that:

> transformational leadership motivates followers to do more than expected by (a) raising followers' levels of consciousness about the importance and value of specified and idealized goals, (b) getting followers to transcend their own self-interest for the sake of the team or organization, and (c) moving followers to address high-level needs. (p. 20)

Later, Western Michigan University professor Peter Northouse (2007) expanded on this idea by defining transformational leadership as "a process that changes and transforms people. It is concerned with the emotions, values, ethics, standards, and long-term goals and includes assessing followers' motives, satisfying their needs, and treating them as full human beings" (p. 175).

Robert J. Marzano, Timothy Waters, and Brian McNulty (2005) identified two general types of change that schools can practice.

1. First-order change is incremental in that it moves or shifts the existing system through a series of small steps.

2. Second-order change, on the other hand, represents a more dramatic, transformational shift that serves to create a new system and entails new ways of thinking and behaving.

The leadership traits that are crucial to guiding this transformation can be clearly expressed in the following fundamental practices that empower leaders to accomplish extraordinary things (Kouzes & Posner, 2007).

- **Modeling:** This requires that leaders be clear about their own expectations and values while providing a personal example through their own behaviors. Want healthy students? Create healthy teachers. They are empowered by healthy leaders.

- **Inspiring a shared vision:** Transformational leaders are the ones who are able to visualize positive outcomes and challenge others to transcend the status quo to achieve something great. Transformational educational leaders provide clear direction and vision for a school to follow. In this case, a deep understanding of the school wellness wheel components is necessary.

- **Challenging the process:** Question the status quo through a willingness to be innovative and creative, and by focusing on growth. Transformational leaders are not afraid to take risks in order to improve the current system. Becoming part of a cohort of other school leaders who are implementing the school wellness wheel in their own setting is invaluable, because it provides leaders with a team of like-minded people to help them continue the journey through the inevitable rough patches of evolution.

- **Enabling others to act:** No matter how charismatic or knowledgeable a leader is, that one person simply cannot accomplish all the things necessary to drive change alone. Transformational leaders enable others to act to accomplish a shared vision. This requires creating an environment where others feel empowered to contribute to the organization. Such leaders also provide encouragement, personal attention, and recognition, establish goals and timeframes, and set high performance expectations. As a result, teachers begin to feel empowered through shared decision making, which leads to a belief in their abilities to make a difference in the classroom and in the school as a whole.

- **Encouraging the heart:** Frequent celebrations to recognize positive contributions are an important aspect of driving instructional improvement and giving it an unwavering focus on students' individual learning needs. Celebrating their contributions increases teachers' motivation, healing, and resilience.

Conclusion

All of the research on resilience suggests that one of the primary issues in student resilience is a relationship with at least one significant adult. We think teachers are uniquely positioned to be that one significant adult. Students who have had significant trauma or toxic stress in their lives have these weights that are pulling them down. Connections are the balloons that can pull them up. *It's not what's wrong with you, it's what's happened to you* is worth noting here. We strongly assert that the students we struggle with are not bad, and they're not crazy. They are injured, and part of our job is to help them recover from, or at least work around, their injuries.

Culture of Connection Proficiency Scale

As a team, rate your school on the following skills.

			Sample Evidence
Score 4.0		*In addition to score 3.0, in-depth inferences and applications that go beyond what was taught.* Students and teachers actively cultivate connections with outside agencies and community groups to enhance student learning and apply it in a real-world setting.	
	3.5	In addition to score 3.0 performance, in-depth inferences and applications with partial success	
Score 3.0		The educators will: • Actively employ a variety of instructional strategies based on the needs of individual students or groups of students and their progress toward mastering identified learning goals. • Demonstrate a demeanor conducive to learning by modeling a positive emotional mindset that enhances learning opportunities. • Facilitate learning communities in classrooms in which taking risks and falling short are celebrated as necessary steps to higher levels of learning. *The educator exhibits no major errors or omissions.*	• *The New Art and Science of Teaching* (Marzano, 2017) • Madeline Hunter's (1967, 1979, 1982) Instructional Theory Into Practice (ITIP) method
	2.5	No major errors or omissions regarding 2.0 content and partial knowledge of the 3.0 content	

Score 2.0		There are no major errors or omissions regarding the simpler details and processes as the educators:
		• Recognize or recall specific terminology, such as *co-regulation, elements, personalized,* and *strategies.*
		• Perform basic processes, such as:
		  + Describe how various strategies provide an array of learning opportunities based on the individual needs and strengths of the students in their care.
		  + Understand how teacher attitudes and mindsets can determine the culture of the classrooms.
		  + Describe how emotions and cognition are inextricably linked.
		  + Utilize an array of grouping strategies to enhance both the input and output literacy of learnings so that every student is able to learn at their highest possible level.
		The educator exhibits major errors or omissions regarding the more complex ideas and processes.
			• *The New Art and Science of Teaching* (Marzano, 2017)
			• Mindprint Learning's Mindprint Assessment (https://bit.ly/3CyIc5J)

	1.5	Partial knowledge of the 2.0 content, but major errors or omissions regarding the 3.0 content	
Score 1.0		With help, a partial understanding of some of the simpler details and processes and some of the more complex ideas and processes	
	0.5	With help, a partial understanding of the 2.0 content, but not the 3.0 content	
Score 0.0		Even with help, no understanding or skill demonstrated	

Chapter 6

Culture of Empowerment

Between stimulus and response there is space . . . and in that space lies our power and our freedom.

—Viktor Frankl

The ultimate purpose of a healing- and resilience-centered model of education is to grow healthy brains and bodies that are empowered to learn and function at their highest possible levels. As such, the twin concepts of *voice* and *choice* are critical elements in terms of healing from trauma as well as strengthening resilience. They are also vitally important for students to help develop their agency as learners, which will help guide them on the road to academic mastery. Exercising guided voice and choice empowers students by encouraging them to take control over certain elements of the learning environment in order to develop confidence and competence.

This chapter discusses the importance of cultivating a culture of empowerment for teachers and students and how enhancing student voice, choice, and agency in order to achieve high-level expectations is a necessary element in all three of the school wellness wheel's pivot points. By empowering students and teachers to reach their full potential academically, socially, and emotionally, building a culture of empowerment directly aligns with level five of Maslow's (1943) hierarchy—self-actualization. You can assess your school's efforts toward this change by using the "Culture of Empowerment Proficiency Scale" (page 122).

Restoring Power Through Guided Voice and Choice

Students who have been victims of trauma or toxic stress have generally experienced abuse of power. Adults or certain people in power in their lives have coerced them, generally not in the best interest of the child, but to meet their own needs. Recovery requires that young people find their own power—and they cannot do that in environments where they are coerced to make the "right" choices. They need to be able to practice decision making. This may mean that we give them some limited choices at first: you can do whichever you prefer of A or B, but that does not mean you can do whatever you want.

Many students are accustomed to having adults do things *to* them or *at* them, and we assert that teachers must shift to doing things *with* them. Ideally, adults are in the role of coaches, and we are helping students to make better choices by guiding and steering them in the right direction. If we take this approach, we can build higher levels of trust, which will also allow us to be more direct when and if the time comes.

The concept of reenactment is important in building a culture of empowerment. If schools operate by coercing students—especially those who have been coerced, bullied, and abused before—those students will respond in the ways they have always responded: they will protect themselves, test adults, push back, and push away. As a result, teachers must not reply to students with default responses. Adults need to intentionally choose their responses rather than just react. Just reacting is always going to promote reenactment. Repeating old patterns is always a feature in trauma and students who have suffered adversity. Their hypervigilance keeps them very focused on threats and they are always scanning for evidence that a teacher or principal is just like everyone else they have encountered. Many students will push very hard to get adults in schools to be coercive, because that is their norm. Unfortunately, many teachers tend to believe that their own success is a product of their student's success. If a student fails, we are failures, which circles back to reenactment.

Typical school systems can tend to display elements of being dysregulated and crisis driven. Teachers need to be able to regulate themselves in the face of challenging institutional issues that impact their work and not pass that along to the students they teach. This is important due to the reality of reenactment. Traumatized people tend to repeat the past. This is an unconscious process. Part of prevention is helping make it conscious. Teachers can unintentionally respond in kind to traumatized students and play the roles that adults have played for the young student's entire life. This is also where self-regulation comes in. If a teacher is reacting to a student's negative behavior using reason, then the teacher is less likely to be drawn into the reenactment and more likely to choose a response that is helpful and productive.

With respect to increased optimism in mastery-based schools: it is effective partly because it shifts the paradigm from adults trying to control students to students taking responsibility for themselves and working at their own pace. It helps eliminate some of the power struggles that come up in school that tend to promote reenactment and escalate affect. Often, the starting point for teachers is wondering how to get students to do what they need them to do. Providing voice and choice can take the air out of these power struggles and prevent reenactment. Voice and choice serve to help students create a new script. This is one of the reasons mastery-based learning is so powerful. It encourages students to move at their pace and puts their hands on the wheel.

Dialogue will help convey that you want to provide a different experience and better understand the students you are standing in front of each day. One way to allow voice and choice is to take a little time with each student to learn something about him or her. That conversation might include the following prompts.

- "Tell me about yourself."
- "What is something that really upsets you?"
- "What are you proud of?"
- "If I have a problem with something you are doing, how would you like me to bring it to your attention?"
- "If you have a problem with something I am doing, how will I know?"

Encouraging voice entails providing all students with authentic opportunities for input and feedback regarding cultural and academic issues. Some additional strategies for encouraging voice and choice follow.

- **Establish class rules with the students:** Be clear that everyone is there to learn, but convey that you know students need to provide input on the conditions that best promote that goal.

- **Ask for feedback:** See how you are doing and how you can do your job better. It is important to act on student suggestions. Soliciting ideas and then failing to act on the input undermines student trust.

- **Focus on strengths and interests:** Use all available resources, as well as the students themselves, to know and understand their stories, cultures, backgrounds, interests, and goals.

- **Emphasize personal choice:** Given that student suggestions should be acted on, teachers should make sure they select areas for student input that they are willing to change.

The purposeful focus on empowering students to build on their strengths provides a healthy foundation for students to actively utilize and rely on throughout their lives. And we should start at the earliest possible moments. For example, although some teachers tend to think of voice, choice, and agency as more appropriate for older students, even the youngest students can benefit by making their own decisions and advocating for themselves. Thus, voice, choice, and agency are critical elements to address at every grade level in the educational experience.

Preschoolers' voices, for example, take shape through looks, words, movements, images, and graphics. Loris Malaguzzi developed the Reggio Emilia approach to education and asserted that listening to preschool students is a fundamental part of their cognitive and social-emotional development (Katz, 1998). In an educational setting, preschool-age students notice that their teachers listen to them while writing, recording, and seriously documenting their interests, preferences, observations, hypotheses, questions, and emotions, with the aim of assessing their knowledge and understanding of a topic they were studying. Furthermore, education professors Alexa Fraley Gardner and Brett D. Jones (2016) suggested that control in a preschool classroom is a shared entity that motivates and empowers students. They asserted that control is an act where the teacher and the student listen to the other's points of view, work cooperatively, share ideas and inspirations, and negotiate to make decisions about the learning process.

Teachers intuitively understand the importance of listening attentively. They therefore invite students to raise their voices to be heard, recommend the use of graphic and artistic tools to present their ideas, and encourage them to respond to questions. The students' own questions can become study projects that arise from the student's initiative. This helps secure their active participation, leads to increased confidence in their abilities, and invites a willingness to continue learning. The teacher, instead of instructing the student in a specific concept from the curriculum, decides how much assistance to provide to ensure progress while also establishing a balance between flexibility and freedom and allowing the student to draw conclusions.

Holding All Learners to High Expectations

How much a teacher expects from his or her students has a great impact on learner engagement and subsequent success. This approach suggests that the students are the ones that are broken and need to be fixed. It is this type of deficit thinking that limits opportunities that are given to students of color and reduces their interactions with the teacher to one of compliance or silence, as it is viewed as the only way to reach the desired outcomes.

Educators Joe Burks and Craig Hochbein (2013) suggested a connection between engagement and student confidence in their ability to be successful, stating, "Interventions specifically designed to improve academic skills might require improvement of academic self-concept, or the belief in one's academic ability" (p. 17). Other research has shown that:

> Student confidence, or self-concept, in terms of their academic abilities often results in stronger student outcomes, and this higher level of achievement can cyclically lead to further increases in academic self-concept, a [phenomenon] that has been referred to as the *reciprocal effects model*. (Marsh & O'Mara, 2008)

The power of high expectations can be profound. In fact, teachers' expectations impact student success more than a student's own motivation (Black & Fernando, 2014; Boser et al., 2014; Siegel, 2013). Unfortunately, students of color and students from low socioeconomic backgrounds often remain at a disadvantage when it comes to teachers' expectations. A number of studies suggest that, on average, teachers tend to be negatively biased about future academic performances of students from these groups (Glock, Krolak-Schwerdt, Klapproth, & Böhmer, 2013). For example, according to a 2014 Center for American Progress report, teachers in U.S. classrooms often have lower teacher expectations for students of color and students from low socioeconomic backgrounds. For instance, high school teachers in this study believed students living in poverty, Black students, and Hispanic students were (respectively) 53, 47, and 42 percent less likely to graduate from college compared to their more affluent or White peers (Boser et al., 2014). On the other end of the spectrum, high school sophomores whose teachers had higher expectations of them were three times more likely to eventually graduate from college than if their teachers had lower expectations of them (Siegel, 2013).

As a result, teacher expectations affected their teaching behavior in the classroom. Teachers who had high expectations for their students created a learning framework, offered feedback, used higher-order questions, and employed positive behavior management strategies. Teachers whose expectations for their students were lower employed such classroom strategies less often, if at all. In addition, teachers often demonstrate a positive bias in evaluating the work of high-expectation students, provide them with more response opportunities, challenging instruction, and praise, and interact with them in ways that are more supportive and caring.

This belief isn't limited to teachers; it can impact students as well. Jerry Z. Park and his colleagues (2015) surveyed White college students regarding how they perceived their non-White peers. A common theme in their research was the misperception by White students that many Hispanic and Black urban students "do not work hard enough to improve their life circumstances" (Lombardi, 2016).

The following steps ensure that high expectations are a nonnegotiable component of the school culture (Lombardi, 2016).

1. Convincing students that they can meet high expectations

2. Communicating reachable, intermediate goals with students

3. Helping students mitigate their fear of failure

4. Using data to foster short-term wins

Convincing Students That They Can Meet High Expectations

Healing- and resilience-centered schools facilitate the pathway to growth by setting the expectation that all students will be college- or career-ready in that they will have mastered the critical skills and knowledge that will help them be successful in life. Teachers communicate through their words and actions that they're present with their students along the entire pathway of their journey. Faculty determine attainable, very short-term goals until the student reaches mastery. Scaffolding these goals by utilizing various strategies—pre-teaching through analogies and metaphors that are congruent with their life experiences, or tapping into their prior knowledge, for example—helps convince students that they *can* attain academic success, that they *can* master content and skills.

Many people in education talk about the importance of having high expectations for students, but not everyone strategizes to reach that end. Schools can easily put high expectations into practice and set the stage for a healthy mindset. Many of the strategies to enhance mindfulness (page 84), as well as helping students understand how proficiency scales provide the blueprint for learning, are perfect steps in this direction.

Communicating Reachable Intermediate Goals to Students

Simply placing a high standard in front of students is not adequate. Those standards and expectations must have reachable, intermediate goals. The expectations must be realistic and students must recognize them. This is the connection between high expectations, optimism, realistic hope, and student growth. The Critical Concepts from Marzano Resources (2019) are a powerful tool for providing high-level learning goals along with solid, clear steps or learning progressions that help guide both teachers and students toward mastery. Students are able to monitor their progress and see how achieving immediate goals will lead them to mastery.

Helping Students Mitigate Their Fear of Failure

In addition, enhancing connections with students by knowing their strengths and areas of growth helps build the trust that encourages students to take risks and continue engaging and focusing on deeper learning. Through this process, we normalize failure as a necessary part of the learning experience. It begins to lose its fearful impact and, thus, its connotation as something to avoid. Athletes, perhaps, understand this concept better than most. It is through their failed attempts that they are able to master their craft. In the classroom, project-based learning provides such opportunities due to its iterative natural. Students are actually not expected to get it right the first time, but expected to learn from their mistakes and revise as needed to end with a comprehensive project. Constantly focusing on short-term wins empowers students to learn that failure is not the ending—it's only the beginning.

Using Data to Foster Short-Term Wins

Healing- and resilience-focused educators constantly strive to use data competently for short-term wins and next-goal planning. They glean data from classroom assessments, academic inventories, and even state tests. They are deeply aware that each data point represents a real student, and they use the data to plan short-term goals so that they can help students take control of their own learning. When teachers actively include student voice in planning for success, student motivation to participate typically increases. In addition, using an array of classroom assessments provides evidence of growth that lets students respond to in a positive manner. Shifting the perspective of assessments from grades to evidence of learning takes some committed, focused effort on the teacher's part, but the results in terms of student engagement and growth can be amazing.

Deepening Awareness

It is important for teachers to understand that being culturally responsive is not a one-off thing that is done, but actually a way to do teaching and learning in general. It is ever evolving and changing based on the learners in the space. It becomes an innate part of how instruction occurs and can look different from year to year.

This understanding allows us to move beyond detached strategies to a much more authentic experience that empowers the learner to take responsibility and ownership of their learning process. So, when we think about why we need to empower students, we have to go back to the goal of establishing a curriculum in the first place. In the case of a social studies curriculum, it was about empowering students to be good citizens:

> In curriculum documents, good citizens are primarily understood to
> be individuals who actively participate in their nation's civic affairs,
> whether by engaging in more traditional practices such as voting or
> more activist means such as boycotting or protesting (Ross, 2012).
> These processes require individuals to be active. Significantly, active
> behavior comes from individuals who are empowered, that is, indi-
> viduals who feel they have the ability to enact social, political, eco-
> nomic, or other change; to manage or to influence others; and/or to
> engage in actions that influence others. (Broom, 2015)

One of the greatest challenges when considering the notion of empowering students is the belief that in doing so, the educator loses some of their (perceived) power. But true empowerment does not stem from a deficit mentality. It comes from the belief that there is enough to go around and the stronger and better prepared our students are, the better off we all are. It also calls for the educator to adopt the role of facilitator—one that supports the brilliance and excellence of each individual student to show up perfectly as they are to participate as directors in their own learning process. This requires confidence in the educator and a clear understanding of the role of educator, to make room for others to lead without feeling threatened. Thus, the responsibility falls on the teacher to deepen their awareness of what their true role is in the educational process:

> Furthermore, and significantly, teachers can see knowledge as liv-
> ing and something acquired by students as they actively engage
> with their experiences (Dewey, [1916] 2008). That is, teachers don't
> "give" their students knowledge, students "acquire" knowledge
> through their interactions with others in what Dewey called "experi-
> ences." Teachers can help students make sense of their experiences
> through reflection, or discussion. In short, teachers can empower
> their students through student-focused lessons that engage them
> in inquiry and reflection and that are nurtured in and through rela-
> tionships. (Broom, 2015)

So, the question becomes, *How* do educators create environments that support students to empower themselves? And this is key: it is not about bestowing empowerment on students but in creating the conditions where empowerment is a determined outcome. Northcentral University (2014) outlined the following list, which can be helpful in achieving the goal:

1. Help students find their passion.

2. Recognize students who participate and share their thoughts.

3. Personalize lessons and make them relevant.

4. Encourage debate and expression of ideas and opinions.

5. Brainstorm with students.

6. Have patience.

7. Help students determine what they want and find their passion.

8. Practice empathy and resilience.

9. Promote leadership and explore different forms of it.

10. Helps students problem solve, analyze, and research issues and ideas.

Each one of the steps share a couple common factors: that teachers make time to truly know who their students are and that they spend quality time helping them navigate the learning process, meeting them where they are and believing they can be where they need to be with the necessary supports in place. Utilizing these steps, along with giving your students a voice in their learning process, will support intellectual and social growth and development necessary for them to take charge of their learning and their lives. Remember, our goal is to prepare students to be complete human beings who have the capacity to direct their lives and experiences in a way that brings them joy in the skin they are in.

Strengthening Student Agency

When a student has more choice and control over their school experience through a collaborative effort with teachers, they are more likely to trust their teachers, engage in schooling more, and learn more effectively (Norford & Marzano, 2016; Ruyle, 2019).

A mastery-based classroom structure enables personalized learning by providing a clear definition of proficiency, along with the corresponding learning progression presented in the form of a proficiency scale. This allows instruction to be student focused and tailored to the learners' specific strengths, needs, and interests. As such, mastery-based learning principles shift the focus of education to the students and their learning, which teachers support with sound instructional practices and resources. This support facilitates student agency, or "the capacity and propensity to take purposeful initiative—the opposite of helplessness" (Ferguson, Phillips, Rowley, & Friedlander, 2015, p. 1).

Student agency serves as a primary goal in mastery-based learning environments. It presents students with the ability to participate in determining what their learning will look like, thereby deepening their belief that they have the capacity for success (Deci & Ryan, 1985, 2012). This also speaks to nurturing a *growth mindset*, which can be defined as the student's belief that their intelligence and ability can be improved through effort (Dweck, 2006). The impact of teaching from a strength perspective is profound in that it can make students more motivated and effective learners.

As a high school student in California said:

> In English, I read the learning goal and look at the proficiency scale until I understand what I need to do. Sometimes we go over the big learning goal as a whole class, and we always point back to it. All the time. My teachers help by talking with me or my group until I'm sure I know it means, then I get to work in my way to show that I "get" it. I love that. And if I don't think that an assignment or assessment is right for me to show my knowledge, then I can change it and show them how I can do it in a better way. (S. Lewis, personal communication, March 2019)

Or, as a middle school student in North Dakota said:

> I hate it when you go into a class and a teacher just tells you the rules. Here I get to understand what I have to do and then do it *my* way. I need more hands-on, and the personal work with the standards allows me to excel. In a regular class, when a teacher is up blabbing, it just goes right through me. (A. Mader, personal communication, March 2019)

The following are powerful elements or actions for cultivating student agency in a mastery-based classroom, as well as specific to trauma- and culturally responsive teaching.

- **Give personal attention:** Although teacher facetime in mastery-based classrooms is no different than in traditional classrooms, students strongly expressed to us that their level of engagement often revolves around the fact that instructors in the mastery-based model teach differently and respect their individual styles of learning more effectively than they had experienced in their traditional classes. This is largely due to the constant use of proficiency scales and aligned assessments, which provide teachers and students with evidence of student learning, and result in teachers using their increased instructional expertise to target strategies specific to student needs (Ruyle, 2019).

- **Ensure predictability:** This element is also based around clearly defined learning goals and proficiency scales. Although activities will certainly vary on a daily basis, the expectation for student demonstration of mastery ultimately drives the daily routine. The element of predictability is also critical in a trauma-responsive classroom.

- **Model and foster positive attitudes:** As mentioned, connection is the antidote to trauma. Teachers displaying positive attitudes about themselves leads to them demonstrating those same attitudes with their learners. Using metacognitive proficiency scales also helps cultivate a positive attitude.

- **Establish high expectations with corresponding support to meet those expectations:** Learning goals aligned with state, provincial, or national standards must be high quality and clearly defined.

- **Empower students to make choices or present options for demonstrating mastery:** This strategy also helps build student capacity to advocate for themselves because they are encouraged to provide options. This can be as simple as providing an array of evidence of mastery as well as participating in classroom- and school-level decisions.

- **Instill a growth mindset:** In traditional academic settings, students learn how to play the game of school instead of focusing on personal growth and development. The shift in student mindsets is critical and will take some time and effort to develop. Authentic learning is more challenging than submitting assignments for grades, but, in our experience and research, student engagement and buy-in raise exponentially once the shift has been made.

- **Develop a shared vision of success:** This element aligns with cultivating learning partnerships, which is a foundational pillar of culturally responsive teaching. By joining in a learning partnership with the teacher, setting goals, and working toward mastery, students in mastery-based classes continually speak about their high engagement and agency.

Making It Happen: Ethical Leadership

Ethical leaders are driven by values and purpose, other people's dignity and rights, the best interests of the teachers and students in their buildings, and a staunch commitment to doing the right thing. These elements, in our experience and research, point to an increase in feelings of empowerment in various stakeholders. This respect for dignity aligns with our view that empowerment is an example of ethical leadership because it is based on the belief that students and teachers will perform at higher levels if they are empowered to do so. For example, an international business study discovered that the psychological empowerment that was cultivated by ethical leaders had a direct correlation with increased creativity (Javed, Khan, Bashir, & Arjoon, 2016). The researchers asserted that ethical leaders promote a culture of respect, dignity, and trust, which provides rich soil for creativity to grow and prosper. Other international studies assert that people are motivated to engage in their work when they are treated with respect and are valued by the organization. They are then more motivated and willing to apply extra effort because they are more committed to delivering high-quality work (Kim & Brymer, 2011; Macey, Schneider, Barbera, & Young, 2009; Metwally, Ruiz-Palomino, Metwally, & Gartzia, 2019).

Empowerment provides people with an active role in their jobs—as teachers or as students—which capitalizes on each person's expertise, judgment, and commitment, and can increase their sense of personal worth. Ethical leaders create systems that will help prepare every learner for the challenges they will face in their futures by building their capacity as learners, as thinkers, and as doers who have faith and trust in their own abilities, voice, and strength. Ethical leaders must set high expectations to make this happen. If students believe that their input is valued, and they are given the power to own their learning, think for themselves, take the initiative, and innovate, they are likely to be more engaged and successful. These are critical components of all three pivot points of the school wellness wheel.

Given the massive, fundamental paradigm shift required to evolve to a healing- and resilience-centered organization, ethical leaders must realize themselves as agents of transformation who are driven by a fundamental, moral commitment to all the learners in their building. It is important to state that educational leaders who assume this responsibility will be challenged often, judged unfairly, and questioned repeatedly by a vast array of voices who would rather revert to the status quo. These could include teacher unions, parent groups, community organizations, and even upper-level educational agencies. The people in these groups usually want what's best for students, but their fear or lack of information can make them extremely resistant to change.

It is easy to acquiesce in such moments. But educational leaders who have assumed the mantle of creating healing- and resilience-centered educational organizations have also assumed the ethical responsibility to lead with courage and resolve to adapt existing school models to more innovative, humane, and robust systems. Leadership experts and Cambridge Leadership Associates co-founders Ronald A. Heifetz and Marty Linsky (2002) spoke to the burden of this style of leadership: "Our values are shaped and refined by rubbing against real problems . . . and in the defining moments of our lives, values count for little without the willingness to put them into practice" (p. 22). The burden of leadership in shifting school systems can be heavy. The temptation to revert to traditional practices during challenging times can become overwhelming, skewing a person's compass.

Continuing to remain informed, engaged, and connected with evolutionary colleagues is the best way to nurture the ethical leadership that is absolutely necessary to maintain momentum during the shift. These leaders constantly deepen their knowledge and commitment through professional reading and collaboration around all the school wellness wheel's components. An important action that ethical leaders can take to maintain and strengthen their resolve is by networking with colleagues and fellow thought leaders from across the world via social network platforms. Professional social networking can help keep leaders informed regarding the most current research, provide support during difficult times, and offer excitement as they continue to engage in innovative and powerful practices alongside colleagues undergoing the same change process.

To cultivate even greater ethical leadership, leaders can also reach out to other leaders and implementation teams on the same journey, forming an implementation cohort. Working together with others on the same journey can reignite passion and keep everyone focused on the goal. As more schools become involved in the implementation process, such teams will become much more common and accessible. We suggest reaching out to the authors of this book to learn where the work is being done and to be placed in contact with like-minded school leaders.

Conclusion

As schools focus on creating and cultivating a culture of empowerment, it is important for educators to more deeply understand the power of high expectations and student voice, choice, and agency. Then, they must act on that understanding. Building a culture of empowerment that provides a focus on beliefs about what teachers and students are capable of achieving with regard to a particular task or situation is critical to self-regulated behavior and learning. When students feel a sense of efficacy, when they believe that they can improve their intelligence and ability through focused effort, and when they feel in control of their learning, they become more motivated to learn and, ultimately, more effective learners (Deci & Ryan, 1985; Dweck & Molden, 2017). These strategies facilitate brain health and ultimately can help align instruction and school design with students' individual capacities and needs, facilitating deeper learning.

Culture of Empowerment Proficiency Scale

As a team, rate your school on the following skills.

			Sample Evidence
Score 4.0		*In addition to score 3.0, in-depth inferences and applications that go beyond what was taught.* Students identify their own learning and healing based on evidence they have provided in their student navigator.	
	3.5	In addition to score 3.0 performance, in-depth inferences and applications with partial success	
Score 3.0		The educators will: • Produce evidence that speaks to higher levels of student engagement and learning ownership based on progress through proficiency scales. • Communicate high-level expectations and produce evidence of students taking ownership of their own learning. • Demonstrate how their role has shifted from purveyors of information to facilitators of learning. *The educator exhibits no major errors or omissions.*	• Critical Concepts • Gooru (www.gooru.org) student navigator tool
	2.5	No major errors or omissions regarding 2.0 content and partial knowledge of the 3.0 content	

Score 2.0		There are no major errors or omissions regarding the simpler details and processes as the educators:
		• Recognize or recall specific terminology, such as *learning expectations, student agency,* and *voice and choice.*
		• Perform basic processes, such as:
		  + Provide official versions of proficiency scales and help students put them in their own language so as to engender student ownership of their own learning.
		  + Consistently tie in the daily lesson, work, or assessment to the previously communicated proficiency scale.
		  + Help students use strategies to monitor their own progress toward mastery using tools such as Gooru Navigator (https://gooru.org/about/navigator).
		The educator exhibits major errors or omissions regarding the more complex ideas and processes.
			• Learning contracts
			• Student-generated proficiency scales

	1.5	Partial knowledge of the 2.0 content, but major errors or omissions regarding the 3.0 content	
Score 1.0		With help, a partial understanding of some of the simpler details and processes and some of the more complex ideas and processes.	
	0.5	With help, a partial understanding of the 2.0 content, but not the 3.0 content	
Score 0.0		Even with help, no understanding or skill demonstrated	

Chapter 7
Culture of Humanity

In the past, jobs were about muscle, now, they're about brains, but in the future, they'll be about heart.

—Minouche Shafik

There is an implicit assumption that schools have designed and maintained educational structures that are the most conducive for human learning and growth. Traditional schooling in reality, however, is not typically centered around authentic learning but rather is usually governed by a system of classes and curricula that are commonly delivered through whole-group instruction to cohorts of same-age students during the same time frame. Arbitrary measures of achievement such as grades, credits, and test scores have resulted in an educational model that relies on seat time over mastery, as well as compliance over deep learning.

We know more about the brain and the act of learning than we ever have before. Educators have access to information to help better understand a variety of factors that dramatically influence the development of the whole child. With this focus has come a deeper understanding of the internal and external factors that impact students' learning readiness and performance.

Neuroscience tells us that emotion and cognition have a particularly powerful connection. Cognition typically involves the processing and evaluating of information, whereas emotion involves behavior and activities based on such processing and evaluations. In this way, cognition and emotion organize all human thought and activity.

Emotions can have a tremendous impact on learning through cultural norms, acute events such as trauma, and systems involved in executive control (Center on the Developing Child, n.d.; Fischer & Bidell, 2006). Emotions further affect engagement and academic success performance through their impact on confidence, self-control, motivation, persistence, anxiety, and curiosity (Immordino-Yang & Damasio, 2007).

The internal resources that children bring to learning—including prior knowledge and experience, integrated neural processes, motivation, and metacognitive skills—also encompass the relational dimensions of learning, including physical and emotional aspects, trust, safety, a sense of belonging and purpose, attachment, and connection with peers and adults. And then, there is the fact that humans are inherently social creatures who are biologically, cognitively, and physically wired to belong. Connections are part of accepting our humanity and the humanity of others.

In an increasingly isolated, digitally dominated world, the profound impact of human connectivity must not be overlooked. In her book, *The Gifts of Imperfection: Let Go of Who You Think You're Supposed to Be and Embrace Who You Are*, researcher Brené Brown (2020) defined *connection* as the "energy that exists between people when they feel seen, heard, and valued; when they can give and receive without judgment; and when they derive sustenance and strength from the relationship" (p. 29). The CDC (n.d.b) defines *connectedness* as the "degree to which a person or group is socially close, interrelated, or shares resources with other persons or groups." Young people who feel connected to someone at school and home are less likely to experience negative health outcomes related to sexual risks, drugs, violence, and mental health. They are thinking carefully about behavior and consequences.

Resilience is strengthened when you give and receive support, which is a gesture that acknowledges another's humanity. The more positive your relationships are, the better you will be able to face challenges. Thus, it is critical for teachers and leaders to actively cultivate and nurture a culture of humanity. This culture is defined largely by adult-student interactions, and most often by consequences that result from poor behavior or breaches of the connection. This chapter looks at the school wellness wheel from the larger organizational structure perspective and presents ways to address subjects such as school discipline and effective implementation of the school wellness wheel model. This chapter also draws from the sixth level in Maslow's (1943) hierarchy—the desire to connect to something greater than oneself. You can assess your school's efforts toward this change by using the "Culture of Ownership Proficiency Scale" (page 134).

Thinking Carefully About Behavior and Consequences

The role of schools in ensuring students have mastered critical responsibility standards that go beyond academics cannot be overstated. Helping young people learn how to adhere to rules, social norms, and appropriate behavior is one of the most important components of an effective educational program. Learning to effectively manage emotions, choices, and behavior has a huge impact on academic as well as subsequent life success. Indeed, the researcher and author Robert Plomin (2018) made the point that student behavior is a much stronger predictor of future success than test scores are. One study of over half a million ninth graders revealed that teachers who helped learners improve their behaviors by focusing on connection and co-regulation saw a decrease in problem behaviors and were also ten times more effective at improving their students' subsequent grade-point averages and graduation rates than teachers who simply focused on improving test scores (Plomin, 2018).

Many students, however, come to school with multiple problems that could include low self-esteem, rejection, a lack of sense of self, relational challenges, trust issues, impaired memory and executive function, and difficulty with emotional control (Bloom & Farragher, 2013; R. Macy, personal communication, September 2019). Many of these problems can result from earlier trauma, stress, or family dysfunction. As a defense mechanism, students may try to protect themselves by acting in a provocative manner to speed up the rejection or dysfunction that they are convinced is coming anyway (Bloom & Farragher, 2013; R. Macy, personal communication, September 2019).

Schools have historically addressed challenging behaviors in a codified manner of punishment, using board-approved guidelines such as behavior codes to spell out specific consequences that correspond with specific infractions. This seems to make sense on a visceral level. When students transgress, break rules, or display behavior that is not in line with established norms, issuing consequences seems to have the effect of making the adults feel as though they are doing something to make the school safe and orderly.

But while simply following traditional policies may feel right on some level, doing so often ignores the real issues. This can also lead to tremendous inequity. For example, Wade Jacobsen and his colleagues (2019) conducted a study of boys who attended schools in large cities between 1998–2000. They discovered that 40 percent of the Black boys had been suspended or expelled by age nine or the end of third grade. Using the same criteria, this number shrank to 8 percent of White or non-Hispanic boys. The researchers assert that the tremendous disparity could be attributed to how teachers interpret interactions—that misbehavior is often perceived as more aggressive and severe when committed by Black and Brown boys than when it is committed by White boys. The same actions resulted in much more severe consequences for Black boys.

In response to these and other stunning data sets, many state legislatures have tried to address the issue. For example, Tennessee H.B. 405/S.B. 170 (2019) has directed the state department of education to examine trauma-informed discipline practices in order to guide school districts and public charter schools toward adopting more trauma-informed discipline policies. The law also requires each local board of education to enact policies requiring schools to submit an assessment of ACEs before bringing a student up for suspension, expulsion, in-school suspension, or alternative schooling.

While policies and procedures regarding punishment are common and certainly serve a role in overall school behavior protocols, we assert that best educational practice for discipline entails the recognition that consequences for challenging behavior must be tailored to the needs of the individual student. School is the time for students to learn how to behave in a productive and appropriate manner and schools can achieve this goal by working from a proactive rather than a reactive perspective. It's not about the punishment—it's about the learning.

Applying Trauma-Responsive Consequences Instead of Punishment

Traditional punishment protocols tend to be reactive while trauma-competent consequences are more of a proactive way to help students learn how to behave in a more positive way. The difference between punishment and trauma-informed consequences are described in table 7.1.

Instead of a punishment approach, healing- and resilience-centered schools consistently attempt to view disruptive behavior as secondary reactions to the trauma, stress, or personal issues that students have experienced or are still confronting as opposed to intentional rejection of rules and order. Thus, educators should begin addressing inappropriate behaviors with some of the following questions when considering trauma-informed and culturally responsive consequences (Bloom & Farragher, 2013; Marzano, Scott, et al., 2017).

1. What is the purpose of enforcing the rules? Is it to teach a student how to manage emotions and become mindful enough to make wise decisions, or to enforce the rules for the rules' sake?

2. Is this student intentionally trying to frustrate me? What is the student getting in this situation? It is important for educators to remember that for many young people, negative attention is preferable to no attention at all.

3. How much of my response to the student is because I feel personally offended, hurt, disrespected, frightened, or upset? Do I need to prove that I am in control?

4. What assumptions am I making about this young person's behavior? Could there be another explanation for this behavior?

5. What other options do I have as a response to this behavior? Students often expect adults to respond to them in certain ways. It gives them a sense of control when they know what to expect.

6. What options or ideas do I have that align with my intention of building the student's proficiency self-managing intense emotions and learning more effective behavior while also maintaining safety and order?

Table 7.1: Trauma-Responsive Consequences Versus Punishment

Traditional Punishment	Trauma-Responsive Consequences
Enforces compliance to a specific authority Uses words and actions that can escalate conflict	Encourages thinking and reflection when emotions are once again regulated Uses words that foster connections between people and repair mistakes
Designed to assert power and control Often leaves a young student feeling powerless or defensive	Designed to teach, change, or shape behavior Offers options with firm limits. Often seeks offender input into appropriate consequences
Often serves to benefit the punisher or the victim of the misbehavior Not specifically designed to assist the person who needs to correct behavior	Benefits the offender through clear, logical consequences that are obviously related to the behavior Issued with empathy, respect, and, often, offender input

Source: Adapted from R. Macy & B. Farragher, personal communication, September 2019.

A potential and dangerous misconception regarding trauma-competent consequences is that there are no rules or consequences for violation of acceptable behavior. There is also a common fear that centers around the idea that if educators do not issue consequences to students for their misbehavior, the adults are somehow enabling them by not holding them accountable for their actions.

We are not in any way suggesting that adults ignore inappropriate behavior. Instead, we ask staff to consider working with students who are often inexperienced at working through issues. Together, they identify the problematic behavior. The staff person helps the student put the offense in a relatable personal context and find different ways to express their intense feelings. It is critical that the process occur when the student is in a calm (regulated) state. Students cannot communicate well or connect when they are not calm. In a healing- and resilience-centered educational program, it is important that students know that the adults can see far beyond the problem behavior and can embrace the students' capabilities and potential.

In terms of issuing consequences for infractions of the rules, it is essential that educators exhibit flexibility, creativity, and critical thinking in working with traumatized individuals. Students can and should be held to high standards—expecting anything less from them is a symptom of inequity and the dereliction of our professional responsibility. The key is to not allow the adults to become caught up in the moment or part of a power struggle. Putting the offense in context to understand the motivation driving the behavior as opposed to simply reacting to the student ensures that the adult response is trauma competent.

The following scenarios are adapted from real situations in schools. They are examples of how to view a specific incident from both a traditional punishment perspective as well as a trauma-responsive perspective. As you read, you can see that working from a trauma-informed perspective and implementing trauma-competent education demands much thought, patience, and perseverance on the part of adults. We have seen educators become so paralyzed due to fears of retraumatizing students or doing something wrong that it leads to a sense of no rules or follow through, but creating boundaries and holding students accountable is exactly what healing- and resilience-centered schooling is all about—but they must be built on a foundation of human connection and understanding.

Incident One

Two fourth-grade students are found passing notes in class. On inspection, the teacher discovers that the students were expressing their disdain for the teacher personally and were plotting ways to get her fired.

Interpretation Through the Punishment Lens:

"The students are being disrespectful!"

"They don't appreciate the school or me."

"We need to set a firm example that we don't allow this type of abuse, disrespect, and demeaning behavior."

Reactive Response:

Teacher threatens to lower grade, send to time-out study hall, or assign in-school suspension

Teacher asks that student leave (or be removed from) class

Interpretation Through the Trauma-Responsive Lens:

"What could be triggering this behavior—fear, shame, a power struggle, avoidance, or overstimulation?"

"What's going on in the school environment that is setting the kids off?"

"Could this behavior be adaptive given the students' life histories?"

"The students need to understand why it's inappropriate and disrespectful and develop constructive self-regulation skills."

Proactive Response:

Teacher engages in co-regulation response, maintaining a regular calm heartbeat

Teacher asks students to cool off in a safe place and to use mindfulness exercises

Available staff member processes experience with the students after they determine the students have calmed down enough to engage

Staff member shares observations with the students about the interaction and asks for feedback, exploring alternative prosocial ways of communicating feelings

Students can be assigned some sort of detention time with the teacher doing something positive, such as helping in the garden, but the teacher personally and actively works with the students in the repair process

Incident Two

A middle school student was caught writing racist graffiti on the bathroom stall doors.

Interpretation Through the Punishment Lens:

"The boy is defacing school property. It's vandalism."

"We must come down hard on him, or other kids will think that it's OK to be racist or vandalize."

Reactive Response:

Suspension, student can no longer be in the bathroom area alone

Suspension or a series of detentions

Interpretation Through the Trauma-Responsive Lens:

"I need to explore why this student was writing racist graffiti on the walls."

"Was the student reacting to something? What kind of attention is he seeking?"

Proactive Response:

As soon as possible, a discussion occurs with student about the incident

Teacher explores why he wrote on the wall

Staff or teacher discusses the rules about graffiti and hate language

Student is assigned to clean or repaint the stall doors

Staff help the student find alternative ways to express feelings

Incident Three

During group work time, two high school students are verbally aggressive, using inappropriate language toward a staff member, acting out in class, and storming out.

Interpretation Through the Punishment Lens:

"These young people are disrespecting me and disrespecting the class."

"I can't create a cohesive group when they feel free to leave whenever they feel like it."

"This isn't fair to the other group members."

Reactive Response:

Students are assigned to in-school suspension or out-of-school suspension

Interpretation Through the Trauma-Responsive Lens:

"Did something in the group trigger these students?"

"What else could I do to help these kids engage in the group?"

Proactive Response:

If another adult is available, they leave the group to check in with the students, determine whether there is ongoing conflict, and see if students can rejoin the group

Teacher may have to call for another adult to take the students out of the room to regulate

Teacher connects with students during or after class to find out what happened

Teacher lets the students know that they can leave the group if they are feeling upset or anxious, but that they are always welcome to rejoin the group

Bringing the School Wellness Wheel to Life

As schools make the fundamental paradigm shift away from simply teaching curriculum "at" students to becoming healing- and resilience-centered organizations that empower all students to learn at their highest possible levels, it is necessary that all stakeholders embrace the concept of creating and nurturing a healthy, humanized organization before anything else. This organization will provide the structure in which all other efforts will grow and prosper. This shift entails the following.

- Ensuring all people in the organization have an intimate understanding of the vision and mission of the school purpose

- Committing continually to deepening the understanding of the three pivot points of the school wellness wheel

- Taking purposeful steps to address the impact of debilitating factors such as trauma and stress on the brain

- Working with a focus on cultivating resilience for every person in the organization based on a strength-based approach to education

No single educator can adequately incorporate personalized education along with trauma-informed care and cultural sensitivity by themselves. Changing the culture of a school is a process that requires the commitment of the staff and leaders to continually hone their educational practice and become experts in learning, brain research, and the impact of various factors on the learning process. Educators are not just purveyors of curriculum and content, but experts who can guide learners in the journey of academic-growth schools. They must be given the time and support to engage in the dynamic process of culture change needed to become a healing- and resilience-centered school.

Making It Happen: Resilient Leadership

To build and sustain a healing- and resilience-centered educational organization, the leaders who guide and develop such organizations must, themselves, exemplify resilience. Resilient leadership theory is a relatively new leadership orientation that emerged in response to the serious nature of the threats and challenges of the modern world. Researchers Bhaggie Patel (2011) and Alfred Faustenhammer and Martin Gössler (2011) asserted that the volatile, uncertain, complex, and ambiguous (Bennis & Nanus, 1985) world demands a new leadership approach that entails qualities such as strategic thinking, emotional intelligence, flexibility, a learning mindset, and the ability to develop others. Such qualities are a necessity for the dedicated and passionate leader who seeks to implement the school wellness wheel.

This resilience is important during implementation, specifically, since there will be resistance and because a culture shift is so difficult. Drawing on that resilience will be crucial in order to exhibit the following skills and characteristics so crucial during second-order change in schools: being knowledgeable about the curriculum, instruction, and assessment; optimizing (such as situations and resources); seeking intellectual stimulation; monitoring and evaluating change; showing flexible ideals and beliefs; and, of course, being a change agent (Marzano et al., 2005).

In an important corollary, four of the behaviors have a negative, or inverse, relationship when evolutionary change is occurring: (1) communication, (2) culture, (3) input, and (4) order (Marzano et al., 2005). This means that although a leader may be doing everything correctly, this person will almost assuredly receive pushback and be accused of not effectively demonstrating the four listed behaviors. For example, communicating a clear vision is an important behavior for a leader when implementing the school wellness wheel. Despite best efforts, teachers may perceive the principal as not communicating as well as he or she could during implementation. Quite often, people equate communication with getting their way, and if that isn't happening during the process, teachers tend to feel the principal does not hear them or is not communicating with them (Marzano et al., 2005).

If a leader goes into the change process armed with knowledge and is prepared for what is to come, when the inevitable obstacles and accusations present themselves, it is easier for a leader to maintain resolve and momentum to keep things moving forward. Resilience is important during this kind of friction, because it will help you continue trying to meet staff's needs. This can be a crucial turning point in the process. Understanding this mindset can help leaders maintain course. Remember: resilience is a buffer, helping one cope with stress, to bend but not break.

Some practical ways leaders can accomplish this is by increasing their visibility in and around school, sending regular text-based communications, consistently engaging colleagues through personal conversations and check-ins, and consciously soliciting feedback from teachers, support staff, and students. This is, in effect, modeling trauma-responsive behaviors as well. In all of these cases, it is impossible to overcommunicate.

Conclusion

The growing movement to empower schools to recognize and be more responsive to the needs of all learners, but especially trauma-exposed students, is critical given the prevalence of trauma and toxic stress. Unprocessed trauma and long-term activation of the stress-response system can hinder brain development.

But what does that look like on the ground? The school wellness wheel encompasses the broad spectrum of skills, attitudes and values that promote success in school and in life—things like managing emotions, setting and achieving goals, persevering through adversity, and working in a team. Healing- and resilience-centered schools benefit students whether or not they have experienced traumatic events. *All* students benefit from safety and positive connections at and to school. All students benefit when learning in an inclusive, respectful environment in which their voice, choice, and agency are valued and encouraged.

Understanding trauma's impact on learning can rally educators around their students' shared need for safety and connection to the school community. This calls for a whole-school approach that is inclusive of all, while recognizing that there are those who are especially vulnerable. Simply stated, schools can be designed to address the individual needs of the most vulnerable students while leveraging their strengths and, simultaneously, creating conditions and opportunities that support all students' engagement and learning.

Culture of Humanity Proficiency Scale

As a team, rate your school on the following skills.

		Sample Evidence
Score 4.0	*In addition to score 3.0, in-depth inferences and applications that go beyond what was taught.* Archive the implementation process in order to share their journey and help guide other schools that will eventually follow a similar path.	• High Reliability Schools (HRS) level 5 certification (Marzano et al., 2014) • Articles, books, or presentations
3.5	In addition to score 3.0 performance, in-depth inferences and applications with partial success	
Score 3.0	The educators: • Structure behavioral boundaries around student needs and educational opportunities for learner growth. • Implement the components of the school wellness wheel using an overarching plan to address the wellness and learning of adults so that they subsequently pass on those lessons to students and grow the system organically from within. *The educator exhibits no major errors or omissions.*	• Professional development plan with experts in the three critical pivot points • Dedicated space in building for mindfulness • Professional learning for all segments of the school including office and cafeteria staff, janitors, bus drivers, and more
2.5	No major errors or omissions regarding 2.0 content and partial knowledge of the 3.0 content	
Score 2.0	There are no major errors or omissions regarding the simpler details and processes as the educators: • Recognize or recall specific terminology, such as *behavior, consequences, follow-up, humanity, implementation, mission, resilient leadership,* and *vision.* • Perform basic processes, such as: 　+ Understand the three pivot points of the school wellness wheel. 　+ Explain how trauma and culture impact learning. 　+ Discuss how to monitor successful implementation of the various components. *The educator exhibits major errors or omissions regarding the more complex ideas and processes.*	• HRS level 5 survey data (Marzano et al., 2014) • Vision statement • Mission statement
1.5	Partial knowledge of the 2.0 content, but major errors or omissions regarding the 3.0 content	
Score 1.0	With help, a partial understanding of some of the simpler details and processes and some of the more complex ideas and processes	
0.5	With help, a partial understanding of the 2.0 content, but not the 3.0 content	
Score 0.0	Even with help, no understanding or skill demonstrated	

Implementation Plan

Each school's journey to implementing the wellness wheel is personal. In our experience, schools typically focus on traditional practices, adopting some new initiatives annually, and engaging in an array of professional learning options. Schools often, for example, concentrate efforts on something like prioritizing standards or a new reading program. They may even consider an element from the school wellness wheel, such as cultural competency, and then have staff complete additional training in that area.

What is less common is when schools maintain focus on a specific initiative or framework for a number of consecutive years and monitor their progress toward mastering the goal's overarching initiative or framework. Implementing the school wellness wheel happens best when it is a long-term approach. Although the diagram of the wheel is straightforward (refer back to figure 1.2, page 19), the complexity of the construct is profound and deep.

Schools currently involved in implementation carry out the process in a variety of ways. For example, in Arkansas, one middle school has been operating independently and has reported positive results by adopting the school wellness wheel as their instructional framework as they work through the High Reliability Schools (HRS) certification process. In California, a K–8 district has been working on implementing the model districtwide, with different schools focusing on different components. Their ultimate plan is to bring their work together. Another California district began implementation with the alternative programs, but the word got out and adoption of the model spread almost immediately to the middle schools and then into the elementary schools with the high schools beginning to understand the big picture.

And a district in North Dakota began the work with the instructional coaching team understanding how the school wellness wheel could serve as their guiding framework as they implemented the *New Art and Science of Teaching* (Marzano, 2017) with their staff. You will read stories from participants in some of these schools in this appendix. All anecdotes from Cloverdale Middle School are shared by Crystal Green-Braswell.

In every case, the people who spearheaded the work have stated that the school wellness wheel can seem daunting at first. They feared overwhelming their teachers. But when they presented it as an overarching framework that defined their mission and vision to become healing- and resilience-centered schools, everything seemed to fall into place.

Implementation Options

Although there is no single method for implementation, we suggest operating in one of two main directions in order to set the stage for success. Figure A.1 displays the foundational pillars of each pivot point, which can help guide the implementation process.

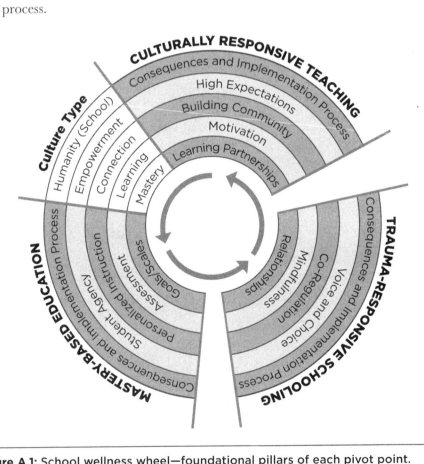

Figure A.1: School wellness wheel—foundational pillars of each pivot point.

Option One

Option one encourages school teams to look at the school wellness wheel from a holistic perspective, beginning with the surface content, then delving deeper and examining the other culture shifts as time moves on.

1. Introduce teams to the school wellness wheel as an overarching vision for schooling. In this scenario, teachers are exposed to the understanding that substantive change begins with the adults in the building.

2. The team takes a deep dive into each culture, beginning with the culture of mastery.

3. Teams dive deeper by engaging with different paradigms one by one, going from a culture of learning to connection, empowerment, and humanity.

Implementation via option one allows teams to maintain focus on the approach as a whole. As stated earlier, we do not encourage focusing on a single pivot point to the detriment of the other two. All three pivot points are critical and equally important. They are intertwined so thoroughly that if a school is engaging with one pivot point, they are also working on the other two as well.

Option Two

Option two encourages schools to implement the school wellness wheel in conjunction with a process such as the HRS certification protocol. In this case, each level of High Reliability Schools™ certification can correspond with a cultural implementation of the school wellness wheel. Examples for each level follow (Marzano et al., 2014).

- HRS level 1 certification—Creating a Safe and Collaborative Culture—can focus on a culture of mastery in the school wellness wheel implementation. Professional learning communities, the critical commitment at level 1, are the perfect place to discuss the wheel as a whole and consider mastery at a deep level.

- HRS level 2 certification—Effective Teaching in Every Classroom— equates with a culture of connection in that *The New Art and Science* (Marzano, 2017) serves as the instructional framework.

- HRS level 3—a Guaranteed and Viable Curriculum—can be accompanied by a culture of learning. The school wellness wheel's assessment piece is an important component in learning and demonstrating mastery of the identified leaning goals.

- HRS level 4—Standards-Referenced Reporting—can align with creating a culture of empowerment in that helping students hone their voice, choice, and agency toward mastery of high-level goals will help teachers move their school toward demonstrated mastery of standards-based learning.

- HRS level 5—Competency-Based Learning—aligns with a culture of humanity in that this level is fundamentally about systems change, while the culture of humanity in the school wellness wheel is fundamentally about schooling's overarching system and structure.

Implementation Steps

No matter which option you choose for implementing the school wellness wheel, we strongly recommend taking these five steps to help the process. In the following sections, we will speak to both implementation methods.

1. Initial planning

2. Kickoff training event

3. Short-term follow-up

4. Long-term follow-up

5. Community involvement

Initial Planning

During initial planning, the leadership staff considers the importance of a healing- and resilience-centered change process. The leadership team should consist of building administration, teacher leaders, and other staff that the administration has carefully selected as being able to help drive the school into the future. Getting the right people on board is vitally important. The team needs people who are respected, who can communicate well, who demonstrate lifelong learning, and are eager to take risks. This team must be able to embody the school wellness wheel components and provide the resilience and energy to bring it to life.

During this phase, the team learns about and discusses the moral imperative to evolve their school. The team takes a deep dive into the central component and actively considers the three pivot points of (1) mastery-based learning, (2) trauma-responsive schooling, and (3) culturally responsive teaching. This is when the fire is sparked in the leadership team. This group will become the heart of the effort, providing the knowledge and passion that will bring the vision to life and grow it over time. This team must commit and embody what a healing- and resilience-centered school looks and feels like.

The following elements are key to successfully planning organizational healing- and resilience-centered change.

- Confirm administrative commitment to and support of the initiative. This is the time to build a moral purpose for the shift.

- Discuss the school and larger community, including an assessment of the capacity for implementation.

- Determine if implementation can align with initiatives such as HRS certification, PLC work, and *The New Art and Science of Teaching* (Marzano, 2017) trainings.

- Form a healing- and resilience-centered group to lead and oversee the change process.

- Gain full representation of each significant stakeholder group in the school operations, including administrators, teachers, support staff, and parents.

- Plan for programmatic awareness of the scope (the entire school and its culture) and timeline (usually up to two years) of the culture shift. Discussions give leaders an opportunity to involve stakeholders in the process.

The following vignette describes how Cloverdale Middle School, in Little Rock, Arkansas, began the journey toward the new model as they shifted to become a healing- and resilience-centered educational program:

> Picking our team members was the first big step in the implementation process. We needed people who understood this work starts in the heart. We could count on this group to help us understand and lead this new model. This was the same team who helped us earn level-1 HRS certification the semester before, so we knew they were dedicated and committed to improving the school.
>
> We knew this would be a heavy lift for us all. So, we planned a four-day training in the mountains outside town. We knew it would be important to get away from our normal surroundings to ensure our sight from different perspectives. Our first activities together were designed as team-building and reflection experiences. We understood the more connection we had as a team, the easier the lift would be as we engaged in this new work. During the day, we worked hard in the new learning of the three pivot points of the school wellness wheel. In the afternoons, we transformed our new learning into actions for our school improvement plan. These actions would also align with the leading indicators of the HRS certification

model. Yes, it was most engaging and mentally exhausting. This stated, it was critical that we learn and practice mindfulness throughout the day. This is when we decided to dedicate a room in the school building as a mindfulness room—a sacred space for adults to go to practice wellness at any time during the day.

During our time together, we exercised, we played (laser tag and go-karts), and had dinners and desserts. This was time to build stronger bonds that our team would need for the journey ahead!

Kickoff Training Event

The goal of the kickoff is to motivate and energize the change process while simultaneously providing a beginning sense of direction. Taking what the leadership team learned in the first step to the school in the form of an inspirational kickoff with the staff is a good way to begin the process of gaining buy-in from all the teachers. As many of the staff as possible attend the kickoff training. During this event, the team presents information about the pivot points of mastery-based education, trauma-responsive schooling, and culturally responsive teaching, emphasizing shifts in both understanding and practice. As they do so, they emphasize the importance of all staff members understanding and embracing the school wellness wheel, ensuring that everyone experiences the same values in the organizational culture that students will need to experience. The kickoff ends with discussion of next steps in the implementation.

It is important that teachers and school staff embrace the concept that the world has shifted and that there is an amazing opportunity to shift our schools, too, into a model that is more personalized, innovative, and optimistic. Presenting the staff with new information leads, in our experience, to a very exciting and energizing message. Once they begin to understand the depth of the framework, it can seem daunting, but it is important that the leaders—right now—present the school wellness wheel not as yet another new thing to absorb or scramble to include, but rather as the foundation of education's entire mission.

Teachers will have opportunities to build their capacity in the model over time through professional learning sessions, collaborative team time, and strong support from the leadership team. Thus, a critical element of the initial kickoff period is to revisit the school's vision and mission and either clarify how the school wellness wheel aligns with the existing vision or create a vision that better represents the new direction.

The following vignette describes how Cloverdale Middle School reconsidered its vision and mission as they shifted their focus to become a healing- and resilience-centered educational program:

After we had an inspirational morning meeting about the new focus, we delved into the research from all the different fields about the impact of trauma, toxic stress, and culture. Our teachers were interested as they recognized the impact of trauma on our community, our kids, and ourselves. The idea of moving to a trauma and healing focus as a school was not a tough philosophical sell, but the *how* was certainly something people struggled with. As a result, the leadership team was ready with short, guided mindful meditations that some of our teachers led in the big-group sessions. Although there was a small amount of initial trepidation, the entire staff participated—especially after they learned about the dramatic impact mindfulness can have on their own brains and bodies—and the room had a different feel almost immediately. We then looked at the big picture—how trauma and stress have impacted our community, city, and country. We had some great discussions. Then we collaboratively came up with what we now refer to as our *central mission*:

Traumatized people have dramatically higher rates of a host of negative health outcomes later in life such as alcoholism, drug abuse, obesity, diabetes, and heart disease. Those exact same factors have a dramatic impact on our larger community as well.

Cloverdale is a traumatized community. This is the result of historical and generational trauma as well as from the effects of continued discrimination and racism. But we now have the science to help mitigate and even reverse these factors in our kids—we know that if we do certain things, people get better. And just as important, the directed activities that can help heal traumatized brains and bodies can also build resilience in non-traumatized brains and bodies. Thus, by healing the brains and bodies of kids in our care, we can help heal and build resilience in our larger community as well. For the present and for generations to come . . . .

In response to this mission, the school adopted the school wellness wheel as their vision to bring the mission to fruition. In adopting this new vision, the faculty collaborated to bring the language of the [school wellness] wheel to the students and the community. Thus, the CUBS poster [figure A.2, page 142] became the Cloverdale version of the school wellness wheel. The CUBS signs were created as our version of the school wellness wheel, made into posters, and placed all around the building. Everyone can speak to it. It made a huge difference.

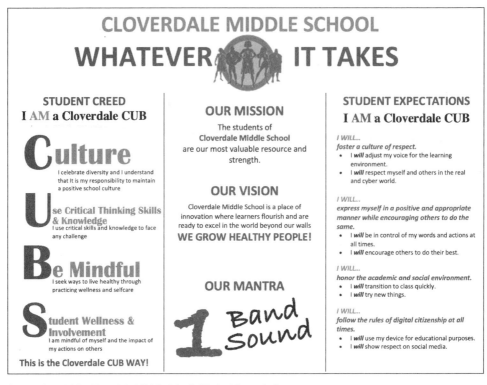

Figure A.2: An adapted version of the school wellness wheel.

Short-Term Follow-Up

Once the kickoff event is over, the gritty work of implementation starts. In the immediate days and months after the kickoff, it is critical to maintain and even increase momentum around the vision. Emphasize professional learning and commitment to mastery-based learning through the classroom implementation of learning goals and proficiency scales. Make mindful practices in staff meetings a norm. Ideally, these training events are offered by experienced consultants and instructional leaders who are able to encourage and teach staff members to improve their practice.

Over the next several months, teachers take the concepts and resources from the trainings and apply them in the classroom. Continued learning and sharing via collaborative teams are crucial, as are detailed feedback and support from the leadership team via walk-throughs and instructional rounds. Discuss any barriers as they arise and help develop strategies to overcome these obstacles. Staff support and care hopefully continue in earnest, emphasizing that a culture shift toward a healing- and resilience-centered model of education rests on staff members' experiences of safety, mindfulness, collaboration, and empowerment.

The following vignette describes how Cloverdale Middle School continued the journey toward the new model:

> It was important to begin the work with the adults in mind. For as far back as we could remember, educators have been conditioned to believe that we always come, at best, second—because the language we hear is that the students always come first. At Cloverdale we understand that the students should reside at the core of what we do. However, realistically, students cannot be first every time. The adults became our primary focus in the critical beginning stages, and we began to see things shift dramatically!
>
> From the trauma-responsive perspective, we conducted a stress audit by asking people about what things were causing them the most stress in the building. We were surprised that the most pressing issue for teachers was being asked to serve as substitutes during their prep time. So, the admin team brainstormed solutions and figured out ways to ensure classes would be covered in other ways than by assigning teachers. The 2020–21 school year was the first year we did not have a single teacher give up a prep time to substitute in a class. We also began to practice mindfulness strategies in every staff meeting. We ultimately wanted our teachers to experience what we would later want them to engage in with their students in their classrooms.
>
> Just doing mindfulness and learning goals with proficiency scales was a big deal for us, so we made sure to focus only on those things and not add anything else that could muddy the waters.

Long-Term Follow-Up

The most important part of long-term follow-up is maintaining momentum. It can be difficult to keep up the same energy that everyone had just after the kickoff. Continue professional learning focused on the components identified as sticking points. On a regular basis, invite experts to meet with staff, reviewing and discussing progress to date. These experts can help the leadership team look at data to monitor progress, identify weak areas, and celebrate victories. At that time, you might initiate ongoing processes to sustain the work. For many schools, this takes them on a deeper dive into the school wellness wheel by focusing on creating a culture of learning (with its emphasis on using assessments as learning tools), as well as building a culture of connection by utilizing an array of instructional strategies to respond to student needs based on the assessment data.

Continued focus on the school wellness wheel—as opposed to chasing the next new initiative—is very important in terms of long-range follow-up. This focused effort will help ensure regular progress, as well as guard against the possibility of decreased morale or dwindling resolve, which can become common over the course of a school year. Leaders must continue to practice trauma-responsive schooling and culturally responsive strategies with their staff by really being able to see, hear, and feel empathy for their teachers.

The following vignette describes how Cloverdale Middle School sustained the vision and grew as a healing- and resilience-centered educational program:

> In previous years, we were pretty accustomed to moving onto new initiatives at this point in the change process. We could easily lose our focus. But the leadership team [members] held each other accountable to continued learning and we never seemed to lose our mojo. In fact, we began to see real, true change in the building . that was so inspiring! The school just felt different. And we heard it from everywhere. Our discipline and attendance data were dramatically better. Also, professional coaching sessions were scheduled once a month to help keep us focused and push us to get better. We needed that outside voice and perspective. We kept looking at data as never before, and that became even more inspiring. It's so liberating to see ourselves improving, as opposed to always chasing the next new thing.

Community Involvement With Service Learning

Once a healing- and resilience-centered school has become fully implemented, there exists a great opportunity to expand the influence of the work in the school to the larger community in which the school lives. This can be accomplished through the effective use of service learning. Service learning has been defined as a:

> Research-based teaching method where guided or classroom learning is applied through action that addresses an authentic community need in a process that allows for youth initiative and provides time for reflection on the service experience and demonstration of acquired skills and knowledge. (Kaye, 2010a, p. 9)

Over the years, service learning has proven to have multiple benefits for schools, many of which fit powerfully not only into mastery-based learning principles, but also trauma- and culturally responsive teaching areas. Some of the immense benefits for students follow (Steffes, 2004, p. 49):

- Developing and applying academic and social-emotional skills

- Increasing motivation and desire to learn
- Appreciating civic responsibility and involving themselves more often in community activities
- Greater cultural awareness and tolerance
- Enhanced social development skill
- Improved interpersonal development
- Better communication skills and ability to work well with others

On top of facilitating a favorable academic and socioemotional experience for the students, the schools that become healing and resilience centers transform all members of their community (students, teachers, administrators, parents, partners) through their interpretation of service learning as an experience of empathy with the world and transformation for humanity, where each member is an agent of change who contributes what they have.

The American School Foundation of Guadalajara (ASFG) in Mexico has developed a service learning program for and by the school called *Aprendiendo Juntos* (Learning Together), a program dedicated to improving the quality of life of the school's maintenance and cleaning personnel that includes English learner classes, developing their reading and writing skills in Spanish, and guidance to continue their education and to receive official recognition for it (ASFG, 2020). The program came into existence after members of this group, who are also part of the community, expressed their desire to learn or improve in these three areas. Middle school and high school students, teachers, administrators from various sections (Mexican program, human resources, material resources, to name a few), and members of the parents' school association teach, design, and create resources for English learner classes, make visits to the library to provide book suggestions based on the level of competence of the student, and assist them in their mission to continue and validate their studies.

The following vignette describes how Cloverdale Middle School and the community strengthened their bond during the shift to becoming a healing- and resilience-centered educational program:

> Once we got this work going, people came out of the woodwork to join us. Our reputation improved and people want to help. They want to be part of it. We are exuding so much energy that people want to come down and teachers want to join our school. This never happened before.
>
> And we want to get out into the community even more.

> Our first mission when we started on this journey was to change Little Rock by building healthy kids here—we are becoming a healing- and resilience-centered organization. It's all now happening in real life!

The reproducible "School Wellness Wheel: Three-Year Initial Planning" (page 149) can help your leadership team begin laying out your long-term plans.

Making It Happen: Resilient Leadership

To build and sustain healing- and resilience-centered educational organizations, the leaders who guide and develop them must themselves exemplify resilience. Resilient leadership theory, a leadership orientation, emerged in response to serious threats and challenges. International researchers Bhaggie Patel (2011), in addition to Alfred Faustenhammer and Martin Gössler (2011), asserted that the volatile, uncertain, complex, and ambiguous (also known as *VUCA*; Bennis & Nanus, 1985) world demands a new leadership approach that entails qualities such as strategic thinking, emotional intelligence, flexibility, a learning mindset, and the ability to develop others. Such qualities are a necessity for the dedicated and passionate leaders who seek to implement the school wellness wheel in their schools.

In their seminal work, *School Leadership That Works: From Research to Results*, Marzano, Waters, and McNulty (2005) shared conclusions gleaned from more than forty years of research demonstrating the impact that building leaders can have on student achievement. The trio identified twenty-one specific leadership responsibilities that each had a statistically significant and positive impact on student achievement, when skillfully tendered (Marzano et al., 2005). Of these leadership responsibilities, the trio asserted that seven are integral to bring about second-order change in schools (Marzano et al., 2005).

1. Change agency
2. Flexibility
3. Ideals and beliefs
4. Intellectual stimulation
5. Optimizing
6. Knowledge of curriculum, instruction, and assessment
7. Monitoring or evaluating

In an important corollary, four of the twenty-one behaviors have a negative relationship when evolutionary change is occurring. This means that although a leader may be doing everything correctly while leading implementation of a new model of schooling, that person will almost assuredly receive pushback and be accused of not effectively demonstrating the four listed behaviors (Marzano et al., 2005).

1. Communication
2. Culture
3. Input
4. Order

For example, communicating a clear vision is an important behavior for a leader to exhibit when implementing the school wellness wheel, but when transformational change is occurring, teachers may perceive the principal as not communicating as well as possible. Quite often, people equate communication with getting their way, and if that isn't happening during the implementation process, teachers tend to feel the principal does not hear them or is not communicating with them (Marzano et al., 2005).

As a result, a resilient leader remembers that constant communication is necessary to implementation of any new vision and that some people who may struggle with the change may often accuse them of not communicating effectively. This can be a crucial turning point in the implementation process and understanding this mindset could help leaders show resilience and maintain course. Some practical ways leaders can accomplish this is by increasing their visibility in and around school, consistently sending communications, constantly engaging colleagues through personal conversations and check-ins, and consciously soliciting feedback from students, teachers, support staff, and other stakeholders. That is actually modeling trauma-responsive behaviors as well. In all of these cases, it is really not possible to overcommunicate, as too much is always better that too little when it comes to conveying a powerful and consistent message.

More important, it is critical for leaders to understand that leading true second-order change will result in pushback and angst from a host of stakeholders who, if not managed well, can hold back progress. Being aware that the four aforementioned behaviors are of particular importance puts the resilient leader in the position to start by focusing on those and being prepared for, despite those efforts, being accused of not communicating or providing opportunities for input, of destroying climate and culture, and of allowing the school to operate in a disorderly fashion. A resilient leader remembers that just because people are anxious or do not understand the direction doesn't mean the work being undertaken is not the right work (or that they are not doing a fine job leading that work). If a leader goes into the change process armed with knowledge and is prepared for what is to come, when the inevitable obstacles and accusations present themselves, it is easier for a leader to show resilience and maintain resolve and momentum.

Conclusion

The growing movement to empower schools to recognize and be more responsive to the needs of all learners, but especially trauma-exposed students, is critical given the prevalence of trauma and toxic stress. Unprocessed trauma and long-term activation of the stress response system can hinder brain development.

But what happens now?

The school wellness wheel encompasses the broad spectrum of skills, attitudes, and values that promote success in school and in life, things like managing emotions, setting and achieving goals, persevering through adversity, and working in a team. Healing- and resilience-centered schools benefit students whether or not they have experienced traumatic events. *All* students benefit from safety and positive connections to school. All students benefit when being taught and learning in an inclusive, respectful environment in which their voice, choice, and agency are valued and encouraged. Understanding trauma's impact on learning can rally educators around their students' shared need for safety and connection to the school community. This calls for a whole-school approach that is inclusive of all, while recognizing that there are those who are especially vulnerable. Simply stated, resilient leaders can design schools that address the individual needs of the most vulnerable students while leveraging their strengths and, simultaneously, creating conditions and opportunities that support all students' engagement and learning.

School Wellness Wheel: Three-Year Initial Planning

Identify each stakeholder team's corresponding tasks as you plan school wellness wheel implementation for each year.

Year One			
	Principal	Teachers	Other Staff
Task One: Confirm a team and confirm administrative commitment to and support of the initiative.			
Task Two: Form a trauma initiative group to lead and oversee the change process.			
Task Three: List here and then seek full representation of each significant stakeholder group in the school operations, including administrators, teachers, support staff, and parents.			
Task Four: Draft agreed-on programmatic awareness of the scope and timeline (usually up to two years) of the culture shift.			

Page 1 of 3

Year Two			
	Principal	Teachers	Other Staff
Task One:			
Task Two:			
Task Three:			
Task Four:			

Year Three			
	Principal	Teachers	Other Staff
Task One:			
Task Two:			
Task Three:			
Task Four:			

References and Resources

Acevedo, T. L. M., Solís, N. R., Caballero, S. S., Bustamante, E. R., Bocanegra, G. M., Espinoza, M. L. A., et al (2007). Habilidades sociales en la formación profesional del docente. *Investigación Educacional, 11*(20), 115–128.

Ali, R. (2019). *Show what you know: A landscape analysis of competency-based education.* Oakland, CA: XQ Institute. Accessed at https://xqsuperschool.org/competency-based-education -cbe/part1 on February 8, 2021.

Altman, D. (2016). *101 mindful ways to build resilience: Cultivate calm, clarity, optimism and happiness each day.* Eau Claire, WI: PESI Publishing.

Amabile, T., & Kramer, S. (2011). *The progress principle: Using small wins to ignite joy, engagement, and creativity at work.* Boston: Harvard Business Review Press.

American Academy of Pediatrics. (2011). *Early childhood adversity, toxic stress, and the role of the pediatrician: Translating developmental science into lifelong health.* Accessed at DOI: 10.1542 /peds.2011-266 on July 19, 2021.

American College Health Association. (2018). *Undergraduate student reference group: Data report fall 2018.* Silver Spring, MD: Accessed at www.acha.org/documents/ncha/NCHA-II _Fall_2018_Undergraduate_Reference_Group_Data_Report.pdf on August 13, 2021.

American Psychiatric Association. (2013). *Diagnostic and statistical manual of mental disorders: DSM-5* (5th ed.). Washington, DC: Author.

American Psychological Association. (2006). *Stereotype threat widens achievement gap.* Accessed at www.apa.org/research/action/stereotype# on February 8, 2021.

American School Foundation of Guadalajara, AC. (2020, December 11). *Aprendiendo Juntos ASFG.* Accessed at https://aprendiendojuntosasfg.weebly.com on March 29, 2021.

Anda, R. F., Felitti, V. J., Bremner, J. D., Walker, J. D., Whitfield, C., Perry, B. D., et al. (2006). The enduring effects of abuse and related adverse experiences in childhood: A convergence of evidence from neurobiology and epidemiology. *European Archives of Psychiatry Clinical Neuroscience, 256*(3), 174–186.

Anderson, S. A. (1994). *Synthesis of research on mastery learning.* Accessed at https://files.eric .ed.gov/fulltext/ED382567.pdf on August 13, 2021.

Artiles, A. J., & Harry, B. (2006). *Addressing culturally and linguistically diverse student overrepresentation in special education: Guidelines for parents.* Washington, DC: National Center for Culturally Responsive Educational Systems.

Aspen Institute. (2018). *From a nation at risk to a nation at hope: Recommendations from the National Commission on Social, Emotional, and Academic Development.* Washington, DC: Author. Accessed at www.nationathope.org on February 9, 2021.

Avenell, G. K. (2014). *Road-testing Robinson et al: Does the "theory" work in practice?* [Unpublished doctoral dissertation]. Griffith University, Queensland, Australia. Accessed at https://research-repository.griffith.edu.au/handle/10072/366760 on August 13, 2021.

Ayoub, C. C., Fischer, K. W., & O'Connor, E. E. (2003). Analyzing development of working models for disrupted attachments: The case of hidden family violence. *Attachment & Human Development, 5*(2), 97–119.

Babad, E., Bernieri, F., & Rosenthal, R. (1989). Nonverbal communication and leakage in the behavior of biased and unbiased teachers. *Journal of Personality and Social Psychology, 56*(1), 89–94.

Bakermans-Kranenburg, M. J., & van Ijzendoorn, M. H. (2007). Research review: Genetic vulnerability or differential susceptibility in child development: The case of attachment. *Journal of Child Psychology and Psychiatry, 48*(12), 1160–1173.

Bandura, A. (1993). Perceived self-efficacy in cognitive development and functioning. *Educational Psychologist, 28*(2), 117–148.

Bandura, A. (1997). *Self-efficacy: The exercise of control.* New York: Freeman.

Banks, J. A. (1988). *Approaches to multicultural curriculum reform.* Accessed at www .teachingforchange.org/wp-content/uploads/2015/11/Banks_James.pdf on February 8, 2021.

Barlow, D. H. (2002). *Anxiety and its disorders.* New York: Guilford Press.

Bass, B. M. (1985). *Leadership and performance beyond expectations.* New York: Free Press.

Bath, H. (2008). The three pillars of trauma-informed care. *Reclaiming Children & Youth, 17*(3), 17–21.

Bauer, C. C. C., Caballero, C., Scherer, E., West, M. R., Mrazek, M. D., Phillips, D. T., et al. (2019). Mindfulness training reduces stress and amygdala reactivity to fearful faces in middle-school children. *Behavioral Neuroscience, 133*(6), 569–585.

Beers, L. S., Szilagyi, M., Seigel, W. M., Davis, W. S., Fukuda, Y., Joseph, M., et al. (2021). *Immunizing against hate: Overcoming Asian American and Pacific Islander racism.* Accessed at https://pediatrics.aappublications.org/content/pediatrics/148/1/e2021051836.full.pdf on September 2021.

Belcourt, A. (2018a, January 25). *The hidden health inequalities that American Indians and Alaskan Natives face.* Accessed at https://theconversation.com/the-hidden-health- inequalities -that-american-indians-and-alaskan-natives-face-89905 on February 8, 2021.

Belcourt, A. (2018b, January 26). *Native Americans are fighting against health inequality*. Accessed at www.good.is/articles/native-american-health-care on February 8, 2021.

Bennis, W., & Nanus, B. (1985). *Leaders: The strategies for taking charge*. New York: Harper Perennial.

Bergstrom, A., Cleary, L. M., & Peacock, T. D. (2003). *The seventh generation: Native students speak about finding the good path*. Charleston, WV: ERIC Clearinghouse on Rural Education and Small Schools.

Berkowitz, R., Moore, H., Astor, R. A., & Benbenishty, R. (2016). A research synthesis of the associations between socioeconomic background, inequality, school climate, and academic achievement. *Review of Educational Research, 87*(2), 425–469.

Bethell, C. D., Newacheck, P., Hawes, E., & Halfon, N. (2014). Adverse childhood experiences: Assessing the impact on health and school engagement and the mitigating role of resilience. *Health Affairs, 33*(12), 2106–2115.

Bezdek, K., & Telzer, E. (2017). *Have no fear, the brain is here! How your brain responds to stress*. Accessed at doi: 10.3389/frym.2017.00071 on July 21, 2021.

Bhushan, D., Kotz, K., McCall, J., Wirtz, S., Gilgoff, R., Dube, S. R., et al. (2020). *Roadmap for resilience: The California Surgeon General's report on adverse childhood experiences, toxic stress, and health*. Sacramento, CA: Office of the California Surgeon General.

Black, D. S., & Fernando, R. (2014). Mindfulness training and classroom behavior among lower income and ethnic minority elementary school children. *Journal of Child and Family Studies, 23*(7), 1242–1246.

Bloom, B. S. (Ed.). (1954). *Taxonomy of educational objectives: Book 1—Cognitive domain*. Boston: Addison-Wesley Longman.

Bloom, B. S. (1968). *Learning for mastery*. Durham, NC: National Laboratory for Higher Education.

Bloom, B. S. (1971). Mastery learning. In J. H. Block (Ed.), *Mastery learning: Theory and practice* (pp. 47–63). New York: Holt, Rinehart, and Winston.

Bloom, B. S. (1977). Favorable learning conditions for all. *Teacher, 95*(3), 22–28.

Bloom, S. L., & Farragher, B. (2013). *Restoring sanctuary: A new operating system for trauma-informed systems of care*. New York: Oxford University Press.

Boser, U., Wilhelm, M., & Hanna, R. (2014). *The power of the Pygmalion effect: Teachers' expectations strongly predict college completion*. Accessed at www.americanprogress.org /issues/education-k-12/reports/2014/10/06/96806/the-power-of-the-pygmalion-effect on February 8, 2021.

Bramante, F., & Colby, R. (2012). *Off the clock: Moving education from time to competency*. Thousand Oaks, CA: Corwin Press.

Brave Heart, M. Y. H. (1998). The return to the sacred path: Healing the historical trauma and historical unresolved grief response among the Lakota through a psychoeducational group intervention. *Smith College Studies in Social Work, 68*(3), 287–305.

Brave Heart, M. Y. H. (2000). Wakiksuyapi: Carrying the historical trauma of the Lakota. *Tulane Studies in Social Welfare, 21*(22), 245–266.

Brave Heart, M. Y. H. (2003). The historical trauma response among natives and its relationship with substance abuse: A Lakota illustration. *Journal of Psychoactive Drugs, 35*(1), 7–13.

Brave Heart, M. Y. H., & Deschenie, T. (2006). Resource guide: Historical trauma and post-colonial stress in American Indian populations. *Tribal College Journal of American Indian Higher Education, 17*(3), 24–27.

Brave Heart, M. Y. H., Elkins, J., Tafoya, G., Bird, D., & Salvador, M. (2012). Wicasa Was'aka: Restoring the traditional strength of American Indian boys and men. *American Journal of Public Health, 102*(2), S177–S183.

Bray, B. (2019). *Maslow's hierarchy of needs and Blackfoot (Siksika) Nation beliefs.* Accessed at https://barbarabray.net/2019/03/10/maslows-hierarchy-of-needs-and-blackfoot-nation-beliefs on August 13, 2021.

Brenhouse, H. C., Lukkes, J. L., & Andersen, S. L. (2013). Early life adversity alters the developmental profiles of addiction-related prefrontal cortex circuitry. *Brain Science, 3*(1), 143–158.

Brookhart, S. M. (2011). Educational assessment knowledge and skills for teachers. *Educational Measurement: Issues and Practice, 30*(1), 3–12.

Broom, C. (2015). *Empowering students: Pedagogy that benefits educators and learners.* Accessed at https://journals.sagepub.com/doi/pdf/10.1177/2047173415597142 on February 9, 2021.

Brown, B. (2020). *The gifts of imperfection: Let go of who you think you're supposed to be and embrace who you are* (10th anniversary ed.). New York: Random House.

Brown, K. W., Creswell, J. D., & Ryan, R. M. (Eds.). (2015). *Handbook of mindfulness: Theory, research, and practice.* New York: Guilford Press.

Brown v. Board of Education, 347 U.S. 483 (1954).

Bucci, M., Marques, S. S., Oh, D., & Harris, N. B. (2016). Toxic stress in children and adolescents. *Advances in Pediatrics, 63*(1), 403–428.

Burks, J., & Hochbein, C. (2013). The students in front of us: Reform for the current generation of urban high school students. *Urban Education, 50*(3), 1–31, 346–376.

Bush, G. H. W. (1990, July 17). *Presidential proclamation 6158.* Accessed at www.loc.gov/loc/brain/proclaim.html on October 1, 2021.

Caballero, C., Scherer, E., West, M. R., Mrazek, M. D., Gabrieli, C. F. O., & Gabrieli, J. D. E. (2019). *Greater mindfulness is associated with better academic achievement in middle school.* Accessed at www.cmhp.ucsb.edu/sites/default/files/2019-06/Caballero%20et%20al.%20(2019)%20Mindfulness%20and%20achievement%20in%20middle%20school.pdf on August 13, 2021.

California State Department of Education. (1986). *Beyond language: Social and cultural factors in schooling language minority students.* Los Angeles: Evaluation, Dissemination and Assessment Center, California State University.

Call, C., Purvis, K., Parris, S. R., & Cross, D. (2014). *Creating trauma-informed classrooms.* Accessed at https://adoptioncouncil.org/publications/adoption-advocate-no-75 on February 8, 2021.

Cannon, W. B. (1927). The James-Lange theory of emotions: A critical examination and an alternative theory. *American Journal of Psychology, 39*, 106–124.

Cantor, C., Osher, D., Berg, J., Steyer, L., & Rose, T. (2019). *Malleability, plasticity, and individuality: How children learn and develop in context.* Accessed at www.tandfonline.com /doi/full/10.1080/10888691.2017.1398649 on July 21, 2021.

Catalino, L. I., Algoe, S. B., & Fredrickson, B. L. (2014). Prioritizing positivity: An effective approach to pursuing happiness? *Emotion, 14*(6), 1155–1161.

Center on the Developing Child. (n.d.). *Resilience.* Accessed at https://developingchild .harvard.edu/science/key-concepts/resilience on October 4, 2021.

Center on the Developing Child. (2007). *A science-based framework for early childhood policy: Using evidence to improve outcomes in learning, behavior, and health for vulnerable children.* Cambridge, MA: Author.

Center on Innovations in Learning. (2015). *High school competency-based education and post-secondary success: A solution-finding report.* Accessed at www.centeril.org/reports /resources/2015_02.04HSCompetencyBasedEducationAndPostSecondarySuccess.pdf on February 8, 2021.

Centers for Disease Control and Prevention. (n.d.a). *About the CDC-Kaiser ACE study.* Accessed at www.cdc.gov/violenceprevention/aces/about.html on February 9, 2021.

Centers for Disease Control and Prevention. (n.d.b). *Youth connectedness is an important protective factor for health and well-being.* Accessed at www.cdc.gov/nchs/fastats /american-indian-health.htm on February 8, 2021.

Centers for Disease Control and Prevention. (2019). *Preventing adverse childhood experiences (ACEs): Leveraging the best available evidence.* Accessed at www.cdc.gov/violenceprevention /pdf/preventingACES-508.pdf on February 8, 2021.

Chua, H. F., Boland, J. E., & Nisbett, R. E. (2005). *Cultural variation in eye movements during scene perception.* Accessed at www.pnas.org/cgi/doi/10.1073/pnas.0506162102 on February 8, 2021.

Clay, R. A. (2020). *Self-care has never been more important: Clinicians, researchers, professors and other psychologists need to continue to prioritize self-care.* Accessed at www.apa.org/monitor/2020 /07/self-care on October 4, 2021.

Clayton, H. (2012). The changing leadership landscape. *Strategic HR Review, 11*(2), 78–83.

Cleare, S., Wetherall, K., Clark, A., Ryan, C., Kirtley, O. J., Smith, M., et al. (2018). *Adverse childhood experiences and hospital-treated self-harm.* Accessed at doi:10.3390 /ijerph15061235 on July 20, 2021.

Cohen, S., & Janicki-Deverts, D. (2012). Who's stressed? Distributions of psychological stress in the United States in probability samples from 1983, 2006, and 2009. *Journal of Applied Social Psychology, 42*(6), 1320–1334.

Cole, M., & Scribner, S. (1974). *Culture and thought: A psychological introduction*. New York: Wiley.

Cole, S. F., Eisner, A., Gregory, M., & Ristuccia, J. (2013). *Helping traumatized children learn: Creating and advocating for trauma-sensitive schools* (Vol. 2). Boston: Massachusetts Advocates for Children, Trauma and Learning Policy Initiative.

El Colegio de México. (2018). *Desigualdades en México 2018*. Accessed at https:// desigualdades.colmex.mx/informe-desigualdades-2018.pdf on March 29, 2021.

Coleman, J. S., Campbell, E. Q., Hobson, C. J., McPartland, J., Mood, A. M., Weinfeld, F. D., et al. (1966). *Equality of educational opportunity*. Washington DC: U.S. Government Printing Office. Accessed at https://eric.ed.gov/?id=ED012275 on February 8, 2021.

Conley, D. T., & French, E. M. (2013). *Student ownership of learning as a key component of college readiness*. Accessed at https://doi.org/10.1177/0002764213515232 on July 20, 2021.

Conradi, L., & Wilson, C. (2010). Managing traumatized children: A trauma systems perspective. *Current Opinion in Pediatrics, 22*(5), 621–625.

Cornell Health. (n.d.). *Building resilience*. Accessed at https://health.cornell.edu/resources /health-topics/building-resilience on July 20, 2021.

Crick, N. R., & Dodge, K. A. (1994). A review and reformulation of social information-processing mechanisms in children's social adjustment. *Psychological Bulletin, 115*(1), 74–101.

Crosnoe, R., & Benner, A. D. (2015). Children at school. In R. M. Lerner (Ed.), *Handbook of child psychology and developmental science: Vol. 4—Ecological settings and processes* (7th ed., pp. 268–304). Hoboken, NJ: Wiley.

Csikszentmihalyi, M. (1997). *Finding flow: The psychology of engagement with everyday life*. New York: Three Rivers Press.

Csikszentmihalyi, M., Rathunde, K., & Whalen, S. (1996). *Talented teenagers: The roots of success and failure*. Cambridge, UK: Cambridge University Press.

Darling-Hammond, L. (2007). Race, inequality and educational accountability: The irony of "No Child Left Behind." *Race Ethnicity and Education, 10*(3), 245–260.

Darling-Hammond, L., Goldhaber, D., Strunk, K. O., & Sutcher, L. (2018). *Teacher supply falls short of demand in high-need fields, locations*. Accessed at https://files.eric.ed.gov/fulltext /ED594728.pdf on October 4, 2021.

Dartey-Baah, K. (2015). Resilient leadership: A transformational-transactional leadership mix. *Journal of Global Responsibility, 6*(1), 99–112.

Davidson, R. J., Dunne, J., Eccles, J., Engle, A., Greenberg, M., Jennings, P., et al. (2012). Contemplative practice and mental training: Prospects for American education. *Child Development Perspectives, 6*(2), 146–153.

Davidson, R. J., Kabat-Zinn, J., Schumacher, J., Rosenkranz, M., Muller, D., & Santorelli, S. F. (2003). Alterations in brain and immune function produced by mindfulness meditation. *Psychosomatic Medicine, 65*(4), 564–570.

Deci, E. L., & Ryan, R. M. *(1985). Intrinsic motivation and self-determination in human behavior.* New York: Plenum.

Deci, E. L., & Ryan, R. M. (2012). Self-determination theory. In P. A. M. Van Lange, A. W. Kruglanski, & E. T. Higgins (Eds.), *Handbook of theories of social psychology* (p. 416–436). Los Angeles: SAGE.

DeLorenzo, R. A., Battino, W. J., Schreiber, R. M., & Carrio, B. G. (2009). *Delivering on the promise: The education revolution.* Bloomington, IN: Solution Tree Press.

Delpit, L. (1993). The silenced dialogue: Power and pedagogy in educating other people's children. In L. Weis & M. Fine (Eds.), *Beyond silenced voices: Race, gender and class in United States schools* (pp. 119–139). Albany: State University of New York Press.

Delpit, L. (2013). *Multiplication is for white people: Raising expectations for other people's children.* New York: The New Press.

Delpit, L. (2016). *Other people's children: Cultural conflict in the classroom.* New York: The New Press.

Dewey, J. (1916). *Democracy and education: An introduction to the philosophy of education.* New York: Macmillan.

Dewey, J. (1938). *Experience and education.* New York: Macmillan.

Divine, M. (2014). *Unbeatable mind: Forge resiliency and mental toughness to succeed at an elite level.* Encinitas, CA: Author.

Downey, L. (2013). *Calmer classrooms: A guide to working with traumatised children.* Melbourne, Australia: State of Victoria, Child Safety Commissioner.

Duckworth, A. L., Kim, B., & Tsukayama, E. (2013). Life stress impairs self-control in early adolescence. *Frontiers in Psychology, 11*(3), 608.

DuFour, R., DuFour, R., Eaker, R., Many, T. W., & Mattos, M. (2016). *Learning by doing: A handbook for Professional Learning Communities at Work* (3rd ed.). Bloomington, IN: Solution Tree Press.

Duran, E. (2019). *Healing the soul wound: Trauma-informed counseling for Indigenous communities.* New York: Teachers College Press.

Dweck, C. S. (2006). *Mindset: The new psychology of success.* New York: Random House.

Dweck, C. S., & Molden, D. C. (2017). Mindsets: Their impact on competence motivation and acquisition. In A. J. Elliot, C. S. Dweck, & D. S. Yeager (Eds.), *Handbook of competence and motivation: Theory and application* (pp. 135–154). New York: Guilford Press.

Dyer, K. (2015). *Research proof points—Better student engagement improves student learning.* Accessed at www.nwea.org/blog/2015/research-proof-points-better-student-engagement -improves-student-learning on August 2, 2021.

Eisenberg, D., Lipson, S. K., Heinze, J., & Zhou, S. (2020). *The healthy minds study.* Accessed at https://healthymindsnetwork.org/wp-content/uploads/2021/02/HMS-Fall-2020 -National-Data-Report.pdf on July 19, 2021.

Ellis, A. K., & Fouts, J. T. (1997). *Research on educational innovations.* Larchmont, NY: Eye on Education.

Evans-Campbell, T. (2008). Historical trauma in American Indian/Native Alaska communities: A multilevel framework for exploring impacts on individuals, families, and communities. *Journal of Interpersonal Violence, 23*(3), 316–338.

Every Student Succeeds Act of 2015, Pub. L. No. 114-95, 20 U.S.C. § 1177 (2015).

Fallot, R. D., & Harris, M. (2008). Trauma-informed services. In G. Reyes, J. D. Elhai, & J. Ford (Eds.), *The encyclopedia of psychological trauma* (pp. 660–662). Hoboken, NJ: Wiley.

Fallot, R. D., & Harris, M. (2011). *Creating cultures of trauma-informed care (CCTIC): A self-assessment and planning protocol.* Accessed at www.researchgate.net/publication /272167009_Creating_Cultures_of_Trauma-Informed_Care_A_Self-Assessment _and_Planning_Protocol on February 9, 2021.

Faustenhammer, A. & Gössler, M. (2011). Preparing for the next crisis: What can organisations do to prepare managers for an uncertain future? *Business Strategy Series, 12*(2), 51–55.

Feinstein, S. (2007). *Teaching the at-risk teenage brain.* Lantham, MD: Rowman & Littlefield Education.

Felitti, V. J., Anda, R. F., Nordenberg, D., Williamson, D. F., Spitz, A. M., Edwards, V., et al. (1998). Relationship of childhood abuse and household dysfunction to many of the leading causes of death in adults: The Adverse Childhood Experiences (ACE) Study. *American Journal of Preventive Medicine, 14*(4), 245–258.

Ferguson, R. (2002). *Ed-excel assessment of secondary school student culture, tabulations by school district and race/ethnicity.* Cambridge, MA: Wiener Center for Social Policy, J. F. Kennedy School of Government, Harvard University.

Ferguson, R. F. (2015). *The influence of teaching: Beyond standardized test scores—Engagement, mindsets, and agency.* Accessed at www.agi.harvard.edu/projects /TeachingandAgency.pdf on May 1, 2018.

Ferguson, R. F., Phillips, S. F., Rowley, J. F., & Friedlander, J. W. (2015). *The influence of teaching beyond standardized test scores: Engagement, mindsets, and agency.* Accessed at www .hks.harvard.edu/publications/influence-teaching-beyond-standardized-test-scores -engagement-mindsets-and-agency on August 13, 2021.

Finkelhor, D., Shattuck, A., Turner, H., & Hamby, S. (2013). Improving the adverse childhood experiences study scale. *JAMA Pediatrics, 167*(1), 70–75.

Finkelhor, D., Turner, H., Ormrod, R., & Hamby, S. L. (2010). Trends in childhood violence and abuse exposure: Evidence from 2 national surveys. *Archives of Pediatric and Adolescent Medicine, 164*(3), 238–242.

Fischer, K. W., & Bidell, T. R. (2006). Dynamic development of action, thought, and emotion. İn R. M. Lerner (Ed.), *Handbook of child psychology: Vol. 1—Theoretical models of human development* (6th ed., pp. 313–399). New York: Wiley.

Flavell, J. H. (1979). Metacognition and cognitive monitoring: A new area of cognitive-developmental inquiry. *American Psychologist, 34*(10), 906–911.

Fleming, J., & Ledogar, R. J. (2008). Resilience, an evolving concept: A review of literature relevant to aboriginal research. *Pimatisiwin: A Journal of Aboriginal & Indigenous Community Health, 6*(2), 7–23.

Fleming, S. (2019, January 14). *This is the world's biggest mental health problem—And you might not have heard of it.* Accessed at www.weforum.org/agenda/2019/01/this-is-the-worlds -biggest-mental-health-problem on February 9, 2021.

Fraley, A. F., & Jones, B. D. (2016). *Examining the Reggio Emilia approach: Keys to understanding why it motivates students.* Accessed at www.redalyc.org/pdf/2931/293149308010.pdf on February 9, 2021.

Freeman, M. A., Johnson, S. L., Staudenmaier, P. J., & Zisser, M. R. (2015). *Are entrepreneurs "touched with fire"?* Accessed at www.michaelafreemanmd.com on February 9, 2021.

Freeman, J., Simonsen, B., McCoach, D. B., Sugai, G., Lombardi, A., & Horner, R. (2016). Relationship between school-wide positive behavior interventions and supports and academic, attendance, and behavior outcomes in high schools. *Journal of Positive Behavior Interventions, 18*(1), 41–51.

Freire, P. (1970a). *Pedagogy of the oppressed.* New York: Continuum International.

Freire, P. (1970b). The banking model of education. In E. F. Provenzo (Ed.), *Critical issues in education: An anthology of readings* (pp. 105–117). Thousand Oaks, CA: SAGE.

Fullan, M. (2003). *The moral imperative of school leadership.* Thousand Oaks, CA: Corwin Press.

Fullan, M. (2007). *The new meaning of educational change* (4th ed.). New York: Teachers College Press.

Fullan, M. (2008). *The six secrets of change: What the best leaders do to help their organizations survive and thrive.* San Francisco: Jossey-Bass.

Fullan, M. (2010). *All systems go: The change imperative for whole system reform.* Thousand Oaks, CA: Corwin Press.

Fullan, M. (2011). *Change leader: Learning to do what matters most.* San Francisco: Jossey-Bass.

Gardner, A. F., & Jones, B. D. (2016). Examining the Reggio Emilia approach: Keys to understanding why it motivates students. *Electronic Journal of Research in Educational Psychology, 14*(3), 602–625.

Garner, A. S., & Shonkoff, J. P. (2012a). *Mitigate 'toxic' stress: A new science of early childhood reveals urgency of protecting developing brains.* Accessed at www.aap.org/en-us/advocacy-and -policy/aap-health-initiatives/EBCD/Documents/NewScienceArticle2012.pdf on March 26, 2021.

Garner A. S., & Shonkoff, J. P. (2012b). Early childhood adversity, toxic stress, and the role of the pediatrician: Translating developmental science into lifelong health. *Pediatrics. 129*(1), e224–e231.

GBD 2017 Disease and Injury Incidence and Prevalence Collaborators. (2018). Global, regional, and national incidence, prevalence, and years lived with disability for 354 diseases and injuries for 195 countries and territories, 1990–2017: A systematic analysis for the Global Burden of Disease Study 2017. *Lancet, 392*(10159), 1789–1858.

George, A. (2018). *The 1968 Kerner Commission got it right, but nobody listened.* Accessed at www.smithsonianmag.com/smithsonian-institution/1968-kerner-commission-got-it-right-nobody-listened-180968318 on August 13, 2021.

Getting Smart. (2018). *Show what you know: A landscape analysis of competency-based education.* Accessed at www.gettingsmart.com/2018/10/show-what-you-know-landscape-of-competency-based-education on August 13, 2021.

Ginsberg, M. B. (2015). *Excited to learn: Motivation and culturally responsive teaching.* Thousand Oaks, CA: Corwin Press.

Gladwell, M. (2000). *The tipping point: How little things can make a big difference.* New York: Back Bay Books.

Gleason, S. C., & Gerzon, N. (2013). *Growing into equity: Professional learning and personalization in high-achieving schools.* Thousand Oaks, CA: Corwin Press.

Glock, S., Krolak-Schwerdt, S., Klapproth, F., & Böhmer, M. (2013). Beyond judgment bias: How students' ethnicity and academic profile consistency influence teachers' tracking judgments. *Social Psychology of Education: An International Journal, 16*(4), 555–573.

Greenberg, J., Romero, V. L., Elkin-Frankston, S., Bezdek, M. A., Schumacher, E. H., & Lazar, S. W. (2019). Reduced interference in working memory following mindfulness training is associated with increases in hippocampal volume. *Brain Imaging and Behavior, 13*(2), 366–376.

Greenberg, M. T., Domitrovich, C. E., Weissberg, R. P., & Durlak, J. A. (2017). Social and emotional learning as a public health approach to education. *The Future of Children, 27*(1), 13–32.

Gregory, G., & Kaufeldt, M. (2015). *The motivated brain: Improving student attention, engagement, and perseverance.* Alexandria, VA: Association for Supervision and Curriculum Development.

Guskey, T. R. (1997). *Implementing mastery learning* (2nd ed.). Belmont, CA: Wadsworth.

Guskey, T. R. (2007). Closing achievement gaps: Revisiting Benjamin S. Bloom's "Learning for Mastery." *Journal of Advanced Academics, 19*(1), 8–31.

Guskey, T. R. (2008). Mastery learning. In T. L. Good (Ed.), *21st century education: A reference handbook* (vol. 1, pp. 194–202). Thousand Oaks, CA: SAGE.

Guskey, T. R. (2010). Lessons of mastery learning. *Educational Leadership, 68*(2), 52–57.

Guskey, T. R. (2011). Five obstacles to grading reform. *Educational Leadership, 69*(3), 16–21.

Hall, G. E., & Hord, S. M. (2011). *Implementing change: Patterns, principles, and potholes* (3rd ed.). Upper Saddle River, NJ: Pearson Education.

Hallinger, P. (2012). *School leadership that makes a difference: Lessons from 30 years of international research.* Accessed at www.utsbasilicata.it/attachments/article/810 /03a_Leadership_21st_century_schools[1].pdf on January 19, 2018.

Hallinger, P., & Murphy, J. (1985). Assessing the instructional management behavior of principals. *Elementary School Journal, 86*(2), 217–247.

Hambrick, E. P., Brawner, T. W., Perry, B. D., Brandt, K., Hofmeister, C., & Collins, J. (2018). Beyond the ACE score: Examining relationships between timing of developmental adversity, relational health and developmental outcomes in children. *Archives of Psychiatric Nursing, 33*(3).

Hammond, Z. (2015). *Culturally responsive teaching and the brain: Promoting authentic engagement and rigor among culturally and linguistically diverse students.* Thousand Oaks, CA: Corwin Press.

Hamoudi, A., Murray, D. W., Sorensen, L., & Fontaine, A. (2015). *Self-regulation and toxic stress: A review of ecological, biological, and developmental studies of self-regulation and stress* (OPRE Report 2015–30). Washington, DC: Office of Planning, Research and Evaluation.

Hamre, B. K., & Pianta, R. C. (2005). *Can instructional and emotional support in the first-grade classroom make a difference for children at risk of school failure?* Accessed at www.jstor.org /stable/3696607 on February 9, 2021.

Hamre, B. K., & Pianta, R. C. (2010). Classroom environments and developmental processes. In J. L. Meece & J. S. Eccles (Eds.), *Handbook of research on schools, schooling, and human development* (pp. 25–41). London: Routledge.

Harris, N. B. (2018). *The deepest well: Healing the long-term effects of childhood adversity.* Boston: Houghton Mifflin Harcourt.

Harris, N. B., Marques, S. S., Oh, D., Bucci, M., & Cloutier, M. (2017). Prevent, screen, heal: Collective action to fight the toxic effects of early life adversity. *Academic Pediatrics, 17*(7), S14–S15.

Harvard Health Publishing. (n.d.). *Understanding the stress response.* Accessed at www.health. harvard.edu/staying-healthy/understanding-the-stress-response on July 22, 2021.

Hattie, J. (2009). *Visible learning: A synthesis of over 800 meta-analyses relating to achievement.* New York: Routledge.

Hattie, J. (2015a). *What doesn't work in education: The politics of distraction.* London: Pearson.

Hattie, J. (2015b). *What works best in education: The politics of collaborative expertise.* London: Pearson.

Heflebower, T., Hoegh, J. K., Warrick, P. B., & Flygare, J. (2019). *A teacher's guide to standards-based learning.* Bloomington, IN: Marzano Resources.

Heifetz, R. A., & Linsky, M. (2002). *Leadership on the line: Staying alive through the dangers of leading.* Boston: Harvard Business School Press.

Heron, M. (2019, June 24). *Deaths: Leading causes for 2017*. Accessed at www.cdc.gov/nchs/data/nvsr/nvsr68/nvsr68_06-508.pdf on October 4, 2021.

Hoegh, J. K. (2020). *A handbook for developing and using proficiency scales in the classroom*. Bloomington, IN: Marzano Resources.

Hölzel, B. K., Carmody, J., Vangel, M., Congleton, C., Yerramsetti, S. M., Gard, T., et al. (2011). Mindfulness practice leads to increases in regional brain gray matter density. *Psychiatry Research, 191*(1), 36–43.

Howard, T. C. (2003). Culturally relevant pedagogy: Ingredients for critical teacher reflection. *Theory Into Practice, 42*(3), 195–202.

Hoy, W. K. (2005a). *Academic optimism of schools*. Accessed at www.waynekhoy.com on February 9, 2021.

Hoy, W. K. (2005b). *SAOS*. Accessed at www.waynekhoy.com/pdfs/saos.pdf on September 9, 2021.

Hoy, W. K., Tarter, C. J., & Bliss, J. R. (1990). Organizational climate, school health, and effectiveness: A comparative analysis. *Educational Administration Quarterly, 26*(3), 260–279.

Hoy, W. K., Tarter, C. J., & Hoy, A. W. (2006a). Academic optimism of schools: A force for student achievement. *American Educational Research Journal, 43*(3), 425–446.

Hoy, W. K., Tarter, C. J., & Hoy, A. W. (2006b). Academic optimism of schools: A second-order confirmatory factor analysis. In W. K. Hoy & C. Miskel (Eds.), *Contemporary issues in educational policy and school outcomes* (pp. 135–157). Greenwich, CT: Information Age.

Hoy, W. K., Tarter, C. J., & Kottkamp, R. B. (1991). *Open schools/healthy schools: Measuring organizational climate*. Newbury Park, CA: SAGE.

Hunter, M. (1967). *Teach more—Faster!* El Segundo, CA: TIP Publications.

Hunter, M. (1979). Teaching is decision making. *Educational Leadership, 37*(1), 62–65.

Hunter, M. (1982). *Mastery teaching*. El Segundo, CA: TIP Publications.

Hunter, R. G., Gray, J. D., & McEwen, B. S. (2018). *The neuroscience of resilience*. Accessed at www.journals.uchicago.edu/doi/10.1086/697956 on July 19, 2021.

Iberlin, J., & Ruyle, M. (2017). *Cultivating mindfulness in the classroom*. Bloomington, IN: Marzano Resources.

Immordino-Yang, M. H., & Damasio, A. (2007). We feel, therefore we learn: The relevance of affective and social neuroscience to education. *Mind, Brain, and Education, 1*(1), 3–10.

Immordino-Yang, M. H., Darling-Hammond, L., & Krone, C. (2018). *The brain basis for integrated social, emotional, and academic development: How emotions and social relationships drive learning*. Washington, DC: Aspen Institute.

Individuals With Disabilities Education Act of 1990, Pub. L. No. 101-476 (1990).

Individuals With Disabilities Education Improvement Act of 2004, Pub. L. No. 108-446 § 300.115 (2004).

Jacobsen, W. C., Pace, G. T., & Ramirez, N. G. (2019). Punishment and inequality at an early age: Exclusionary discipline in elementary school. *Social Forces, 97*(3), 973–998.

Javed, B., Khan, A. A., Bashir, S., & Arjoon, S. (2016). *Impact of ethical leadership on creativity: The role of psychological empowerment.* Accessed at http://dx.doi.org/10.1080/13683500 .2016.1188894 on July 19, 2021.

Jensen, E. (2009). *Teaching with poverty in mind. What being poor does to kids' brains and what schools can do about it.* Alexandria, VA: Association for Supervision and Curriculum Development.

Johnson, D. C., Thom, N. J., Stanley, E. A., Haase, L., Simmons, A. N., Pei-An, S., et al. (2014). Modifying resilience mechanisms in at-risk individuals: A controlled study of mindfulness training in Marines preparing for deployment. *American Journal of Psychiatry, 171*(8), 844–853.

Johnson, S. B., Riis, J. L., & Noble, K. G. (2016). State of the art review: Poverty and the developing brain. *Pediatrics, 137*(4), 1–16.

Johnson, S. B., Riley, A. W., Granger, D. A., & Riis, J. (2013). *The science of early life toxic stress for pediatric practice and advocacy.* Accessed at https://doi.org/10.1542/peds.2012-0469 on July 19, 2021.

Jones, C. M., Merrick, M. T., & Houry, D. E. (2020). Identifying and preventing adverse childhood experiences: Implications for clinical practice. *Journal of the American Medical Association, 323*(1), 25–26.

Jones, S. M., Bailey, R., Barnes, S. P., & Partee, A. (2016). *Executive function mapping project: Untangling the terms and skills related to executive function and self-regulation in early childhood.* Washington, DC: Office of Planning, Research and Evaluation.

Jones, S. M., & Bouffard, S. M. (2012). *Social and emotional learning in schools: From programs to strategies and commentaries.* Accessed at www.srcd.org/sites/default/files/documents /spr_264_final_2.pdf on February 9, 2021.

Juneau, D., & Broaddus, M. S. (2006). And still the waters flow: The legacy of Indian education in Montana. *Phi Delta Kappan, 88*(3), 193–197.

Kabat-Zinn, J. (1990). *Full catastrophe living: Using the wisdom of your body and mind to face stress, pain, and illness.* New York: Delacorte Press.

Kabat-Zinn, J. (2005a). *Coming to our senses: Healing ourselves and the world through mindfulness.* New York: Hyperion.

Kabat-Zinn, J. (2005b). *Full catastrophe living: Using the wisdom of your body and mind to face stress, pain, and illness.* New York: Delta Trade Paperbacks.

Kaplan, M., Silver, N., Lavaque-Manty, D., & Meizlish, D. (Eds.). (2013). *Using reflection and metacognition to improve student learning.* Sterling, VA: Stylus Publishing.

Katz, L. G. (1998). What can we learn from Reggio Emilia? In C. Edwards, L. Gandini, & G. Forman (Eds.), *The hundred languages of children: The Reggio Emilia approach—Advanced reflections* (2nd ed., pp. 27–45). Westport, CT: Greenwood Publishing Group.

Kaye, C. B. (2010a). *The complete guide to service learning: Proven, practical ways to engage students in civic responsibility, academic curriculum, and social action* (2nd ed.). Minneapolis: Free Spirit Publishing.

Kaye, C. B. (2010b). *Service learning: Engagement, action, results!* Accessed at https://scholarworks.gvsu.edu/colleagues/vol5/iss1/5 on October 4, 2021.

Kellam, S. G., Mackenzie, A. C. L., Brown, C. H., Poduska, J. M., Wang, W., Petras, H., et al. (2011). The good behavior game and the future of prevention and treatment. *Addiction Science & Clinical Practice, 6*(1), 73–84.

Kerr, C. E., Sacchet, M. D., Lazar, S. W., Moore, C. I., & Jones, S. R. (2013). Mindfulness starts with the body: Somatosensory attention and top-down modulation of cortical alpha rhythms in mindfulness meditation. *Frontiers in Human Neuroscience, 7*, 12.

Kerrigan, D., Johnson, K., Stewart, M., Magyari, T., Hutton, N., Ellen, J. M., et al. (2011). Perceptions, experiences, and shifts in perspective occurring among urban youth participating in a mindfulness-based stress reduction program. *Complementary Therapies in Clinical Practice, 17*(2), 96–101.

Khoury, L., Tang, Y. L., Bradley, B., Cubells, J. F., & Ressler, K. J. (2010). *Substance use, childhood traumatic experience, and Posttraumatic Stress Disorder in an urban civilian population.* Accessed at www.ncbi.nlm.nih.gov/pmc/articles/PMC3051362 on May 5, 2021.

Kim, W. G., & Brymer, R. A. (2011). The effects of ethical leadership on manager job satisfaction, commitment, behavioural outcomes, and firm performance. *International Journal of Hospitality Management, 30*(4), 1020–1026.

Kingston, J. (2020). *American awakening: Eight principles to restore the soul of America.* Grand Rapids, MI: Zondervan.

KnowledgeWorks Foundation. (2016). *Recommendations for advancing personalized learning under the Every Student Succeeds Act (ESSA).* Accessed at https://knowledgeworks.org/wp-content/uploads/2018/01/personalized-learning-essa-recommendations.pdf on August 13, 2021.

Kouzes, J. M., & Posner, B. Z. (2007). *The leadership challenge* (4th ed.). San Francisco: Jossey-Bass.

Ladson-Billings, G. (1995). Toward a theory of culturally relevant pedagogy. *American Educational Research Journal, 32*(3), 465–491.

Ladson-Billings, G. (2009). *The dreamkeepers: Successful teachers of African-American children* (2nd ed.). San Francisco: Jossey Bass.

Ladson-Billings, G. (2014). Culturally relevant pedagogy 2.0: a.k.a. the remix. *Harvard Educational Review, 84*(1), 74–84.

Lai, E. R. (2011). *Motivation: A literature review.* London: Pearson.

Lazar, S. W., Bush, G., Gollub, R., Fricchione, G., Khalsa, G., & Benson, H. (2000). Functional brain mapping of the relaxation response and meditation. *Neuroreport, 11*(7), 1581–1585.

Lazar, S. W., Kerr, C. E., Wasserman, R. H., Gray, J. R., Greve, D. N., Treadway, M. T., et al. (2005). Meditation experience is associated with increased cortical thickness. *Neuroreport, 16*(17), 1893–1897.

Leider, R. J. (2015). *The power of purpose: Find meaning, live longer, better* (3rd ed.). Oakland, CA: Berrett-Koehler.

Leithwood, K., & Sun, J. (2012). The nature and effects of transformational school leadership: A meta-analytic review of unpublished research. *Educational Administration Quarterly, 48*(3), 387–423.

Lesley University. (n.d.). *The psychology of emotional and cognitive empathy.* Accessed at https://lesley.edu/article/the-psychology-of-emotional-and-cognitive-empathy on August 12, 2021.

Levine, E., & Patrick, S. (2019). *What is competency-based education? An updated definition.* Accessed at https://aurora-institute.org/wp-content/uploads/what-is-competency -based-education-an-updated-definition-web.pdf on August 13, 2021.

Lindsay, R., & Lindsay, D. (2020). *Overcoming the barriers: The Center for Culturally Proficient Educational Practice.* Accessed at https://ccpep.org/home/what-is-cultural-proficiency /overcoming-barriers on February 9, 2021.

Listenbee, R. L., Torre, J., Boyle, G., Cooper, S. W., Deer, S., Durfee, D. T., et al. (2012). *Report of the Attorney General's National Task Force on Children Exposed to Violence.* Washington, DC: U.S. Department of Justice. Accessed at www.justice.gov /defendingchildhood/cev-rpt-full.pdf on February 9, 2021.

Lombardi, J. D. (2016, June 14). *The deficit model is harming your students.* Accessed at www .edutopia.org/blog/deficit-model-is-harming-students-janice-lombardi on October 7, 2021.

Lyubomirsky, S., King, L. L., & Diener, E. (2005). The benefits of frequent positive affect: Does happiness lead to success? *Psychological Bulletin, 131*(6), 803–855.

Macey, W. H., Schneider, B., Barbera, K. M., & Young, S. A. (2009). *Employee engagement: Tools for analysis, practice, and competitive advantage.* London: Wiley-Blackwell.

Macy, R. D., Behar, L., Paulson, R., Delman, J., Schmid, L., & Smith, S. (2004). *Community-based, acute posttraumatic stress management: A description and evaluation of a psychosocial-intervention continuum.* Accessed at https://internationaltraumacenter.files .wordpress.com/2015/10/macy-ptsm-pub-2.pdf on August 12, 2021.

Marcovitch, S., & Zelazo, P. D. (2009). A hierarchical competing systems model of the emergence and early development of executive function. *Developmental Science, 12*(1), 1–18.

Marsh, H. W., & O'Mara, A. (2008). Reciprocal effects between academic self-concept, self-esteem, achievement, and attainment over seven adolescent years: Unidimensional and multidimensional perspectives of self-concept. *Personality and Social Psychology Bulletin, 34*(4), 542–552.

Martin, A. J. (2012). The role of personal best (PB) goals in the achievement and behavioral engagement of students with ADHD and students without ADHD. *Contemporary Educational Psychology, 37*(2), 91–105.

Martin, A. J., & Liem, G. A. D. (2010). Academic personal best (PBs), engagement, and achievement: A crosslagged panel analysis. *Learning and Individual Differences, 20*(3), 265–270.

Martin, A. J., & Liem, G. A. D. (2011). Personal best (PB) approaches to academic development: Implications for motivation and assessment. *Educational Practice and Theory, 33*(1), 93–99.

Marzano, R. J. (2000). *Transforming classroom grading.* Alexandria, VA: Association for Supervision and Curriculum Development.

Marzano, R. J. (2006). *Classroom assessment and grading that work.* Alexandria, VA: Association for Supervision and Curriculum Development.

Marzano, R. J. (2009). Setting the record straight on "high-yield" strategies. *Phi Delta Kappan, 91*(1), 30–37.

Marzano, R. J. (2010). *Formative assessment and standards-based grading.* Bloomington, IN: Marzano Resources.

Marzano, R. J. (2017). *The new art and science of teaching.* Bloomington, IN: Solution Tree Press.

Marzano, R. J. (2018). *Making classroom assessments reliable and valid.* Bloomington, IN: Solution Tree Press.

Marzano, R. J., & Heflebower, T. (2011). Grades that show what students know. *Educational Leadership, 69*(3), 34–39.

Marzano, R. J., & Marzano, J. S. (2015). *Managing the inner world of teaching: Emotions, interpretations, and actions.* Bloomington, IN: Marzano Resources.

Marzano, R. J., Norford, J. S., Finn, M., & Finn, D. (2017). *A handbook for personalized competency-based education.* Bloomington, IN: Marzano Resources.

Marzano, R. J., Norford, J. S., & Ruyle, M. (2019). *The new art and science of classroom assessment.* Bloomington, IN: Solution Tree Press.

Marzano, R. J., Scott, D., Boogren, T. H., & Newcomb, M. L. (2017). *Motivating and inspiring students: Strategies to awaken the learner.* Bloomington, IN: Marzano Resources.

Marzano, R. J., Warrick, P., & Simms, J. A. (2014). *A handbook for high reliability schools: The next step in school reform.* Bloomington, IN. Marzano Resources.

Marzano, R. J., & Waters, T. (2009). *District leadership that works: Striking the right balance.* Bloomington, IN: Solution Tree Press.

Marzano, R. J., Waters, T., & McNulty, B. A. (2005). *School leadership that works: From research to results.* Alexandria, VA: Association for Supervision and Curriculum Development.

Marzano, R. J., Yanoski, D. C., Hoegh, J. K., & Simms, J. A. (2013). *Using Common Core standards to enhance classroom instruction and assessment.* Bloomington, IN: Marzano Resources.

Marzano Resources. (n.d.). *The Critical Concepts.* Accessed at www.marzanoresources.com /educational-services/critical-concepts on September 9, 2021.

Maslow, A. H. (1943). A theory of human motivation. *Psychological Review, 50*(4), 370–396.

Masten, A. S., & Coatsworth, J. D. (1998). *The development of competence in favorable and unfavorable environments: Lessons from research on successful children.* Accessed at http://dx.doi.org/10.1037/0003-066X.53.2.205 on July 21, 2021.

Mayo Clinic Staff. (2014). *Stress management.* Accessed at www.mayoclinic.org/tests-procedures/stress-management/basics/definition/prc-20021046 on July 29, 2016.

Mayo Clinic Staff. (2021). *Chronic stress puts your health at risk.* Accessed at www.mayoclinic.org/healthy-lifestyle/stress-management/in-depth/stress/art-20046037 on October 4, 2021.

McGonigal, J. (2015). *Superbetter: A revolutionary approach to getting stronger, happier, braver and more resilient—powered by the science of games.* New York: Penguin Books

Medin, D. L., & Bang, M. (2014a). The cultural side of science communication. *Proceedings of the National Academy of Sciences, 111*(4), 13621–13626.

Medin, D. L., & Bang, M. (2014b). *Who's asking? Native science, Western science, and science education.* Cambridge, MA: MIT Press.

Medina, J. (2014). *Brain rules: 12 principles for surviving and thriving at work, home, and school* (Updated and expanded ed.). Seattle: Pear Press.

Meiklejohn, J., Phillips, C., Freedman, M. L., Griffin, M. L., Biegel, G., Roach, A., et al. (2012). Integrating mind-fulness training into K–12 education: Fostering the resilience of teachers and students. *Mindfulness, 3*(4), 291–307.

Merrick, M. T., Ford, D. C., Ports, K. A., & Guinn, A. S. (2018). Prevalence of adverse childhood experiences from the 2011–2014 behavioral risk factor surveillance system in 23 states. *JAMA Pediatrics, 172*(11), 1038–1044

Merrick, M. T., Ford, D. C., Ports, K. A., Guinn, A. S., Chen, J., & Klevens, J. (2019). *Estimated proportion of adult health problems attributable to adverse childhood experiences and implications for prevention: 25 states, 2015–2017.* Accessed at www.cdc.gov/mmwr/volumes/68/wr/mm6844e1.htm?s_cid=mm6844e1_w on February 9, 2021.

Metwally, D., Ruiz-Palomino, P., Metwally, M., & Gartzia, L. (2019). *How ethical leadership shapes employees' readiness to change: The mediating role of an organizational culture of effectiveness.* Accessed at www.frontiersin.org/article/10.3389/fpsyg.2019.02493 on August 1, 2021.

Michel, K. L. (2014, April 19). *Maslow's hierarchy connected to Blackfoot beliefs* [Blog post]. Accessed at https://lincolnmichel.wordpress.com/2014/04/19/maslows-hierarchy-connected-to-blackfoot-beliefs on August 13, 2021.

Mindprint Learning. (n.d.). *Mindprint toolbox.* Accessed at https://my.mindprintlearning.com/product/12877?page=1&name=cognitive+screen on September 21, 2021.

Morales, K. (2018). *La marginación en México, retrospectiva de una década.* Accessed at http://bibliodigitalibd.senado.gob.mx/bitstream/handle/123456789/3932/2018_La%20marginaci%C3%B3n%20en%20M%C3%A9xico-retrospectiva%20de%20una%20d%C3%A9cada%20VF%20040618.pdf?sequence=34&isAllowed=y on September 8, 2021.

Müller-Lyer, F. C. (1889). Optische urteilstäuschungen. Archiv für Anatomie und Physiologie, *Physiologische Abteilung, 2*(Supplement), 263–270.

Murphy, M. (2016). *The tug of war between change and resistance.* Accessed at www.ascd.org /el/articles/the-tug-of-war-between-change-and-resistance on July 21, 2021.

National Academies of Sciences, Engineering, and Medicine. (2018). *How people learn II: Learners, contexts, and cultures.* Washington, DC: National Academies Press.

National Center for Education Statistics. (n.d.). *NAEP data explorer.* Accessed at https:// nces.ed.gov/nationsreportcard/naepdata on February 9, 2021.

National Center for Education Statistics. (2012). *National Indian Education Study 2011: The educational experiences of American Indian and Alaska Native students at grades 4 and 8.* Washington, DC: U.S. Department of Education.

National Center for Learning Disabilities. (2019). *Forward together: Helping educators unlock the power of students who learn differently.* Washington, DC: Author. Accessed at www.ncld. org/wp-content/uploads/2019/05/Forward-Together_NCLD-report.pdf on February 9, 2021.

National Council on Measurement in Education. (n.d.). *Assessment glossary.* Accessed at www.ncme.org/resources/glossary on February 9, 2021.

Native Hope. (2021). *How trauma gets passed down through generations.* Accessed at https:// blog.nativehope.org/how-trauma-gets-passed-down-through-generations on August 13, 2021.

Nesbit, J., & Graham, E. (2020, August 7). *13 ways to build school community.* Accessed at www.ptotoday.com/pto-today-articles/article/5949−5-ways-to-build-school -community on February 9, 2021.

Nestor, J. (2020). *Breathe: The new science of a lost art.* New York: Riverhead Books.

Nisbett, R. E. (2003). *The geography of thought: How Asians and Westerners think differently. . . and why.* New York: Free Press.

No Child Left Behind (NCLB) Act of 2001, Pub. L. No. 107-110, § 115, Stat. 1425 (2002).

Noguera, P. A. (2008). *The trouble with Black boys: And other reflections on race, equity, and the future of public education.* San Francisco: Jossey-Bass.

Norford, J. S., & Marzano, R. J. (2016). *Personalized competency-based education: Creating a cohesive and coherent system.* Accessed at http://soltreemrls3.s3-website-us-west-2 .amazonaws.com/marzanoresearch.com/media/documents/Personalized_CBE _Whitepaper_September_2016.pdf on May 5, 2021.

Northcentral University. (2014, October 21). *10 ways to empower your students in the classroom* [Blog post]. Accessed at www.ncu.edu/blog/10-ways-empower-your-students -classroom#gref on February 9, 2021.

Northern Plains Reservation Aid. (n.d.). *History and culture.* Accessed at www .nativepartnership.org/site/PageServer?pagename=airc_hist_boardingschools on March 26, 2021.

Northouse, P. G. (2007). *Leadership: Theory and practice* (4th ed.). Thousand Oaks, CA: SAGE.

Oral, R., Ramirez, M., Coohey, C., Nakada, S., Walz, A., Kuntz, A., et al. (2016). Adverse childhood experiences and trauma informed care: The future of health care. *Pediatric Research, 79*(1–2), 227–233.

Osher, D., Cantor, P., Berg, J., Steyer, L., & Rose, T. (2018). Drivers of human development: How relationships and context shape learning and development. *Applied Developmental Science, 24*(1), 6–36.

Osher, D., & Kendziora, K. (2010). Building conditions for learning and healthy adolescent development: Strategic approaches. In B. Doll, W. Pfohl, & J. Yoon (Eds.), *Handbook of youth prevention science* (pp. 121–140). New York: Routledge.

Oyserman, D. (2009). Identity-based motivation and consumer behavior. *Journal of Consumer Psychology, 19*(3), 276–279.

Park, J. Z., Martinez, B. C., Cobb, R., Park, J. J., & Wong, E. R. (2015). Exceptional outgroup stereotypes and White racial inequality attitudes toward Asian Americans. *School Psychology Quarterly, 78*(4), 399–411.

Patel, B. (2011). *The importance of resilience in leadership.* Accessed at https://nfpsynergy.net /press-release/importance-resilience-leadership on August 1, 2021.

Patrick, S., Kennedy, K., & Powell, A. (2013). *Mean what you say: Defining and integrating personalized, blended and competency education.* Accessed at https://aurora-institute.org /wp-content/uploads/mean-what-you-say-1.pdf on August 1, 2021.

Pember, M. A. (2019). *Death by civilization.* Accessed at www.theatlantic.com/education /archive/2019/03/traumatic-legacy-indian-boarding-schools/584293 on May 5, 2021.

Perfect, M., Turley, M., Carlson, J. S., Yohannan, J., & Gilles, M. S. (2016). School-related outcomes of traumatic event exposure and traumatic stress symptoms in students: A systematic review of research from 1990 to 2015. *School Mental Health, 8,* 7–43.

Perry, A. M. (2014, July 7). *Zero-tolerance policies are destroying the lives of Black children.* Accessed at www.washingtonpost.com/posteverything/wp/2014/07/07/zero-tolerance-policies -are-destroying-the-lives-of-black- children on February 9, 2021.

Perry, B. D. (1994). Neurobiological sequelae of childhood trauma: Post-traumatic stress disorders in children. In M. Murburg (Ed.), *Catecholamine function in post-traumatic stress disorder: Emerging concepts* (pp. 253–276). Washington, DC: American Psychiatric Press.

Perry, B. D. (2006). Applying principles of neurodevelopment to clinical work with maltreated and traumatized children: The neurosequential model of therapeutics. In N. B. Webb (Ed.), *Social work practice with children and families: Working with traumatized youth in child welfare* (pp. 27–52). New York: Guilford Press.

Perry, B. D. (2008). *Relational poverty and the modern world : The importance of early childhood relationships for child, community and culture.* Houston, TX: Child Trauma Academy.

Perry, B. D. (2009). *Examining child maltreatment through a neurodevelopmental lens: Clinical applications of the neurosequential model of therapeutics.* Accessed at https://childtrauma org /wp-content/uploads/2013/09/TraumaLoss_BDP_Final_7_09 pdf on February 9, 2021.

Perry, B. D., & Child Trauma Academy. (2008). *Relational poverty and the modern world: The importance of early childhood relationships for child, community and culture* [Video.]. Houston, TX: Child Trauma Academy.

Peterson, C., Florence, C., & Klevens, J. (2018). The economic burden of child maltreatment in the United States, 2015. *Child Abuse and Neglect; 86*,178–183.

Petrides, L., Jimes, C., & Karaglani, A. (2014). Assistant principal leadership development: A narrative capture study. *Journal of Educational Administration, 52*(2), 173–192.

Philadelphia ACE Project. (2019). *Philadelphia ACE survey.* Accessed at www .philadelphiaaces.org/philadelphia-ace-survey on February 9, 2021.

Pickersgill, M. (2020). *Epigenetics, education, and the plastic body: Changing concepts and new engagements.* Accessed at https://journals.sagepub.com/doi/full/10.1177 /0034523719867102 on April 21, 2021.

Pink, D. H. (2011). *Drive: The surprising truth about what motivates us.* New York: Riverhead Books.

Pink, D. H. (2018). *When: The scientific secrets of perfect timing.* New York: Riverhead Books.

Pintrich, P. R. (2003). A motivational science perspective on the role of student motivation in learning and teaching contexts. *Journal of Educational Psychology, 95*(4), 667–686.

Plomin, R. (1994). *SAGE series on individual differences and development: Vol. 6—Genetics and experience—The interplay between nature and nurture.* Thousand Oaks, CA: SAGE.

Plomin, R. (2018). *Blueprint: How DNA makes us who we are.* London: Allen Lane.

Porche, M. V., Costello, D. M., & Rosen-Reynoso, M. (2016). Adverse family experiences, child mental health, and educational outcomes for a national sample of students. *School Mental Health, 8*(1), 44–60.

Powell, C. (2012). *It worked for me: In life and leadership.* New York: Harper.

Prewitt, E. (2016, January 7). *New elementary and secondary education law includes specific "trauma- informed practices" provisions.* Accessed at www.acesconnection.com/g/aces-in -education/blog/new-elementary-and-secondary-education-law-includes-specific -trauma-informed-practices-provisions on February 9, 2021.

Priest, N., Rudenstine, A., & Weisstein, E. (2012). *Making mastery work: A close-up view of competency education.* Quincy, MA: Nellie Mae Education Foundation.

RAND Corporation. (2014). *Early progress: Interim research on personalized learning.* Accessed at http://k12education.gatesfoundation.org/student-success/personalized-learning/early- progress-interim-report-on-personalized-learning-rand on February 9, 2021.

RAND Corporation. (2015). *Continued progress: Promising evidence on personalized learning.* Accessed at www.rand.org/pubs/research_reports/RR1365.html on February 9, 2021.

Responsive Classroom. (2015, August 18). *Strong communities build strong schools.* Accessed at www.responsiveclassroom.org/strong-communities-build-strong-schools on February 9, 2021.

Robinson, V. M. J., Hohepa, M., & Lloyd, C. (2009). *School leadership and student outcomes: Identifying what works and why—Best Evidence Synthesis iteration [BES]*. Wellington, New Zealand: New Zealand Ministry of Education.

Rodriguez, R. (1998). California has another proposition: This one would prohibit bilingual education. *Black Issues in Higher Education, 14*(23), 11.

Rolfsnes, E. S., & Idsoe, T. (2011). School-based intervention programs for PTSD symptoms: A review and meta-analysis. *Journal of Traumatic Stress, 24*(2), 155–165.

Rosenberg, L. (2012). Behavioral disorders: The new public health crisis. *The Journal of Behavioral Health Services and Research, 39*(1), 1–2.

Rushton, J. P. (1990). Sir Francis Galton, epigenetic rules, genetic similarity theory, and human life-history analysis. *Journal of Personality, 58*(1), 117–140.

Ruyle, M. (with O'Neil, T. W., Iberlin, J. M., Evans, M. D., & Midles, R.). (2019). *Leading the evolution: How to make personalized competency-based education a reality*. Bloomington, IN: Marzano Resources.

Ryan, R. M., & Deci, E. L. (2020). Intrinsic and extrinsic motivation from a self-determination theory perspective: Definitions, theory, practices, and future directions. *Contemporary Educational Psychology, 61*.

Saeri, A. K., Cruwys, T., Barlow, F. K., Stronge, S., & Sibley, C. G. (2018). Social connectedness improves public mental health: Investigating bidirectional relationships in the New Zealand Attitudes and Values Survey. *Australia and New Zealand Journal of Psychiatry, 52*(4), 365–374.

Schenck, J. (2011). *Teaching and the adolescent brain: An educator's guide*. New York: Norton.

Schonert-Reichl, K. A., & Lawlor, M. S. (2010). The effects of mindfulness-based program on pre- and early adolescents' well-being and social and emotional competence. *Mindfulness, 1*(3), 137–151.

Schonert-Reichl, K. A., Oberle, E., Lawlor, M. S., Abbott, D., & Thomson, A. (2015). Enhancing cognitive and social-emotional development through a simple-to-administer mindfulness-based school program for elementary school children: A randomized controlled trial. *Developmental Psychology, 51*(1), 52–66.

Schunk, D. H. (2012). *Learning theories: An educational perspective* (6th ed.). Boston: Pearson.

Schwahn, C., & McGarvey, B. (2012). *Inevitable: Mass customized learning, learning in the age of empowerment*. Lexington, KY: CreateSpace.

Schwahn, C., & McGarvey, B. (2014). *Inevitable too! The total leader embraces mass customized learning*. Lexington, KY: CreateSpace.

Schwantes, M. (2016, November 22). *Google's insane approach to management could transform your company*. Accessed at www.inc.com/marcel-schwantes/googles-insane-approach-to-management-could-transform-your-company.html on February 9, 2021.

Scott, D., & Marzano, R. J. (2014). *Awaken the learner: Finding the source of effective education*. Bloomington, IN: Marzano Resources.

Segall, M. H., Campbell, D. T., & Herskovits, M. J. (1966). *The influence of culture on visual perception.* New York: Bobbs-Merrill.

Sege, R., Bethell, C., Linkenbach, J., Jones, J. A., Klika, B., & Pecora, P. J. (2017). *Balancing adverse childhood experiences (ACEs) with HOPE: New insights into the role of positive experience on child and family development.* Accessed at https://cssp.org/wp-content/uploads/2018/08 /Balancing-ACEs-with-HOPE-FINAL.pdf on February 9, 2021.

Seligman, M. E. P. (2002). Positive psychology, positive prevention, and positive therapy. In C. R. Snyder & S. J. Lopez (Eds.), *Handbook of positive psychology* (pp. 3–9). New York: Oxford University Press.

Sevinc, G., Greenberg, J., Hölzel, B. K., Gard, T., Calahan, T., Brunsch, V., et al. (2020). *Hippocampal circuits underlie improvements in self-reported anxiety following mindfulness training.* Accessed at www.ncbi.nlm.nih.gov/pmc/articles/PMC7507558 on August 21, 2021.

Shonkoff, J. P. (2012). Leveraging the biology of adversity to address the roots of disparities in health and development. *Proceedings of the National Academy of Sciences, 109*(2), 17302–17307.

Shonkoff, J. P. (2016). Capitalizing on advances in science to reduce the health consequences of early childhood adversity. *JAMA Pediatrics, 170*(10), 1003–1007.

Siegel, D. J. (2007). *The mindful brain: Reflection and attunement in the cultivation of well-being.* New York: Norton.

Siegel, D. J. (2010). *The mindful therapist: A clinician's guide to mindsight and neural integration.* New York: Norton.

Siegel, D. J. (2012). *The developing mind: How relationships and the brain interact to shape who we are* (2nd ed.). New York: Guilford Press.

Siegel, R. D. (2013). *Positive psychology: Harnessing the power of happiness, personal strength, and mindfulness.* Boston: Harvard Health Publications.

Simms, J. A. (2016). *The critical concepts (final version: English language arts, mathematics, and science).* Centennial, CO: Marzano Resources.

Spencer, M. B. (2007). Phenomenology and ecological systems theory: Development of diverse groups. In R. M. Lerner (Ed.), *Handbook of child psychology and developmental science: Vol. 1—Theory and method* (6th ed., pp. 829–893). Hoboken, NJ: Wiley.

Srinivasan, M. (2014). *Teach, breathe, learn: Mindfulness in and out of the classroom.* Berkeley, CA: Parallax Press.

Stafford-Brizard, K. B. (2016). *Building blocks for learning: A framework for comprehensive student development.* New York: Turnaround for Children. Accessed at www.turnaroundusa.org /wp-content/uploads/2016/03/Turnaround-for-Children-Building-Blocks-for -Learningx-2.pdf on February 9, 2021.

Stafford-Brizard, K. B., Cantor, P., & Rose, L. T. (2017). *Building the bridge between science and practice: Essential characteristics of a translational framework.* Accessed at https://doi.org /10.1111/mbe.12153 on February 9, 2021.

Steele, C. M. (2010). *Whistling Vivaldi: And other clues to how stereotypes affect us.* New York: W. W. Norton.

Steffes, J. S. (2004). Creating powerful learning environments beyond the classroom. *Change, 36*(3), 46–50.

Steiner, R. J., Sheremenko, G., Lesesne, C., Dittus, P. J., Sieving, R. E., & Ethier, K. A. (2019). *Adolescent connectedness and adult health outcomes.* Accessed at https://doi.org /10.1542/peds.2018-3766 on August 13, 2021.

Steinke, P., & Fitch, P. (2017). Minimizing bias when assessing student work. *Research and Practice in Assessment, 12,* 87–95.

Strong, R., Silver, H. F., & Robinson, A. (1995). Strengthening student engagement: What do students want (and what really motivates them)? *Educational Leadership, 53*(1), 8–12.

Sturgis, C. (2016b, September 8). *NYC big takeaways* [Blog post]. Accessed at https://aurora -institute.org/blog/nyc-big-takeaways on February 9, 2021.

Substance Abuse and Mental Health Services Administration. (2014). *SAMHSA's concept of trauma and guidance for a trauma-informed approach.* Accessed at https://ncsacw.samhsa.gov /userfiles/files/SAMHSA_Trauma.pdf on August 13, 2021.

Substance Abuse and Mental Health Services Administration. (2017). *Key substance use and mental health indicators in the United States: Results from the 2016 National Survey on Drug Use and Health.* Accessed at www.samhsa.gov/data/sites/default/files/NSDUH-FFR1-2016 /NSDUH-FFR1-2016.htm on August 13, 2021.

Sutherland, K. S., & Oswald, D. (2005). The relationship between teacher and student behavior in classrooms for students with emotional and behavioral disorders: Transactional processes. *Journal of Child and Family Studies, 14*(1), 1–14.

Szalavitz, M., & Perry, B. D. (2010). *Born for love: Why empathy is essential—And endangered.* New York: HarperCollins.

Tanner, K. (2012). *Promoting student metacognition.* Accessed at www.researchgate.net /publication/225186579_Promoting_Student_Metacognition on September 7, 2021.

Tavris, C., & Aronson, E. (2007). *Mistakes were made (but not by me): Why we justify foolish beliefs, bad decisions, and hurtful acts.* Orlando, FL: Harcourt.

Tedeschi, R. G. (2020, July–August). *Growth after trauma.* Accessed at https://hbr.org/2020 /07/growth-after-trauma on February 9, 2021.

Tedeschi, R. G., Shakespeare-Finch, J., Taku, K., & Calhoun, L. G. (2018). *Posttraumatic growth: Theory, research, and applications.* New York: Routledge.

Teicher, M. H., & Samson, J. A. (2016). Annual research review: Enduring neurobiological effects of childhood abuse and neglect. *Journal of Child Psychology and Psychiatry, 57*(3), 241–266.

Teicher, M. H., Samson, J. A., Anderson, C. M., & Ohashi, K. (2016). The effects of childhood maltreatment on brain structure, function and connectivity. *Nature Reviews Neuroscience, 17,* 652–666.

Tennessee H.B. 405/S.B. 170. (2019). Accessed at www.capitol.tn.gov/Bills/111/Bill/HB0405.pdf on August 1, 2021.

Terry, R., Townley, G., Brusilovskiy, E., & Salzar, M. S. (2019). The influence of sense of community on the relationship between community participation and mental health for individuals with serious mental illnesses. *Journal of Community Psychology, 47*(1), 163–175.

U.S. Department of Education. (n.d.). *Competency-based learning or personalized learning.* Accessed at www.ed.gov/oii-news/competency-based-learning-or-personalized-learning on August 1, 2021.

Van der Kolk, B. A. (2003). The neurobiology of childhood trauma and abuse. *Child and Adolescent Psychiatric Clinics of North America, 12*(2), 293–317.

Van der Kolk, B. A. (2006). Clinical implications of neuroscience research in PTSD. *Annals of the New York Academy of Sciences, 40*, 1–17.

Van der Kolk, B. A. (2015). *The body keeps the score: Brain, mind, and body in the healing of trauma.* New York: Penguin.

Van der Kolk, B. A. (2017). Developmental trauma disorder: Toward a rational diagnosis for children with complex trauma histories. *Psychiatric Annals, 35*(5), 401–408.

Vander Ark, T., & Liebtag, E. (2020). *Difference making at the heart of learning: Students, schools, and communities alive with possibility.* Thousand Oaks, CA: Corwin Press.

Vander Ark, T., Liebtag, E., & McClennen, N. (2020). *The power of place: Authentic learning through place-based education.* Alexandria, VA: Association for Supervision and Curriculum Development.

Vygotsky, L. S. (1978). *Mind in society: The development of higher psychological processes.* Cambridge, MA: Harvard University Press.

Wade, R., Shea, J. A., Rubin, D., & Wood, J. (2014). Adverse childhood experiences of low- income urban youth. *Pediatrics, 134*(1), e13–e20.

Walker, P. (2013). *Complex PTSD: From surviving to thriving.* Lafayette, CA: Azure Coyote.

Walker, T. (2019). *'I didn't know it had a name': Secondary traumatic stress and educators.* Accessed at www.nea.org/advocating-for-change/new-from-nea/i-didnt-know-it-had-name-secondary-traumatic-stress-and on August 8, 2021.

Wallace Foundation. (2007). *Getting principal mentoring right: Lessons from the field.* New York: Author. Accessed at www.wallacefoundation.org/knowledge-center/pages/getting-principal-mentoring-right.aspx on February 9, 2021.

Wallace Foundation. (2009). *Assessing the effectiveness of school leaders: New directions and new processes.* Accessed at www.wallacefoundation.org/knowledge-center/Documents/Assessing-the-Effectiveness-of-School-Leaders.pdf on February 9, 2021.

Wallace Foundation. (2013). *The school principal as leader: Guiding schools to better teaching and learning.* Accessed at www.wallacefoundation.org/knowledge-center/Documents/The-School-Principal-as-Leader-Guiding-Schools-to-Better-Teaching-and-Learning-2nd-Ed.pdf on February 9, 2021.

Waziyatawin, A. W., & Yellow Bird, M. (2012). *For Indigenous minds only: A decolonization handbook*. Santa Fe, NM: School for Advanced Research Press.

White, M. (2013). *Building a resilient organizational culture*. Accessed at http://execdev.kenan -flagler.unc.edu/hubfs/White%20Papers/UNC-EXECUTIVE-DEVELOPMENT -Building-a-Resilient-Organizational-Culture-final.pdf on August 13, 2021.

Willink, J., & Babin, L. (2015). *Extreme ownership: How U.S. Navy SEALS lead and win*. New York: St. Martins Press.

Wlodkowski, R. J., & Ginsberg, M. B. (1995). *A framework for culturally responsive teaching*. Accessed at www.ascd.org/publications/educational-leadership/sept95/vol53/num01 /A-Framework-for-Culturally-Responsive-Teaching.aspx on February 9, 2021.

Wong, C. A., Gachupin, F. C., Holman, R. C., MacDorman, M. F., Cheek, J. E., Holve, S., et al. (2014). American Indian and Alaska Native infant and pediatric mortality, United States, 1999–2009. *American Journal of Public Health, 104*(3), S320–S328.

World Economic Forum. (2020). *Global Risks Report 2020*. Accessed at http://reports. weforum.org/global-risks-report-2020 on February 9, 2021.

World Health Organization. (2020). *Violence against children*. Accessed at www.who.int /news-room/fact-sheets/detail/violence-against-children#:~:text=Globally%2C%20 it%20is%20estimated%20that,lifelong%20health%20and%20well%2Dbeing. on March 12, 2021.

World Health Organization. (2021). *World health statistics: Monitoring health for the SDGs, sustainable development goals*. Accessed at https://cdn.who.int/media/docs/default-source /gho-documents/world-health-statistic-reports/2021/whs-2021_20may.pdf?sfvrsn =55c7c6f2_8 on June 1, 2021.

Wycoff, S., Tinagon, R., & Dickson, S. (2011). Therapeutic practice with Cambodian refugee families: Trauma, adaptation, resiliency, and wellness. *The Family Journal, 19*(2), 165–173.

Yehuda, R., Daskalakis, N. P., Bierer, L. M., Bader, H. N., Klengel, T., Holsboer, F., et al. (2016). Holocaust exposure induced intergenerational effects on FKBP5 methylation. *Biological Psychiatry, 80*(5), 372–380.

Yehuda, R., Spiegel, D., Southwick, S., Davis, L. L., Neylan, T. C., & Krystal, J. H. (2016). What I have changed my mind about and why. *European Journal of Psychotraumatology, 7*, 33768.

Zelazo, P. D. (2015). Executive function: Reflection, iterative reprocessing, complexity, and the developing brain. *Developmental Review, 38*, 55–68.

Zelazo, P. D., Blair, C. B., & Willoughby, M. T. (2016). *Executive function: Implications for education*. Accessed at https://files.eric.ed.gov/fulltext/ED570880.pdf on August 11, 2021.

Index

"Ruyle and colleagues provide the much-needed road map to transform schools from organizations that teach content to organizations that teach learning. With an approach that is both evidence based and practical for classrooms, the school wellness wheel provides a framework that is, and should be, accessible to all."

—Nancy Weinstein
CEO, MindPrint Learning

"[*The School Wellness Wheel* is] a compelling resource for stakeholders in the educational field who are determined to embrace the wealth of knowledge and hard data currently available on the experiences that affect brain development, overall health, student behavior, and learning to translate them into classroom practice and responsive school environments in order to enhance individual development and contribute to a more just educational system for all. The humane yet intellectually rigorous school wellness wheel model provides a framework that will enable stakeholders to make the necessary cultural shift to accomplish the desired transformation."

—Carmen A. Castillo
International Educational Consultant, Co-author of the Winner of the Academics' Choice Award Book *Picturing the Project*

"What I appreciate about *The School Wellness Wheel* is that it gets right to the heart of the matter—it's not about just changing one thing, but changing everything we do in schools for the success of all of our students. It is big work, but it is essential work!"

—Cale VanVelkinburgh
Principal, Bozeman Charter School, Bozeman, Montana

"The school wellness wheel helps us meet the needs of our most challenging students. Healing trauma and building resilience in our students will be the goal for all educators moving forward. This research-based program provides educators with a well-developed road map on how to accomplish these goals.

—Jason M. Oden
Principal, Canton City Public Schools, Cuyahoga Falls, Ohio

"*The School Wellness Wheel* provides teachers, counselors, principals, and superintendents a framework to both understand the impact of trauma on an entire school community and take concrete steps to meet the needs of all our students. Deeply rooted in research, the authors present a compelling paradigm of what our schools could be. A great reminder that SEL is not "another thing" to add to the plate, but the foundation everything else is built upon."

—Michael Evans
Director of Student Services, Neosho School District, Neosho, Missouri

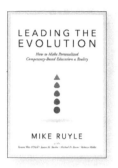

Leading the Evolution
Mike Ruyle With Tamera Weir O'Neill, Jeanie M. Iberlin, Michael D. Evans, and Rebecca Midles
Take action to evolve the existing model of schooling into one that is more innovative, relevant, and effective. *Leading the Evolution* introduces a three-pronged approach to driving substantive change—called the *evolutionary triad*—that connects transformational leadership, student engagement, and teacher optimism around personalized competency-based education.
BKL042

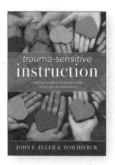

Trauma-Sensitive Instruction
John F. Eller and Tom Hierck
Confidently and meaningfully support your trauma-impacted students with this accessible resource. The authors draw from their personal and professional experiences with trauma, mental health, and school culture to provide real insight into what you can do now to help learners build resilience and achieve at high levels.
BKF847

The Metacognitive Student
Richard K. Cohen, Deanne Kildare Opatosky, James Savage, Susan Olsen Stevens, and Edward P. Darrah
What if there were one strategy you could use to support students academically, socially, and emotionally? It exists—and it's simple, straightforward, and practical. Dive deep into structured SELf-questioning and learn how to empower students to develop into strong, healthy, and confident thinkers.
BKF954

The Wraparound Guide
Leigh Colburn and Linda Beggs
Your school has the power to help students overcome barriers to well-being and achievement—from mental health issues to substance abuse to trauma. With this timely guide, discover actionable steps for launching and sustaining wraparound services embedded in your school that support the whole child.
BKF956

MARZANO Research

Visit MarzanoResources.com or call 888.849.0851 to order.

Professional Development Designed for Success

Empower your staff to tap into their full potential as educators. As an all-inclusive research-into-practice resource center, we are committed to helping your school or district become highly effective at preparing every student for his or her future.

Choose from our wide range of customized professional development opportunities for teachers, administrators, and district leaders. Each session offers hands-on support, personalized answers, and accessible strategies that can be put into practice immediately.

Bring Marzano Resources experts to your school for results-oriented training on:

- Assessment & Grading
- Curriculum
- Instruction
- School Leadership

- Teacher Effectiveness
- Student Engagement
- Vocabulary
- Competency-Based Education

LEARN MORE at MarzanoResources.com/PD